CADET POCKET BOOK

By Dave Hazlewood

Published and Distributed by:
Cadet Direct Ltd
www.cadetdirect.com

ISBN: 978-1-7393617-0-9

Cadet Pocket Book - 2023 onwards

© Copyright 2023 - Cadet Direct Ltd

All rights reserved. No part of this publication may be reproduced, stored in a retrieval system, or transmitted in any form or by any means, electronic, mechanical, photocopying, recording or otherwise, without the prior permission of the copyright holder.

This publication is not sponsored by either the Ministry of Defence or the Reserve Forces & Cadet Associations. The publishers take no responsibility whatsoever, for any inaccurate information contained within.

Written by Dave Hazlewood

Published and distributed by Cadet Direct Ltd
www.cadetdirect.com

Contains images and text courtesy of Cadet Books
www.cadetbooks.com

Cover image by Peter Russell
www.peterrussellphotography.com

Contains public sector information licensed under the Open Government Licence v3.0.

INTRODUCTION

The first Cadet Pocket Book, written by John Harris, was published in 1981 and was designed to help cadets and Cadet Force Adult Volunteers (CFAVs) get the most out of their time with the Army Cadets. It has gone on to sell over 100,000 copies and is still extremely popular today.

UPDATE 2023

Since its first release, there have been many revisions as the Cadet Forces have changed to keep up with the modern world but 2020 saw one of the biggest periods of change as a global pandemic stopped face to face training for the first time in over a hundred years. This pause on training brought about a whole array of changes to the Army Cadets, from new systems for booking and running events, right through to a completely new syllabus.

This release has been completely re-written by Dave Hazlewood to bring the pocketbook right up to date and continue the good work started by John Harris over 30 years ago.

AIDE MEMOIR

This pocket book provides general information and revision only and is not a substitute for the official training manuals and resource centre training aids. Instructors are encouraged to make full use of the official materials provided and create lesson plans for all training.

At the time of publication, after extensive research, all information contained in this publication is accurate to the best of our knowledge and belief. Any feedback, comments or suggestions are always welcome, so please feel free to contact us via our website: www.cadetdirect.com

Dedicated to Major John Hobbis Harris (1927-2015)
Original author and creator of the Cadet's Pocket Book

THE CHARTER OF THE ARMY CADET FORCE

The Army Cadet Force is a national voluntary youth organisation. It is sponsored by the Army and provides challenging military, adventurous and community activities. Its aim is to inspire young people to achieve success in life with a spirit of service to the King, their country and their local community, and to develop in them the qualities of good citizens.

This aim is achieved by:
- Providing progressive cadet training, often of a challenging and exciting nature, to foster confidence, self reliance, initiative, loyalty, and a sense of service to other people.
- Encouraging the development of personal powers of practical leadership and the ability to work successfully as a member of a team.
- Stimulating an interest in the Army, its achievements, skills and values.
- Advising and preparing those considering a career in the Services or with the Reserve Forces.

The motto of the Army Cadet Force
'TO INSPIRE TO ACHIEVE'

The Cadet Training Centre, Frimley Park, Camberley, Surrey

CONTENTS

CHAPTER ONE
GETTING STARTED — 1
Uniformed Youth Organisations	2
Becoming an Army Cadet	3
The ACF Detachment	6
Values & Standards	8
Security	10
Welfare	11
The Cadet Portal	12
Becoming an Adult Volunteer	14

CHAPTER TWO
STRUCTURE & ORGANISATION — 19
ACF Structure	20
ACF Staff	22
CCF Structure	25
CCF Staff	26
Affiliation	28
Structure of the British Army	29
Organisation of the British Army	30

CHAPTER THREE
UNIFORM & APPEARANCE — 33
What is Issued	34
Preparing Uniform	35
Wearing Uniform	38
Maintaining Uniform	39
Dress Regulations	40
Inspections	42

CHAPTER FOUR
TRAINING & EVENTS — 43
Army Cadet Activities	44
Army Cadet Events	45
Getting Involved	46
Staying Away	50

CHAPTER FIVE
KIT & EQUIPMENT — 53
Overview	54
Wash Kits	55
First Aid Kits	56
Boot cleaning & sewing kits	57
Full Kit List - Camp	58
Full Kit List - Field	60
Full Kit List - Expedition	62

CHAPTER SIX
PROGRESSION — 65
Overview	66
Cadet Star Levels	67
Cadet Rank Structure	68
Cadet Qualifications	69
Cadet Badges	71
Advanced Cadet Roles	73
Adult Rank Structure	74
Adult Qualifications	77

CHAPTER SEVEN
ARMY CADET SYLLABUS — 81
Introduction	82
Recruit Cadet	83
Basic Cadet	84
One Star Cadet	85
Two Star Cadet	86
Three Star Cadet	87
Four Star Cadet	88

CHAPTER EIGHT
INSTRUCTIONAL TECHNIQUES — 89
Intro to CFIT	90
Overview of CFIT Lessons	91
Identify & Plan Training	93
Deliver Training	97
Assess Cadets & Evaluate	98

CHAPTER NINE
MILITARY KNOWLEDGE — 99
Introduction & Basic Overview	100
One Star Training MK Overview	102
Two Star Training MK Overview	103
Three & Four Star Training	104

CHAPTER TEN
DRILL & TURNOUT — 105
Introduction	106
Drill Timing	107
Basic Training DT Overview	108
One Star Training DT Overview	114
Two Star Training DT Overview	118
Three Star Training DT Overview	122
Four Star Training DT Overview	128

CONTENTS (continued)

CHAPTER ELEVEN
FIELDCRAFT & TACTICS — 129
Introduction	130
Basic Training FC Overview	131
One Star Training FC Overview	135
Two Star Training FC Overview	145
Three Star Training FC Overview	151
Four Star Training FC Overview	153

CHAPTER TWELVE
NAVIGATION — 155
Introduction	156
Basic Training Nav Overview	157
One Star Training Nav Overview	160
Two Star Training Nav Overview	166
Three Star Training Nav Overview	177
Four Star Training Nav Overview	182

CHAPTER THIRTEEN
EXPEDITION — 187
Introduction	188
Basic Training Exp Overview	189
One Star Training Exp Overview	192
Two Star Training Exp Overview	204
Three Star Training Exp Overview	208
Four Star Training Exp Overview	213

CHAPTER FOURTEEN
SKILL AT ARMS — 217
Introduction & Basic Overview	218
One Star Training SAA Overview	223
Two - Four Star Training	230

CHAPTER FIFTEEN
SHOOTING — 231
Introduction	232
Firing Ranges	233
Grouping & Zeroing	237
The Marksmanship Principles	238
Basic Training SH Overview	242
One Star Training SH Overview	243
Two Star Training SH Overview	244
Three Star Training SH Overview	245
Four Star Training SH Overview	246

CHAPTER SIXTEEN
FIRST AID — 247
Introduction & Primary Survey	248
Syllabus First Aid	254
Basic Training FA Overview	255
One Star Training FA Overview	256
Two Star Training FA Overview	257
Three Star Training FA Overview	260
Four Star Training FA Overview	261

CHAPTER SEVENTEEN
COMMUNITY ENGAGEMENT — 263
Introduction & Basic Overview	264
One Star Training CE Overview	266
Two Star Training CE Overview	268
Three Star Training CE Overview	270
Four Star Training CE Overview	272

CHAPTER EIGHTEEN
KEEPING ACTIVE — 273
Introduction & Basic Overview	274
One - Three Star Training KA	277

CHAPTER NINETEEN
ADVENTUROUS TRAINING — 281
Introduction & Basic Overview	282
One Star Training AT Overview	285
Two Star Training AT Overview	286
Three Star Training AT Overview	288
Four Star Training AT Overview	290

CHAPTER TWENTY
COMMUNICATIONS — 291
Introduction	292
Basic Training CIS Overview	293
One Star Training CIS Overview	297
Two Star Training CIS Overview	305
Three Star Training CIS Overview	307
Four Star Training CIS Overview	308

CHAPTER TWENTY ONE
MUSIC — 309
Overview	310

CHAPTER TWENTY TWO
INITIALS, ACRONYMS & SLANG — 311
Overview	312

CHAPTER ONE
GETTING STARTED

CONTENTS:
- Uniformed Youth Organisations
- Becoming An Army Cadet
- The ACF Detachment
- Values & Standards Of The Army Cadets
- Security
- Welfare
- The Cadet Portal
- Becoming An Adult Volunteer

REFERENCES:
- *Army Cadet Force regulations - AC14233 (Version 3.2.0 - November 2022)*
- *Army Cadet Syllabus - AC71101 (Version 1.2 - July 2022)*
- *Army Cadets Military Knowledge Training Manual - AC72158 (Version 1 - 2021)*
- *Army Cadet Resource Centre via Westminster*

CHAPTER ONE: GETTING STARTED

UNIFORMED YOUTH ORGANISATIONS

There are five national voluntary uniformed youth organisations sponsored by the Ministry Of Defence (MOD) in the UK. Each have their own identity and specialise in skills practiced by their relevant service but all of them do exceptionally good work in assisting young people develop confidence and skills such as teamwork, leadership and discipline.

1. **The Army Cadet Force (ACF) - Army**
2. **The Royal Air Force Air Cadets (RAFAC) - Air Force**
3. **The Marine Society and Sea Cadets (MSSC) - Navy**
4. **The Volunteer Cadet Corps (VCC) - Navy**
5. **The Combined Cadet Force (CCF) - Army, Navy & Air Force**

The first four organisations focus on just one of the three Armed Forces whereas the Combined Cadet Force has elements of all three.

Note: Although sponsored by the MOD, the cadet forces are not part of the Armed Forces. Cadets and instructors are not expected to take part in any military action and cannot be called up for service.

ARMY CADETS IN THE ACF AND THE CCF

ACF: The ACF specialises in Army related training and is open to anyone above the age of 12, local to one of the 1,600 detachments spread out over the UK.

CCF: CCF units can run Army, Navy and Air Cadet sections and are based in schools. Not all schools run all three options but pupils can choose which they would like to join out of what is available.

The ACF Logo

Army Cadets in the CCF are almost exactly the same as those in the ACF and use the same syllabus and are governed by the same authorities. They both carry out the same military style training as well as activities such as expeditions and Adventurous Training (AT). Information in this book relates more to the ACF but most of it will be the same for the CCF.

The CCF Logo

CHAPTER ONE: GETTING STARTED

BECOMING AN ARMY CADET

Anyone between the ages of 12 and 18 can become an Army Cadet and join either the ACF or the CCF.

If you are lucky enough to have a CCF contingent in your school, you will be able to join there and can apply to join direct.

JOINING THE ACF

If you do not have access to a CCF unit in your school, there is likely to be an ACF unit very close to where you live that you can join instead. The joining process is all done online and is extremely easy.

APPLICATION

- Go to **www.armycadets.com**
- Click on 'Join Now'.
- Enter your postcode and hit return. This will bring up a map of your local area marked with the detachments (venues) closest to where you live along with parade nights and times.
- Find the one you would like to join and click 'Join as a cadet'.
- Here you will need to fill in the details for the person wanting to join along with their parent/guardian details.
- Once this has been done an email will be sent to the parent/guardian which has the next steps of the joining process.

It is important to remember that this process is dealt with at a national level before being sent on to the relevant county to process so it might be a few days before you hear anything back.

For more info or to join go to the official ACF website:

CHAPTER ONE: GETTING STARTED

VISIT

Once your application has filtered down to your local area, you will receive an email from the person in charge of the detachment you want to join (called a Detachment Commander or DC). They will explain a bit more about the detachment and invite you in for an evening to meet the staff and cadets and see how a normal cadet night runs. This is always a bit daunting and requires some courage to go along but once there, everyone does their best to make all potential new cadets feel welcome and at ease.

TRIAL PERIOD

The first few parade nights are a great time to see how you enjoy it and decide if it is something you want to continue with. Anyone can leave or change detachment at any time so there is no pressure to commit. Remember, everyone there has been through the same thing.

UNIFORM

Once you have decided to continue as an Army Cadet the process moves along and you can be measured for your uniform. Measurements can be done at home or at detachment and the sizes will then be sent off to have your uniform ordered. Availability of certain items can change so waiting times can vary.

Unless the detachment has some spare, you will not be issued boots so you need to buy your own.

Note: More information on how to prepare, wear and look after your uniform is in Chapter Three.

CHAPTER ONE: GETTING STARTED

BASIC TRAINING

As soon as you start as an Army Cadet you will take part in lessons at detachment. You start as a recruit or 'basic training cadet' and you will take part in lessons and assessments on the following subjects:

• Military Knowledge	• Shooting
• Drill & Turnout	• First Aid
• Fieldcraft & Tactics	• Community Engagement
• Navigation	• Keeping Active
• Expedition	• Adventurous Training
• Skill At Arms	• Communications

Training is progressive and is measured in star levels. It should take around three to six months to pass basic training and then start One Star training. Initially most of your training and assessments can be done at your detachment but, as you progress, more training will take place at other locations on training weekends.

Note: More information about training and events can be found in chapter four. More information about lessons and assessments can be found from Chapter Nine onwards.

CHAPTER ONE: GETTING STARTED

THE ACF DETACHMENT

As you progress as an Army Cadet you will get lots of opportunities to go away on training weekends and other activities but, initially, you will do most of your training at your local detachment.

STAFF

The ACF is a non-profit organisation and most of the staff within it are volunteers. Most staff have day jobs and are only part of the Army Cadet Force in their spare time. On training events away from detachment, volunteers receive a small payment called a volunteer allowance, but the majority of what they do is unpaid. A lot of time and effort goes into making sure things go as smoothly as possible and create as many opportunities for the cadets as possible, but please be patient if things don't always go to plan.

COSTS

All Army Cadet activities are heavily subsidised by the Ministry Of Defence (MOD) which means they are always a lot cheaper than you would find within other organisations. Any money taken after expenses goes back into cadet funds which helps pay for extra equipment, stationary and other items needed by the cadets.

Approximate Costs

- **Enrolment fee:** A one off initial payment of around £10 may be required to join.
- **Subs:** Some detachments charge a small amount to parade each night called 'subs'. This is normally no more than £1 - £2.
- **Snacks & drinks:** 50p - £1.
- **Local events:** Free or specific to activity.
- **Weekend training (all inclusive):** £15 - £25.
- **Annual Camp 1 - 2 weeks: (all inclusive):** £75 - £150.

WELFARE FUND

A welfare fund is also available for cadets parents/guardians that may have difficulty to pay for events and can be applied for via Area or County Headquarters.

CHAPTER ONE: GETTING STARTED

NAAFI

There will be a break around the middle of each evening to get snacks and drinks. This is called NAAFI which stands for Navy, Army, Air Force Institute and refers to the organisation that has provided catering, retail and leisure to the Armed Forces for many years.

FORMAT

Evenings will be taken up mainly with training, but can also include social events, sports nights and other variations. Each night will have similar timings and format though:

- **Arrival:** Meet up with friends and check uniform is looking good.
- **First parade:** Normally led by a senior cadet, everyone forms up to pay their subs (if required), have a uniform inspection and receive a briefing on the evening's activities and any other important updates.
- **Training period one:** Lesson or other activity.
- **NAAFI break:** Chance to chat to friends and relax.
- **Training period two:** Another lesson or activity.
- **Clear up:** Taking time to keep the detachment clean and tidy.
- **Final parade:** Similar to the first parade, cadets receive feedback on the evening and get details of upcoming parade nights and events.
- **Leave:** Instructors always wait until all cadets have been collected (or set off on their journeys if they walk home).

POINT OF CONTACT (POC)

As volunteers, staff are not required to give out their personal phone numbers so communication is generally done via email (staff all have Army-Mail email accounts), closed social media groups and at detachment. If you have serious issues, you can also contact the detachment's Area Headquarters or the County Headquarters.

HOLIDAYS & DETACHMENT CLOSURES

All detachments are different but quite a few close during school and national holidays and detachment staff will advise you of that. If staff are sick or held up at work, there may also be the occasion when a parade night is cancelled last minute so it is always worth checking before leaving home that there are no last minute updates.

CHAPTER ONE: GETTING STARTED

VALUES & STANDARDS OF THE ARMY CADETS

The British Army has a set of Values and Standards that form the basis of how soldiers and officers at all levels should behave and act in all situations. The ACF has a similar set of Values and Standards.

VALUES

Values are the beliefs that we need to adopt to help us make the right decisions and do the right thing. Some may not seem natural to you, so it is important to learn what they are and allow them to develop who you are.

Use **C DRILS** to help remember the six values.

C: Courage: Have the physical courage to push on and not give up when things are tough or scary such as a long expedition or using a climbing wall for the first time. Have the moral courage to stand up for what is right even if you think it will make you unpopular, such as not allowing bad conduct from other cadets.

D: Discipline: Be self disciplined with things like looking after your uniform and getting out of bed and ready on time. Stick to the rules and regulations laid down to you when taking part in cadet activities and respond to direction from instructors and officers.

R: Respect for Others: Treat others as you would like to be treated. Avoid any discrimination against people of different gender, race, religion etc. Listen to other people's views and keep an open mind.

I: Integrity: Always be honest and truthful and trust team members. Admitting a mistake is much better than trying to hide it.

L: Loyalty: Being loyal to the people around you will help build trust and allow you to achieve a lot more. Back team decisions and learn how to work through differences. However, loyalty does not mean accepting poor behaviour or conduct from friends or peers.

S: Selfless Commitment: Putting the needs of others ahead of your own. This means looking out for those that are less fortunate than you or that struggle with tasks that you find easy.

These values help us by building trust within ourselves and others we come into contact with. Trust is broken when we let others know our values but then do not stick to them.

CHAPTER ONE: GETTING STARTED

STANDARDS

Standards are how we put our values into practice. They allow us to act in the correct way to ensure we can always stick to our Values.

Use **PLAD** to remember the four standards.

P: Professional Behaviour: Our conduct should always be of a high standard that shows respect for the uniform we wear. Even when not in uniform, we should still act in a way that does not put the ACFs reputation at risk.

L: Lawful Behaviour: We must abide by the law at all times. With cadets, there are laws in place with regard to drinking alcohol and smoking etc that also must be adhered to.

A: Appropriate Behaviour: Our behaviour must always be appropriate and avoid any conduct that demonstrates a lack of tolerance for any race, religion, gender etc. Bad language and views that are biased must be avoided.

D: Duty of Care: This applies more to instructors and officers within the ACF as they have a Duty of Care to all young people but cadets can still look out for each other and report anything they feel may be affecting the welfare of any fellow cadets.

Learn these values and standards and start to build them into how you act as you develop as an Army Cadet or CFAV. The lessons learnt here will transfer into everyday life, too, and will help in all aspects of your future career and family life.

CHAPTER ONE: GETTING STARTED

SECURITY

Anyone that is part of the military community in the UK has to take security extremely seriously and, although not officially part of the Army, UK Army Cadets wear the same uniform and can therefore be mistaken for Regular or Reserve British Army soldiers. We must therefore also be aware of this and take the necessary precautions.

THREAT LEVELS IN THE UK

In the UK, the government has five levels of threat which let people know how likely a terrorist attack is.

1. **Low** - An attack is highly unlikely.
2. **Moderate** - An attack is possible but not likely.
3. **Substantial** - An attack is likely.
4. **Severe** - An attack is highly likely.
5. **Critical** - An attack is highly likely in the near future.

Note: When writing this book, the UK threat level was 'substantial'.

Threat from terrorists is now always a concern but criminal gangs may also take an interest in someone with military connections.

WHAT CAN YOU DO?

Security is the responsibility of all cadets and CFAVs to protect themselves from any form of attack and to avoid the leak of any sensitive ACF or military information that could compromise security.

- **Uniform** - Everyone feels proud to wear their uniform but there may be occasions when it is not suitable, for example, when walking through a busy town or city on the way to a parade night. If concerned at all, travel in civilian clothing and then change at detachment.

- **Social media** - Being on a Regular Army camp can be quite exciting, especially if there are regular units conducting training. It is important not to take photos of these things and there should definitely not be anything posted on social media.

  Cadets and CFAVs should also be careful if posting photos of themselves in uniform on social media and photos posing with rifles or looking very soldier-like should be avoided.

CHAPTER ONE: GETTING STARTED

- **Talk** - Be careful what you are talking about in public, especially when discussing camps, unit locations and exercises you may have seen. Within the ACF there are also sensitive issues so avoid discussing them in public places where you may be overheard.
- **Documents** - Careful handling of documents is important to avoid information being seen by the wrong people (see page 299 for details on security classification). Data protection rules also have to be followed to keep individuals personal details safe. A breach of this could also lead to legal action being taken.

There are a lot more measures that can be taken and many more examples of situations where security is important, but hopefully this has given a brief insight and will make you think more in the future.

WELFARE

The primary role of all CFAVs, regardless of rank or job role, is to look after the welfare of young people, even if not under their direct supervision. This means that training and cadet activities are secondary to the welfare of the people taking part. CFAVs also have a responsibility to look after the welfare of other adults.

Welfare issues can range from serious problems at home or at school through to general health and safety concerns on training weekends or when at detachment. Full training is given to all CFAVs and this training is revised and assessed annually to make sure they are prepared to deal with anything they may encounter.

TALK

Cadets should feel that they can talk to their instructors about any problems or worries, even if they are happening away from the ACF environment. The ACF is a family and everyone involved is committed to looking out for each other and helping deal with issues.

Cadets can also talk to the following organisations:

- **NSPCC - 0808 800 5000**
- **Childline - 0800 1111**

CFAVs should also feel that they can talk to their fellow instructors or officers that they feel comfortable with.

CHAPTER ONE: GETTING STARTED

THE CADET PORTAL

Cadets and CFAVs have access to the cadet portal which is a great online resource that allows individuals to manage their cadet experience. Available through a computer, tablet or mobile phone there is a whole array of options.

NOTIFICATIONS

- Get news and info on everything that interests you.
- Customise your notifications to only get what you want.
- Choose to receive updates by text or email.

PERSONALISE

- Choose what information you see.
- Set favourites.
- Make it your own.

ACTIVITIES

- Search for events and courses.
- One click to show you're interested in taking part.
- Get event details such as dates, times, location etc.

TRACK YOURSELF

- Track your star level progress.
- View current rank and qualifications.
- See what next steps are available to you.

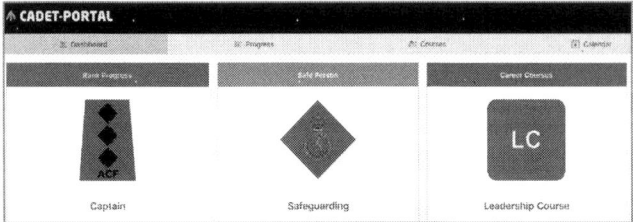

CHAPTER ONE: GETTING STARTED

SIGN UP

CFAVs have automatic access to the cadet portal but cadets will need to register online.

Before starting you will need the following:
- Email address of parent/guardian that can easily be accessed.
- Cadet ACF service number (detachment commander can provide this). Service number will need to have been active for at least 24 hours.

> **Sign up here:**
> **www.portal.cadets.mod.uk**

- Click on 'create account'.
- Click 'yes' to say you are current serving MOD personnel.
- Fill in the relevant details.
- Read and confirm you have read SyOps & JSP740 and submit.
- Check your emails and verify.
- Login using your details but **DO NOT** click 'Continue to defence gateway' after verification.
- Go to www.portal.cadets.mod.uk and login there.

WESTMINSTER

CFAVs are all issued with an Army Mail email account and have access to Westminster which is an online resource available through the MOD Defence Gateway. Full training is given and it is an extremely useful tool to manage everything to do with the ACF.

Here are just a few things that can be done:
- Send and receive emails via Army-Mail.
- Access training manuals, lesson aids and assessments.
- Access event forms, documents and guidelines.
- Book on courses and events and set up your own.
- Do online learning modules and pre-course training via the 'Defence Learning Environment (DLE).
- Record parade night and event attendance and claim VA payments.
- Monitor cadet progress and update records.

CHAPTER ONE: GETTING STARTED

BECOMING AN ADULT VOLUNTEER

Subject to strict background checks and security screening, anyone above the age of 18 can become a Cadet Force Adult Volunteer (CFAV). No military or cadet background is required as full training will be given.

There are three options available:

1. **Non Uniformed Volunteer (NUV)** - Supervise and assist.
2. **Non-Commissioned Officer (NCO)** - Supervise and Instruct.
3. **Officer** - Manage, plan and lead.

The choice between these 3 options is down to personal preference and background which is explained in more detail below.

NON UNIFORMED VOLUNTEER (NUV)

The role of the non uniformed volunteer is not always explained enough to potential new volunteers but it is an extremely important and useful role which requires the least commitment.

Background and security checks are done, as with all volunteers, but beyond that there is very little training. Volunteers do not wear a uniform or receive any VA (Volunteer Allowance) payments, although travel expenses can be claimed. They are not allowed to teach cadets but there are lots of useful tasks that can be carried out such as:

• Supervise cadets	• Shop for detachment items
• Clean & tidy detachments	• Monitor detachment accounts
• Operate the tuck shop (NAAFI)	• Run camp guard rooms
• Help with detachment admin	• Perform fire checks
• Become a minibus driver	• Maintain stores & equipment
• Act as a first aider	• Run closed social media groups

The most suitable people for this role would be parents of cadets, older members of the community, people with busy work schedules that cannot commit to lots of training or anyone who just wants to be involved but does not want to go though the full training to become an instructor.

It is also an ideal way to join the organisation and get a feel for how it works before taking the next step to becoming a full instructor.

CHAPTER ONE: GETTING STARTED

NON-COMMISSIONED OFFICER (NCO)

These are the backbone of the Army Cadets and work tirelessly to make sure our cadets are looked after and have great fun taking part in all of the amazing activities provided.

Background and security checks are done as with all volunteers but then full instructor training is given. No military or cadet experience is required as the comprehensive training package covers all of the lesson material as well as how to teach it.

Those that do have military or cadet experience will normally go through the same process to make sure everyone is at the same standard. It is also important to see how certain lessons are taught from a CFAV perspective rather than that of an ex-soldier or ex-cadet.

Once fully trained and qualified, Sergeant Instructors (SIs), can do all of the things that a NUV can do but can also book, plan and run events, teach cadets up to a reasonable level and move onto more specialist courses in subjects such as Navigation, Shooting or First Aid.

Being an adult volunteer is extremely rewarding and is a great way to make new friends, develop leadership skills and gain qualifications that are recognised in civilian life.

CHAPTER ONE: GETTING STARTED

OFFICER

Officers are senior in rank to other CFAVs and are responsible for planning events, leadership and management of adult instructors and other admin related tasks. They do not always have the time to interact with the cadets as much but make a real difference by ensuring that things run smoothly in the background.

It is possible to join the organisation as an officer but, for anyone that has no previous experience, it is a good idea to spend some time as a Sergeant Instructor first. Ex-Regular or Reserve officers may be able to carry their commission over to the ACF although it may not be at their previous rank.

APPLICATION

Whichever role is being applied for the process starts off the same.

- Go to **www.armycadets.com**
- Click on 'Join now'.
- Enter your postcode and hit return - This will bring up a map of your local area marked with the detachments (venues) closest to where you live along with parade nights and times.
- Find the one you would like to join and click 'Join as a volunteer'.
- Here you will need to fill in the details required and answer a few simple questions.
- Once this has been done an email will be sent to you which has the next steps of the joining process.

It is important to remember that this process is dealt with at a national level before being sent on to the relevant county to process so it might be a few days before you hear anything back.

CHAPTER ONE: GETTING STARTED

ADULT JOINING PROCESS

After your initial application has been submitted things start to get moving behind the scenes. This is a general overview of what happens next:

- Application screened and sent onto the County Headquarters of the requested detachment.
- An open evening may be organised for new applicants at this point.
- County Headquarters process the application and send it onto the Area Headquarters of the requested detachment.
- The Area Headquarters staff make contact with the applicant and arrange a convenient time for an initial interview.
- Initial interview takes place (normally at the Area Headquarters) between the applicant and the Area Commander.
- If all is good at this point, the application is passed back to the County Headquarters for the relevant checks to be done and for the applicant to be set up on the ACF's 'Westminster' computer system.
- Relevant checks such as Disclosure and Barring Service (DBS), security and vetting are carried out which can take quite a long time.
- A familiarisation day or weekend is organised for any new applicants to explain the joining process and training schedule. These are low pressure, fun events that allow applicants to ask questions and meet staff and other new recruits. Those that continue from here sign an Adult Volunteer Agreement and are 'boarded'.

Once all of the above has happened and the relevant checks have been returned with no concerns, applicants are allowed to parade at their chosen detachment. An Army number (PNumber) is allocated, uniform is issued and the applicant is officially a Probationary Instructor (PI) ready to start training.

Probationary Instructor (PI)

PIs are allowed to assist with lessons and supervise cadets but are not permitted to teach alone or plan events.

They wear the first PI rank slide which has a red stripe across it and the initials PI.

CHAPTER ONE: GETTING STARTED

INITIAL CFAV TRAINING

Here is a general outline of the different elements of PI training:

- **Basic Induction Course (BIC):** Run over several weekends or a complete week, this introduces PIs to life in the ACF and covers lessons relevant to basic training cadets.
- **Basic Westminster User Course:** Training on the official Army Cadet website called 'Westminster' which is hosted through the MODs Defence Gateway. Instructors can access resources, perform admin tasks and send/receive emails via an Army-Mail email address.
- **Red Book Test:** All CFAVs are issued a small reference booklet called 'The Red Book' that has important information regarding safety, safeguarding and dealing with emergencies. An annual open book test must be done by all CFAVs.
- **Responsible For Information (RFI):** An online course that deals with security of information which must be completed by all CFAVs annually.
- **Safeguarding:** Made up of an online course and a face to face briefing, all CFAVs need to complete this annually.
- **D of E e-induction:** Introduction to the Duke of Edinburgh award scheme which allows instructors to assist on expeditions.
- **Intermediate Induction Course (IIC):** Further development of instructional techniques and one star lessons. Run over weekends or a full week, once completed, a new rank slide is issued (See page 74).
- **First Aid At Work (FAAW):** This is an official qualification that allows instructors to teach first aid up to two star level and provide first aid cover at events or when on a range etc.
- **Shooting & Coaching course:** A short course to allow CFAVs to assist cadets shooting.
- **Advanced Induction Course (AIC):** This is normally a week long course run by Regular Army Soldiers and experienced CFAVs. It is designed to finish the PI training to a level where they can look after cadets and comfortably teach most subjects up to two star level.

New recruits are given up to 2 years to complete all the above, some of which can be done from home. On successful completion, recruits are promoted to Sergeant Instructor (SI).

CHAPTER TWO
STRUCTURE & ORGANISATION

CONTENTS:
- ACF Structure
- ACF Staff
- CCF Structure
- CCF Staff
- Affiliation
- Structure of the British Army
- Organisation of the British Army

REFERENCES:
- *Army Cadet Force regulations - AC14233*
  (Version 3.2.0 - November 2022)
- *Army Cadet Syllabus - AC71101*
  (Version 1.2 - July 2022)
- *Army Cadets Military Knowledge Training Manual - AC72158*
  (Version 1 - 2021)
- *British Army Website - www.army.mod.uk*
- *Army Cadet Resource Centre*

CHAPTER TWO: STRUCTURE & ORGANISATION

ACF STRUCTURE

The Army Cadet Force in the UK has around 39,000 cadets and 9,000 Cadet Force Adult Volunteers (CFAVs) spread over 1,600 detachments so there needs to be a structure in place to make sure things run smoothly.

COUNTIES

The UK is broken down into 52 main groupings known as **counties, battalions** or **sectors**. Staff at County Headquarters do not often interact directly with cadets but instead provide support and management for the units under their control.

AREAS

Each county is further broken down into several smaller areas. These areas are referred to as **areas, companies, groups** or **squadrons** dependant on the affiliation of the cadets in that area.

A small number of Area Headquarters staff are the link between the County Headquarters staff and the detachment staff and cadets.

DETACHMENTS

Each area is made up of around ten detachments which is where cadets do all of their main weekly training.
Cadets and CFAVs parade (attend) once or twice per week at a detachment near to where they live. This detachment is normally named after the town or district it is in and has anywhere up to around 50 cadets and up to around four to eight adult instructors.

EXAMPLE

This is how one of the 52 counties, Kent ACF, is organised.
36 detachment have been broken down into four areas, each made up of eight to ten detachments.

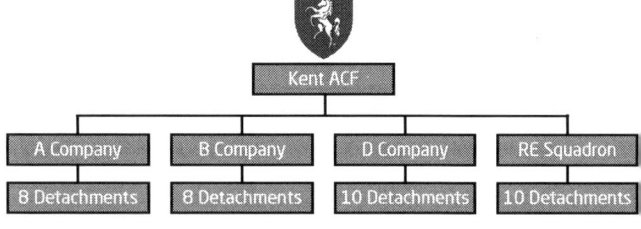

CHAPTER TWO: STRUCTURE & ORGANISATION

YOUR LOCATION

Find out about your detachment and area and fill in the boxes below.

Your County (County, Battalion, Sector)

Your Area (Area, Company, Group, Sector)

Your Detachment

Other Areas in Your County

Other Detachments in Your Area

CHAPTER TWO: STRUCTURE & ORGANISATION

ACF STAFF

There are thousands of people involved in creating the Army Cadet experience, all of whom go out of their way to look after our cadets and make sure they develop as young adults. Most of the people involved are volunteers (CFAVs) who give up their free time for very little or no pay. There are a small number of Permanent Support Staff (PSS) who are employees and are paid to assist the volunteers, look after kit and equipment and maintain buildings and military premises.

ACF DETACHMENT

Here are the people that make the Detachment run.

- **DC - Detachment Commander:** Responsible for the running of the detachment. Looks after all cadets and staff and ensures all training and admin happens.
- **2IC - Second in Command:** Backs up the DC and helps to make sure everything goes according to plan.
- **DI - Detachment Instructor:** Instructors at the detachment that deliver lessons and help to look after the welfare of cadets.
- **NUV - Non Uniformed Volunteer:** Volunteers that don't go through the same training as instructors, but help out with other general admin duties.
- **Staff Cadets:** Cadets that have reached the upper age limit to continue as cadets but are allowed to stay on until they are 20 years old to assist with teaching and cadet supervision. They also have the opportunity to finish training in areas such as DofE.
- **Senior Cadets:** Advanced cadets at the detachment that help with the day to day running and may even deliver some of the lessons.

ACF AREA/COMPANY/GROUP/SECTOR

To support the detachments, there are other NCOs and Officers.

- **OC - Officer Commanding:** Responsible for all detachment staff and cadets within the area's detachments.
- **SO - Staff Officer:** Responsible for all admin and accounts for the area and is quite often the area 2IC (second in command).

CHAPTER TWO: STRUCTURE & ORGANISATION

- **TO - Training Officer:** Responsible for planning detachment training and booking and running all area training events.
- **Area SM - Area Sergeant Major:** Responsible for standards and discipline throughout the area. May also assist the other area officers.
- **Subject Lead:** Instructors that specialise in a specific subject such as shooting or first aid etc. to help plan training and advise DCs and DIs.
- **CAA - Cadet Administrative Assistant:** A Permanent Support Staff (PSS) member of staff that assists with administration, stores, equipment and premises.

ACF COUNTY/BATTALION/SECTOR

Here are some of the key people at county/battalion/sector level:

- **Commandant:** Over all in command of the county/battalion/sector.
- **Deputy Commandant:** Second in charge (can be more than one).
- **RSM - Regimental Sergeant Major:** Responsible for discipline and standards of staff and cadets within the county/battalion/sector.
- **CEO - Cadet Executive Officer:** (PSS) Professional advisor to the Commandant, and responsible for the running of the County/Battalion/Sector HQ.
- **MSO - Medical Support Officer:** Ensures adequate First Aid cover is in place throughout the county and all relevant paperwork is in place and correct.
- **CTO - County Training Officer:** Oversees all training for the county.
- **CQM - Cadet Quarter Master:** (PSS) Responsible for all stores and equipment issued with the help of the CAAs (Cadet Admin Assistants) and CSAs (Cadet Stores Assistants).
- **Chaplain:** Under guidance from the Senior Chaplain, they cater to all faiths and visit detachments and training events so provide advice on spiritual and moral well-being to all.
- **Subject Leads:** Other positions such as Shooting Officer or Sports Officer can also be in place to take lead on specific areas of training and advise sub-units.

CHAPTER TWO: STRUCTURE & ORGANISATION

YOUR STAFF - ACF

Find out about the people in your area and fill in the boxes below.

ACF DETACHMENT	
Detachment Commander (DC):	
Second in Command (2IC):	
Instructors & Non Uniformed Volunteers (NUV):	
Senior Cadets & Staff Cadets:	

ACF AREA	
Area Commander (OC):	
Staff Officer (SO):	
Training Officer (TO):	
Area Sergeant Major (ASM):	
Cadet ASM:	

ACF COUNTY	
Commandant:	
Deputy Commandant(s):	
County Training Officer (CTO):	
Regimental Sergeant Major (RSM):	
Cadet Executive Officer (CEO):	
Medical Support Officer (MSO):	
Cadet RSM:	

CHAPTER TWO: STRUCTURE & ORGANISATION

CCF STRUCTURE

The structure of the CCF is slightly different from that of the ACF as cadets parade in school 'contingents' instead of local detachments. Instead of being organised into areas and counties, it is all managed through HQ Regional Command in Aldershot. This works through London District and nine Regional Points of Command (RPoCs) spread over the UK to provide, support, training and management to contingents in their local area. (Some of these RPoC HQs are also Brigade HQs).

Each RPoC/Brigade has a Cadet Training Team made up of Regular and Reserve Soldiers that support contingents by planning and running events and assisting with senior cadet and recruit staff training. They also assist with ACF units but not to the same extent.

Brigade/RPoC Structure

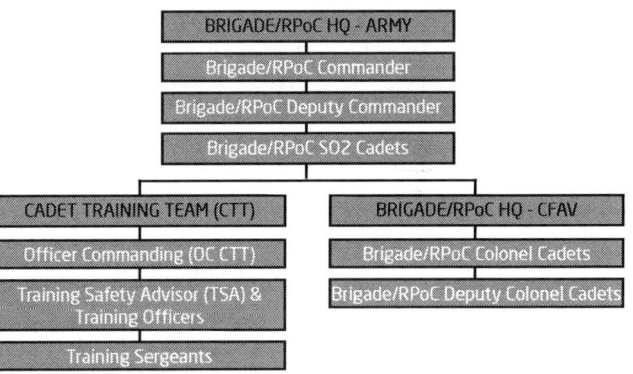

CHAPTER TWO: STRUCTURE & ORGANISATION

CCF STAFF

As with the ACF, there are lots of people involved in running the CCF.

CCF CONTINGENT

A CCF unit based in a school is known as a contingent. The organisation is similar to that of an ACF area with a lot of the roles fulfilled by teachers at the school backed up with one or two PSS.

- **Contingent Commander:** Overall command of the contingent. Similar in role to a Company Commander (OC).
- **SSI - School Staff Instructor:** (PSS) Responsible for planning all cadet training and activities. Includes any Sea or Air cadets.

CADET TRAINING TEAMS (CTT)

Assists and supports contingents in their region.

- **Officer Commanding Cadet Training Team (OC CTT):** Oversees and co-ordinates all training delivered by the Cadet Training Team staff.
- **Training Safety Advisor (TSA):** Responsible for making sure all training that takes place is safe and in line with current guidelines. Reports back to the OC CTT and advises CTT and contingent staff.
- **Training Officer:** Supports Army sections within the CCF by organising training and allocating support where needed.
- **Training Sergeants:** Deliver training and advise contingent staff.
- **Company Quartermaster Sergeant (CQMS):** Manages and allocates resources for CCF training.

CCF BRIGADE/RPOC (REGIONAL POINTS OF COMMAND)

- **Commander:** Oversees the Cadet Forces in their region.
- **Deputy Commander:** Supports the Commander and deputises on occasions.
- **Colonel Cadets:** Works closely with CCF contingents and advises the Brigade/RPoC Commander and Deputy Commander.
- **Deputy Colonel Cadets:** Assists the Colonel Cadets with all duties.
- **Staff Officer Cadets (SO2 Cdts):** Deals with finances and admin and liaises with Regional Command.

CHAPTER TWO: STRUCTURE & ORGANISATION

YOUR STAFF - CCF

Find out about the people in your area and fill in the boxes below.

CCF CONTINGENT	
Contingent Commander:	
School Staff Instructor:	
Army Section Commander:	
Army Section Instructors:	

CADET TRAINING TEAM (CTT)	
Officer Commanding:	
Training Safety Advisor (TSA):	
Training Officer (TO):	
Training Sergeant:	
Company Quartermaster Sgt (CQMS):	
Colonel Cadets:	
Deputy Colonel Cadets:	

OTHER ORGANISATIONS

There are also other organisations that support the ACF:

- **ACCT - Army Cadet Charitable Trust:** Formerly known as the Army Cadet Force Association (ACFA). This is a registered charity dedicated to promoting the ideals and activities of the ACF.
- **RFCA - Reserve Forces & Cadet Association:** Looks after a lot of the infrastructure of the ACF and Reserve Forces.
- **The British Army:** Provides operational command and funding for the ACF as well as assisting where possible with training support.
- **MOD - Ministry Of Defence:** Overall sponsors of all uniformed volunteer youth organisations.

CHAPTER TWO: STRUCTURE & ORGANISATION

AFFILIATION

Although there is a standard uniform worn by cadets and CFAVs, the headdress and cap badge varies around the country. Each ACF detachment and CCF contingent is affiliated to a regiment or corps of the British Army that is normally based in the same area and will therefore wear the same headdress and cap badge that they do.

This helps to create a bond between the Regular or Reserve Army units and the Army Cadets and gives a real sense of pride to all cadets and CFAVs as they learn their affiliated unit's history.

County and regimental badge for cadets in parts of Kent. Sewn onto the left upper arm blanking plate and worn on combat shirt or smock.

CHAPTER TWO: STRUCTURE & ORGANISATION

STRUCTURE OF THE BRITISH ARMY

The British Army is made up of two elements:

ARMS & SERVICES

1. **Arms:** These are the units trained and equipped to directly fight an enemy. **Combat Arms** are the front line troops that directly engage with the enemy. **Combat Support Arms** provide direct support to the Combat Arms. Arms of the British Army include the following:

- Household Cavalry
- Royal Armoured Corps (RAC)
- Royal Regiment of Artillery (RA)
- Corps of Royal Engineers (RE)
- Royal Corps of Signals
- Infantry
- Army Air Corps (AAC)
- Intelligence Corps

2. **Services:** These units provide essential administrative support. **Combat Service Support** provide support to Combat and Combat Support Arms. Services of the British Army include the following:

- Corps of Royal Electrical and Mechanical Engineers (REME)
- Royal Logistic Corps (RLC)
- Royal Army Medical Corps (RAMC)
- Queen Alexandra's Royal Army Nursing Corps (QARANC)
- Royal Army Dental Corps (RADC)
- Royal Army Veterinary Corps (RAVC)
- Royal Army Chaplains Department (RAChD)
- Royal Army Physical Training Corps (RAPTC)
- Corps of Army Music (CAMus)
- Adjutant General's Corps (AGC) - The largest corps, made up of the following:
  - Staff & Personnel Support (SPS)
  - Army Legal Services (ALS)
  - Education & Training Services (ETS)
  - Provost (made up of the following 3)
    1. Royal Military Police (RMP)
    2. Military Provost Staff
    3. Military Provost Guard Service (MPGS)

CHAPTER TWO: STRUCTURE & ORGANISATION

ORGANISATION OF THE BRITISH ARMY

REGIMENTS AND CORPS

The individual units that make up the Arms and Services are known as regiments or corps (pronounced as 'core').

Personnel within both are trained as soldiers first so are all capable of combat and can be Regular (full time) or Reserve (part time).

- **Regiments:** Each regiment has its own unique history and heritage, soldiers all wear the same cap badge and carry out a similar role to each other, (e.g. The Parachute Regiment).
- **Corps:** Each Corps also has its own unique history and heritage but is a much larger grouping than a regiment and can actually be made from several regiments (e.g. The Royal Armoured Corps is made up of 14 different regiments).

GROUPINGS

The regiments and corps of the Arms and Services are organised into different sized groupings to allow them to be deployed effectively. On the opposite page is a table to show how the infantry is organised.

Note: Numbers are approximate.

CHAPTER TWO: STRUCTURE & ORGANISATION

Number of Soldiers	Grouping title	Description	Commanded by
2	Battle Partners	2 soldiers working together in the field	-
4	Fire team	4 soldiers working together (2 pairs)	Lance Corporal
8	Section	Smallest group that can carry out a mission. Made up of 2 fire teams	Corporal
30	Platoon	Made up of 3 sections plus platoon IC etc.	Lieutenant & Sergeant
100	Company	Made up of 3 platoons and a headquarters element	Major & Company Sergeant Major
650	Battalion	Made up of 5 companies and associated staff	Lieutenant Colonel & Regimental Sergeant Major
2500 +	Brigade	Made up of 5 battalions with supporting units	Brigadier
40,000	Division	Made up of 2 or more brigades with additional support and services	Major-General

CHAPTER TWO: STRUCTURE & ORGANISATION

DEPLOYMENT

When the Army fights, it deploys brigades under the control of a Divisional Headquarters (HQ).

There are four types of fighting Brigade:

1. **Air Assault Brigade:** Highly mobile and can deploy anywhere at very short notice.
2. **Armoured Infantry Brigade:** Tank Regiments and armoured infantry Battalions.
3. **Strike Brigade:** Lighter and more mobile forces.
4. **Infantry Brigade:** Provide security and carry out operations on the ground.

There are also more specialist brigades that can be called on for specific roles such as Artillery, Engineering, Communications, Aviation, Intelligence, Logistics, Medical, Military Police, Cyber and Cultural.

VISIT WWW.ARMY.MOD.UK TO FIND OUT MORE

CHAPTER THREE
UNIFORM AND APPEARANCE

CONTENTS:
- What Is Issued
- Preparing Uniform
- Wearing Uniform
- Maintaining Uniform
- Dress Regulations
- Inspections

REFERENCES:
- *Army Cadet Force regulations - AC14233*
  (Version 3.2.0 - November 2022)
- *Army Cadet Syllabus - AC71101*
  (Version 1.2 - July 2022)
- *Army Cadets Military Knowledge Training Manual - AC72158*
  (Version 1 - 2021)
- *Army Dress Regulations (all ranks) Part 8 - CCF & ACF*

CHAPTER THREE: UNIFORM & APPEARANCE

WHAT IS ISSUED

All cadets are issued with full uniform which includes everything except boots. The uniform is the same as the British Army wears and is known as MTP-PCS.

- **MTP:** Multi Terrain Pattern (British Military camouflage pattern).
- **PCS:** Personal Clothing System.

Uniform and equipment is given on a long term loan basis which means that it always belongs to the MOD and must be returned when a cadet (or CFAV) leaves the Army Cadet Force.

ISSUED ITEMS

The following items are issued (subject to availability)

• **Socks** x 1 or 2 pairs	• **Beret, flash and badge** x 1
• **Trousers** x 1 or 2 pairs	• **Cadet rank slide** x 1
• **T-shirts** x 1 or 2	• **Belt & clips** x 1
• **Shirts** x 1 or 2	• **Fleece**
• **Combat smock** x 1	• **County/Affiliated unit badge**

BOOTS AND OTHER NON-ISSUED ITEMS

The only major items that are not issued and needs to be purchased are boots. These should ideally be brown but black is also acceptable. If not fully waterproof, boots should at least be water resistant.

Leather boots are good as they have a good resistance to water, offer adequate support and last a long time. For anyone who struggles to afford their own boots, they should talk to their Detachment Commander who may be able to get help through Area/County HQ.

Other items that are good to buy are as follows:

- Trouser twisters (tidies up bottoms of trousers).
- Extra socks suitable for extended wear.
- Boot cleaning kit.
- Hat, gloves & scarf in green or other suitable dark colour.

There are other items that may be required later but that becomes apparent as training progresses.

CHAPTER THREE: UNIFORM & APPEARANCE

PREPARING UNIFORM

When you receive your uniform there will be a few things that need to be done before you can wear it.

CLOTHING (TROUSERS, SHIRT, ETC.)

These should ideally be washed first but will at least require ironing before they can be worn. When ironing, remove ALL creases including straight creases down the front of trousers and sleeves of shirts.

Remove loose threads with some small scissors and use either the ties built in or your own 'twisters' to tidy the bottoms of trousers.

Trouser Twisters

Tucked inside trouser leg so bottom of trouser folds in and looks neat.

BELT SIZING & CLIP FITTING

A sturdy belt is issued with new uniform which needs to be adjusted to fit correctly. To do this hold the belt around your waist and fold the ends under until the folds meet around your middle. There are 2 clips that go left and right of the folds and 2 buckle parts that can then be fitted into the folds. To finish off, the clips can then be crimped into place and some of the excess belt can be cut off.

CHAPTER THREE: UNIFORM & APPEARANCE

BERET SHAPING

A new beret needs to be 'shaped' to get it the correct shape and fit for each individual. This involves dunking the new beret into warm and then cold water repeatedly until thoroughly soaked (avoid getting the leather band wet). It is then placed on the head and pulled over to the right side to create the correct shape. This should then be left to dry naturally before wearing.

CAP BADGE & FLASH

All berets have a cap badge over the left eye to show which regiment or corps they are linked to and some also have coloured 'flashes' behind them which are small pieces of cloth that are also linked to that regiment or corps.

To fit the flash (if required) fold the ends in to hide any rough cut edges and sew onto the front of the beret where the cap badge will go. Next, make small holes through the flash and beret to fix the cap badge. This must line up with a small leather strip inside the beret.

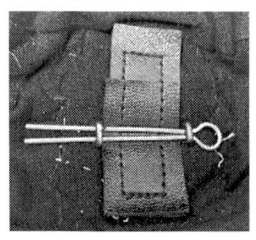

CHAPTER THREE: UNIFORM & APPEARANCE

BLANKING PLATE BADGES

On the sleeves of your combat shirt and smock are Velcro backed MTP patches called blanking plates. These are where you will add badges as you acquire them. The plate with the Union Flag goes on the left sleeve along with any county/area/sector badges you may be provided with. All other badges will then go on the right side.

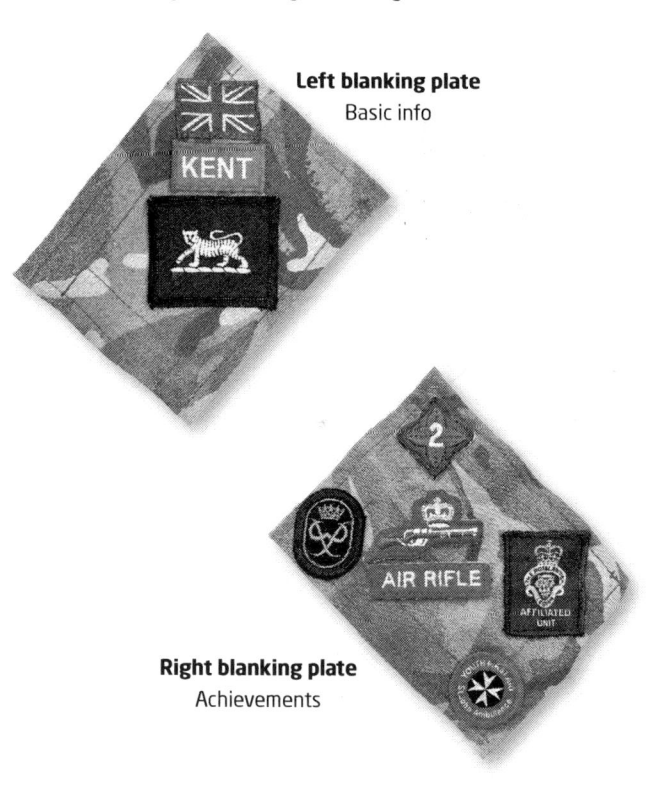

Left blanking plate
Basic info

Right blanking plate
Achievements

CHAPTER THREE: UNIFORM & APPEARANCE

WEARING UNIFORM

Military uniform needs to be looked after and maintained to a high standard and should not be mixed with civilian clothes.

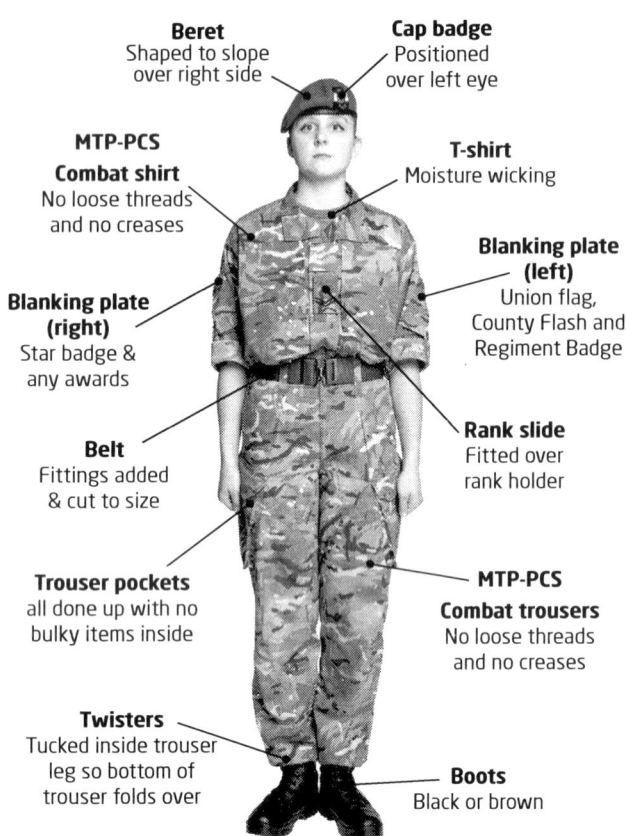

Beret
Shaped to slope over right side

Cap badge
Positioned over left eye

MTP-PCS
Combat shirt
No loose threads and no creases

T-shirt
Moisture wicking

Blanking plate (right)
Star badge & any awards

Blanking plate (left)
Union flag, County Flash and Regiment Badge

Belt
Fittings added & cut to size

Rank slide
Fitted over rank holder

Trouser pockets
all done up with no bulky items inside

MTP-PCS
Combat trousers
No loose threads and no creases

Twisters
Tucked inside trouser leg so bottom of trouser folds over

Boots
Black or brown

CHAPTER THREE: UNIFORM & APPEARANCE

MAINTAINING UNIFORM

Cadets and CFAVs are privileged to be allowed to wear the uniform of the British Army so the utmost respect must be shown.

Uniform must be kept clean and serviceable at all times and turnout and presentation should be impeccable. Regular inspections are carried out on parade nights to monitor this.

CLEANING, POLISHING & IRONING

Wash these in a washing machine on a medium setting:

- **Combat shirt** (empty pockets and remove blanking plates first)
- **Combat trousers** (empty pockets first)
- **Combat smock** (empty pockets and remove blanking plates first)
- **T-Shirts & socks**

Note: Trousers, shirts and jackets should be ironed to remove all creases. Avoid ironing any Velcro sections as these may melt.

Other items:

- **Boots** (use a good brand polish of the correct colour)
- **Beret** (brush off, but don't wash it with your other clothing)

Write your uniform sizes here for future reference:

Height:	Waist:
Seat:	Inside Leg:
Head:	Chest:
Shoe Size:	

CHAPTER THREE: UNIFORM & APPEARANCE

DRESS REGULATIONS

Being smart and well turned out while wearing uniform is essential, but there are a few other guidelines to help us all look our best. Army Dress Regulations and local policies have far more detail, but here are some general points:

SLEEVES

Shirt sleeves can be rolled up or left down depending on what each individual feels comfortable with and how warm the weather is. It is good when possible though, to make sure a group of cadets working together all do the same. When rolled up, sleeves need to be above the elbow. When rolled down, sleeves need to be uncreased with cuff buttons done up.

HEAD DRESS

When in uniform, your beret should be worn at all times except for in a few circumstances. You will remove your beret when going into a dining hall or when given permission to do so in lessons etc but there may also be times when head dress is removed for etiquette or religious reasons. If in doubt, ask!

CHARITY ITEMS

Poppies can be worn during the period of Remembrance. A single wristband from a recognised charity can also be worn when not on a formal parade.

CHAPTER THREE: UNIFORM & APPEARANCE

JEWELLERY

Watches are allowed when not on a formal parade and female cadets only can wear one stud earring in each ear. CFAVs are also allowed to wear wedding rings. No other jewellery is allowed.

HAIR

Hair must be neat, tidy, of a natural colour and must not be extreme or exaggerated. Hair must fit neatly within the beret and must not show below the brow of the beret or over the ears. Styles such as twists, corn rows or locks are acceptable but must be well groomed and conform to the points previously mentioned.

- **Male cadets:** Hair must be short enough to not reach the shirt collar.
- **Female cadets:** can wear their hair in a bun, single pony tail or in a braid. Hair must not be longer than the top of the belt and for certain activities, they may be asked to wear their hair in a more suitable way for safety reasons. Any hair nets, clips etc. must be of a similar colour to the hair.

FACIAL HAIR

Male cadets must be clean shaven at all times. Permission to have a moustache or beard can be granted to cadets or CFAVs by the County/Area/Sector Commandant, but would only normally be for medical or religious reasons.

MAKE UP

Female cadets only can wear subtle make up with no bright coloured nails etc. Male cadets are not allowed to wear any make up.

RELIGIOUS AND CULTURAL CONSIDERATIONS

The rules around wearing uniform are there to make sure we all show the appropriate respect for the uniform and make a good impression when out in public. There is flexibility in the regulations to cater for specific religious and cultural requirements though.

Full guidance and more detail is available in the Dress Regulations document.

CHAPTER THREE: UNIFORM & APPEARANCE

INSPECTIONS

On most parade nights a senior cadet or CFAV will inspect all cadets to make sure their turnout is up to standard. It is good to have two people carry out the inspection so that one can inspect and the other can take notes. Any corrections or improvements can then be monitored. This is not a long process and once everyone knows what is expected, it becomes just a formality with the occasional improvement required.

SEQUENCE

When inspecting start with the front of the front rank. Bring them to attention and then check the left side, centre and then right side of each cadet before moving onto the next.

Check from the top down. Check beret, hair, face and jewellery, t-shirt, shirt, blanking plates, sleeves, belt, trousers, ankles and bottoms of trousers and boots.

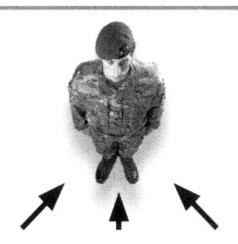

When at the end of the front rank move back along behind to check the back of the cadets.

Once the front rank have been checked front and back, they can then be stood at ease and the next rank bought to attention to repeat the process. Repeat this again for the rear rank (if there is one).

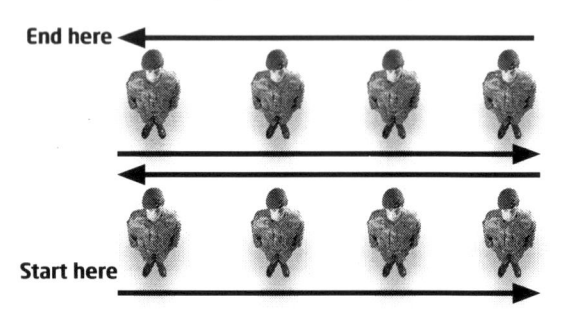

End here ←

Start here

CHAPTER FOUR
TRAINING & EVENTS

CONTENTS:
- Army Cadet Activities
- Army Cadet Events
- Getting Involved
- Staying Away

REFERENCES:
- *Army Cadet Force regulations - AC14233*
  (Version 3.2.0 - November 2022)
- *Army Cadet Syllabus - AC71101*
  (Version 1.2 - July 2022)
- *Army Cadets Military Knowledge Training Manual - AC72158*
  (Version 1 - 2021)
- *Army Cadet Resource Centre*

CHAPTER FOUR: TRAINING & EVENTS

ARMY CADET ACTIVITIES

Army cadets are able take part in a variety of activities locally and at various locations around the UK and abroad, not all of which are strictly military themed.

TYPES OF ACTIVITIES

Here is an overview of the types of activities that Army Cadets do:

- Specific military themed training and assessments in subjects such as Fieldcraft, Drill and Skill At Arms.
- Both military and civilian themed training and assessments in subjects such as First Aid, Navigation and Keeping Active.
- Adventurous Training, Expeditions and sports events.
- Social events, cultural visits and foreign trips.
- Community activities, parades and charity events.
- Specialist courses and qualification opportunities such as Duke of Edinburgh award, BTEC, Radio User and First Aid.
- Leadership and teaching courses.
- Annual camps that run for one or two weeks and combine many of the elements above.

All activities are designed to be enjoyable and engaging but also help to develop young people into confident young adults. Without becoming an Army Cadet, a lot of young people would never have these experiences.

DETACHMENT ACTIVITIES

All detachments around the UK parade once or twice per week. On these parade nights, there are various activities:

- Training and assessments in military and non-military subjects.
- Keeping Active and sports nights.
- Parade and drill practice.
- Social nights.

Most detachments are fairly limited to how much training can be delivered there so more advanced training takes place at other locations.

CHAPTER FOUR: TRAINING & EVENTS

ARMY CADET EVENTS

Some of the activities listed on the previous page can happen locally but more advanced training and bigger events tend to happen further away from home and sometimes even abroad.

DETACHMENT (CONTINGENT) EVENTS

- These can be local community events, parades, fundraising or extra training activities close to your detachment.
- Only open to cadets and staff from one or two detachments.
- Normally take place over just one day.

AREA (REGION) EVENTS

- Combined activities with other detachments in your local area.
- More in depth training events, adventurous training, cultural trips or possibly larger scale parades and fundraising.
- Training events tend to run for a whole weekend (Friday evening to Sunday afternoon) and are generally held on regular Army Camps/Training areas or at Cadet Training Centres.

COUNTY (BRIGADE) EVENTS

- More advanced training events for Senior Cadets.
- Large scale trips, events or parades.
- Annual Camps which run for up to two weeks at a large regular Army Establishment and cover a whole array of activities, training and exercises.
- Foreign visits and cadet exchanges.

NATIONAL EVENTS

- High level training for the most advanced cadets in the country.
- Huge organised trips and events such as battlefield tours and national parades.
- International trips, expeditions and training events in places such as Canada and Europe.

CHAPTER FOUR: TRAINING & EVENTS

GETTING INVOLVED

Apart from weekly parade night training, all events need to be booked onto. Cadets and CFAVs can do this through their Detachment Commander or through the Cadet Portal. There is sometimes a cost involved but this is not often very expensive.

FIND OUT ABOUT EVENTS

Major events are normally well publicised through detachments in the form of briefings, posters, social media posts and mail outs. For more specialist events and courses, some research may be needed.

- Local/Area/County Events: Social media, Cadet Portal, posters etc.
- Senior Cadet courses: Detachment Commander, Cadet Portal.
- Adventurous Training (AT) and Expeditions: Local and national social media, Cadet Portal and the Cadet Centre for Adventurous Training (CCAT) - www.armycadetadventure.co.uk
- CFAV courses: Cadet Portal or Westminster 'Course search'.

BOOKING ONTO EVENTS

For any events you want to take part in, you need to register your interest. Cadets and CFAVs can do this via their Detachment Commander or on the Cadet Portal. For specialist adult courses, CFAVs may need to request a space through their Detachment Commander who will then put this through to the Area Training Officer.

- **Pending:** Once you have been booked onto the event you will be listed as 'Pending' until you have paid (if payment is required). This does not guarantee you a place but lets the organisers know you wish to attend.
- **Accepted:** Once a place has been confirmed or, for events that require payment, once payment has been received your booking will be updated to 'Accepted'. This means that you are booked to attend.
- **CFAV courses:** Booking changes from 'Student' to 'Accepted' if you are accepted onto the course. Keep an eye on this as lots of courses have limited spaces so you may not always get onto the course you want.

CHAPTER FOUR: TRAINING & EVENTS

- **Payment**: Costs of events vary, but for a standard Area Weekend the cost will probably be around £20 and Annual Camp will probably be around £100 which offers extremely good value for money. Methods for payment vary around the country so ask your DC for details.
- **Closing date:** Each event has a cut off date for booking. This allows enough time for the organisers to arrange food, accommodation and transport. No extra bookings can be taken after this date and no refunds can be given as transport, food and accommodation is booked based on the number of cadets listed as attending on the closing date.

EVENT DETAILS - JOINING INSTRUCTIONS (JIs)

The details for each event will be quite different so information around dates, times, locations and kit required is always put into a document called Joining Instructions. This document should be available to download through the Cadet Portal or Westminster. Quite often Detachment Commanders will print copies out for cadets at their detachments.

Joining Instructions normally contain the following information:

- **Point of Contact (POC):** Contact details and address of the person organising the event.
- **Dates:** Start and end date of event.
- **Locations:** Event location along with and any drop off/pick up points for coaches etc. if event is not local. Full addresses with postcode and maps should be included.
- **Timings:** Drop off time for start and pick up time at end of event. Also includes any timings for specific elements that others may need to know (e.g. Parade for parents arrival time).
- **Outline and Aims:** What is happening during the event, what everyone is doing and what the overall aim of the event is.
- **Feeding Plan:** What meals are provided and what food needs to be taken by participants.
- **Bedding:** What the sleeping arrangements are and what bedding, if any, needs to be taken.
- **Kit List:** What to wear and what to pack. (Full kit list examples are in Chapter Five).

CHAPTER FOUR: TRAINING & EVENTS

EVENT PAPERWORK - CADETS

Cadets do not need to complete a lot of paperwork for events as a lot of information is collected on joining through the application process. There are still a few documents that may be required so refer to the Joining Instructions for details on this.

- **Parent Consent Form:** This one page document just asks parents/guardians to confirm that they are happy for their child to take part in the activities outlined. It also asks for up to date information around any medication, allergies and dietary requirements.
- **Physical Activity Readiness Questionnaire (PARQ) Form:** This is to confirm that parents/guardians are happy for their child to take part in activities such as AT and assault courses.
- **Specific forms:** For some activities such as an Adventurous Training package run by an external company, there may be extra consent forms required.

EVENT PAPERWORK - CFAVS

CFAVs do not generally need to complete paperwork when assisting or instructing on events, but there may be requirements when attending courses. There may also be pre-course training modules or other pre-requisites required to take part so make sure to check the Joining Instructions as soon as possible. Sometimes, failure to complete pre-course requisites will result in individuals being removed from the course. This is known as being Returned To Unit (RTU).

For CFAVs to plan and run events there are different levels of paperwork required depending on the complexity of the event. The few documents listed below are required for all events though.

- **Cadet Action Safety Plan (CASP):** This is a comprehensive document that includes all relevant information about an event. It includes basic information that you would find in the Joining Instructions along with a lot more detail around people involved, qualifications, timings, safety etc.
- **Main Event List (MEL):** Detailed timings for all stages of an event including meal times, lesson start/end times, lights out etc. (This can be included in the CASP).

CHAPTER FOUR: TRAINING & EVENTS

- **Risk Assessment (5010C - RA):** A comprehensive and realistic risk assessment document to highlight procedures and equipment needed to run a safe event. (This can be included in the CASP).

MEDICATION, ALLERGIES AND DIETARY REQUIREMENTS

All health issues or concerns need to be administered correctly by CFAVs while cadets are away so it is important that all up to date information is provided along with any medication.

- **Medication:** This need to be in its original packaging with dosage/regularity stated and must be handed directly from a parent/guardian to a CFAV. Cadets are not permitted to hand in medication or self medicate.
- **Dietary requirements:** These should be listed on each cadet's original application form when joining the Army Cadets, but up to date information is required for every event away. Requirements around allergies or religious beliefs can always be catered for but cadets that simply do not like certain foods cannot always be catered for.
- **Allergies:** As with medication, any issues need to be made known to CFAVs when booking onto the event and location of any items such as epipens should be made clear.

CHAPTER FOUR: TRAINING & EVENTS

STAYING AWAY

Going away for training weekends or longer events such as annual camp can be a bit daunting to start with but are so much fun that they soon become the best part of being an Army Cadet. For new cadets it can also be quite confusing knowing what to do, where to be and what to pack so here is a bit more information.

TRAVEL

How cadets get to different events depends entirely on the type and location of the event but, quite often, there will be a central location locally for cadets to be dropped off and minibuses or coaches will then take everyone to the final destination. If the training venue is local, cadets may just need to be dropped off directly.

FEEDING

Meals are always included in the cost of a training weekend or camp and will cover all main meals. If leaving on Friday evening, no meal will normally be provided until Saturday morning though, so it is advisable to take snacks.

Types of meals will depend on the venue and the type of training.

- **In Camp:** If in a regular army camp, meals will be provided in a 'cook house' which normally have various hot and cold meal options.
- **In the Field:** If doing fieldcraft training, meals will be in the form of 24 hour Operational Ration Packs (ORP). Full training is given on how to prepare everything and all meals are nutritionally balanced and filling.
- **Expeditions:** If out walking and potentially camping out, cadets get to choose and prepare their own meals. If cadets are required to take enough food with them for an event, training will be provided to the cadets on what to buy and details will be in the Joining Instructions.
- **NAAFI:** Just the same as when at detachment, there is quite often the opportunity to buy drinks and snacks when away too. It is a good idea to take a small amount of money away for this purpose.
- **Dietary Requirements:** These should be noted in the cadet's application to become an Army Cadet and on the event permission form.

CHAPTER FOUR: TRAINING & EVENTS

SLEEPING

Sleeping arrangements also depend on the type of activity and location.

- **In camp:** Cadets staying in a camp will normally sleep in rooms with multiple beds for up to around 20 people. Male and female accommodation blocks are separated and each have toilet, washing and shower facilities called 'ablutions'.

  Cadets are required to make their own beds and keep their bed spaces tidy. Some bedding may be provided but details of this will be in the joining instructions.

- **In the field:** If doing fieldcraft training, cadets will sleep outside under a 'basha' which is a shelter made from a type of plastic, camouflage sheet. Under the basha they will be in sleeping bags which will also be in waterproof 'bivvy' bags.

  All items are normally issued to cadets to use for the duration of their training. Items such as tent pegs, string or bungee cords which are also required may be issued or cadets may need to bring their own so check the joining instructions for clarification. If cadets want to buy their own sleeping bag, they need to be dark in colour and at least three season specification.

- **Expeditions:** On expeditions cadets normally get to camp out in civilian tents which are issued for the duration of the expedition. Cadets will also need sleeping bags which can be issued, but if cadets buy their own, they need to be at least three season specification.

CHAPTER FOUR: TRAINING & EVENTS

BEHAVIOUR AND CONDUCT

When cadets from different detachments and areas get together in larger numbers, things can be a little harder for CFAVs to manage so good conduct and behaviour needs to be of the highest standard. Younger cadets will be excited to be away and will need guidance from the more senior cadets.

A lot of training takes place on Regular Army training camps where there may well be Regular or Reserve Soldiers also training. It is therefore especially important to act in an appropriate manner and represent the Army Cadet Force in a good way.

With the number of cadets compared to the number of staff, it is not always possible to focus a lot of time on cadets who are disruptive or poorly behaved. <u>If after discussion and warnings, the cadet does not improve, it is likely that their parents/guardians will be called to collect them and disciplinary action can be looked at after the event.</u>

CHAPTER FIVE
KIT & EQUIPMENT

CONTENTS:
- Overview
- Wash Kits
- First Aid Kits
- Boot Cleaning & Sewing Kits
- Full Kit List: In Camp
- Full Kit List: In The Field
- Full Kit List: Expedition

REFERENCES:
- *Army Cadet Force regulations - AC14233*
  (Version 3.2.0 - November 2022)
- *Army Cadets Fieldcraft & Tactics Training manual - AC71966*
  (Version 1 - 2021)
- *Expedition Training Manual for Army Cadet Instructors - AC72149*
  (Version 2 - 2021)

CHAPTER FIVE: KIT & EQUIPMENT

OVERVIEW

Packing for an event can be a bit confusing as you want to have everything you might need but you don't want to pack so much that you can't carry it all, especially if you're going to be walking a long way with it. After a few events, it gets a lot easier as everyone learns through experience, but to start with, it is good to follow a suggested kit list. Remember, if you pack it you need to be able to carry it.

WHAT TO BUY

Uniform and a lot of kit is issued on long term loan or for the duration of an activity/event but there are certain items that cadets and CFAVs need to source themselves. No one is expected to spend a lot of money and there are welfare funds available for anyone who needs help so don't feel under pressure to go out and buy lots of expensive equipment.

Some cadets and CFAVs like to buy their own items to use instead of the issued items which is normally OK but it is worth checking with your detachment commander or event organiser as sometimes it is not permitted. If buying your own equipment make sure to get items that are up to the job and are suitable alternatives to what is issued.

KIT LISTS

A kit list is a list of items required for an event or activity. It can be used as a checklist when preparing and packing to go away and removes a lot of guess work.

This chapter has some suggested kit lists for various standard events. The quantity you pack will depend on the type of activity and the duration of the event. On longer camps there are washing facilities so clothes can be washed and ironed to avoid having to take enough to last the entire trip.

These kit lists will give you a general idea of what is required as well as what to buy and what should be issued. Always check the Joining Instructions for each event carefully though to make sure you have all you need. You may also need items from several different kit lists if you are doing a mixture of activities.

CHAPTER FIVE: KIT & EQUIPMENT

WASH KITS

Army Cadets are trained to be self sufficient and need to take ownership of their own personal hygiene. This is important so it is monitored to make sure it is happening and wash kits should be checked to make sure they are suitable and are being used.

For Army Cadet activities, two different wash kits are required.

1. FULL WASH KIT - IN CAMP

This is for use in camps where you have space in your room to keep a full size wash kit and have everything you will need for a time away. It can be the same as any wash kit you would take away on holiday or when staying away from home and should include the following items:

- Toothbrush
- Toothpaste
- Shower Gel Or Soap
- Deodorant
- Shampoo
- Comb Or Hairbrush
- Nail Clippers
- Towel(s)
- Flip Flops For Showers
- Sun Cream & After Sun
- Boys - Shave Gel & Razor
- Girls - Sanitary Items

2. SMALL WASH KIT - IN THE FIELD OR ON EXPEDITION

This is a small, compact wash kit that has less content and has travel size items that take up less space and weigh less. This is ideal for any activity away from camp where you will need to carry everything with you in a rucksack or bergan and should include the following items:

- Travel Toothbrush & Toothpaste
- Cleaning Wipes For Body & Face
- Deodorant (Odourless)
- Travel Mirror
- Comb Or Hairbrush
- Small Sun Cream & After Sun
- Insect Repellent
- Flannel &/Or Travel Size Towel
- Boys - Shave Gel & Razor
- Girls - Sanitary Items

Note: Foot powder is a good addition to both kits if walking a lot.

CHAPTER FIVE: KIT & EQUIPMENT

FIRST AID KITS

For all activities in the ACF there will be fully trained First Aid Staff along with a comprehensive First Aid Kit large enough for the number of people participating. Cadets and CFAVs simply need to carry a personal First Aid Kit to be able to self treat any minor injuries such as a small cut or graze etc.

Contents can be quite personal and include items that each individual thinks they might need. Contents can include:

- **Sterile wipes**
- **Disposable gloves**
- **Selection of plasters**
- **Blister plasters**
- **Various sized dressings**
- **Rolled bandages**
- **Triangular bandage**

- **Eye wash & eye dressing**
- **Survival (foil) blanket**
- **Mouth shield (for CPR)**
- **Insect bite relief**
- **Small scissors**
- **Tweezers**
- **Safety pins**

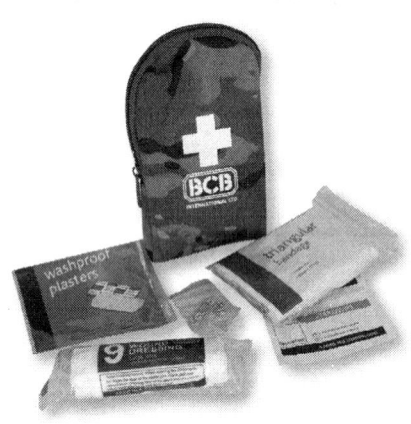

All prescription medication needs to be in the original packaging with dosage and regularity stated and be handed into a member of staff by a parent or guardian before the event.

CHAPTER FIVE: KIT & EQUIPMENT

BOOT CLEANING & SEWING KITS

As well as looking after personal health and hygiene, cadets also need to look after their kit and equipment so will need extra items to assist with this too.

BOOT CLEANING KIT

Keeping boots clean and well maintained will make them last a long time, but also helps waterproof them. When at detachment, on a camp or out in public, it also makes them look smart and professional.

Not much is needed in a boot cleaning kit but it should include the following items:

- **Cleaning cloth**
- **Small brush (to remove dirt)**
- **Polishing cloth**
- **Boot polish**
- **Polish application brush**
- **Polish removal brush**
- **Spare laces**

SEWING & REPAIR KIT

Repairing small rips and tears in clothing or carrying equipment can be quite easy and save a lot of hassle so taking a few items just in case is well worth it.

You only need a very small kit which can include the following items:

- **Needles**
- **Pins**
- **Safety pins**
- **Dark coloured cotton**
- **Various spare buttons**

Plus:

- **Small scissors & tweezers (if not in first aid kit)**
- **Cloth 'scapa' (sniper) tape**
- **Strong string or paracord**

CHAPTER FIVE: KIT & EQUIPMENT

FULL KIT LIST: IN CAMP

When staying in a camp, cadets sleep in large multi-person rooms, eat hot meals in a cook-house and conduct training in classrooms or outside, local to the camp. In the evenings there may be down time to socialise and there may be more than one activity taking place.

This means there are essential items required for any time away in a camp but there may also be specialist items required. As mentioned before, check the Joining Instructions for every specific event to make sure you have the right items with you.

All items should be packed into one large rucksack, bergan or case and a small daysack or rucksack. All personal items and both bags should be clearly labelled with the cadet's name and detachment.

Cadets are responsible for keeping their rooms clean and tidy and should also take responsibility for the security of any personal items.

ESSENTIALS

The following items will be required for almost any overnight activity in a camp.

- **Uniform**
  - Beret
  - T-shirts (enough for each day)
  - Shirt (+ spare if required)
  - Blanking plates
  - Rank slide
  - Smock
  - Belt
  - Trousers (+ spare if required)
  - Fleece
  - Socks (enough for each day)
  - Boots
- **Underwear**
  - Enough for each day
- **Small, Personal First Aid Kit**
- **Bedding** (check what is issued)
  - Sleeping bag or duvet cover and pillow case
- **Wash kit**
  - Full wash kit - see page 55
- **Boot cleaning & repair kits**
  - See page 57
- **Phone & charger**
  - Hand in to staff for security
- **Medication**
  - Handed into staff by parent or guardian
- **Water bottle & mug**
- **Notebook & pens**
- **Appropriate civilian clothing** (for evenings or trips)

CHAPTER FIVE: KIT & EQUIPMENT

OPTIONAL

The following items are optional based on personal preference or weather conditions.

- **Cold weather kit**
  - Hat
  - Gloves
  - Scarf (green, brown or black)
- **Sun cream & after sun**
  - If not already in wash kit
- **Money for NAAFI**
- **Pyjamas**
- **Foot powder**
- **Padlock**
  - For room lockers if available
- **Extension lead**
- **Clothes cleaning kit**
  - Washing machine tabs
    Travel iron
- **Alarm clock**
  - If not available on phone
- **Clothes hangers**

POTENTIAL EXTRAS

The following items may be required for specific activities but will be briefed to cadets beforehand.

- **Sports kit**
  - Trainers
  - Socks
  - Tracksuit bottoms or shorts
  - T-shirts
  - Track top or hoodie
- **Swimming kit**
  - Swimming costume/shorts
  - Towel
- **Adventurous training kit**
  - Old trainers
  - Tracksuit bottoms or similar
  - Old t-shirt/top
  - Towel
  - Items may get wet or damaged so take old items.
- **Waterproof clothing**

CHAPTER FIVE: KIT & EQUIPMENT

FULL KIT LIST: IN THE FIELD

When conducting fieldcraft training, cadets will normally be away from a fixed camp at a military training area usually made up of fields and woodland with the occasional farm building or village mock up. Cadets will therefore need to make shelter and will sleep outside. Full training on how to do this is given as part of the fieldcraft training and a lot of the equipment needed is issued so does not need to be bought. Joining Instructions for each event should give clearer guidance on this though.

ESSENTIALS

The following items will be required for almost any overnight activity out in the field. Extra clothing items may be required if weather is wet.

- **Uniform**
  - Beret
  - Bush hat (camouflage or green)
  - T-shirts (enough for each day)
  - Blanking plates
  - Rank slide
  - Smock
  - Belt
  - Trousers (+ spare if required)
  - Fleece
  - Socks (enough for each day)
  - Boots
- **Underwear & t-shirts**
  - Enough for each day
- **Cold weather kit** *(Dark colour)*
  - Hat
  - Gloves
  - Scarf
- **Dry bags (waterproof bags)**
  - To keep all kit dry
- **Water bottle & mug**
  - May be issued
- **Small, personal first aid kit**
  - See page 56
- **Boot cleaning & repair kit**
  - See page 57
- **Wash kit**
  - Small wash kit - see page 55
- **Medication**
  - Handed into staff by parent or guardian
- **Mobile Phone (safety only)**
  - Hand in to staff for security
- **Emergency whistle**
- **Notebook & pens**
- **Small torch with red filter**
- **20 - 30 meters of paracord**
  For communication cord & other fieldcraft uses
- **Rubbish bag**

CHAPTER FIVE: KIT & EQUIPMENT

All items should be packed into one large rucksack or bergan which can be provided by the cadet or may be issued. Clearly label all items of clothing and bags with full name and detachment. Any purchased items need to be adequate for use and should be dark colours such as green, brown or black.

ISSUED

The following items are normally issued to cadets for the duration of the event but it is a good idea to double check this.

- **Sleeping & shelter**
  - Sleeping bag - Dark colour and 3 - 4 season
  - Bivvy bag - Waterproof sleeping bag cover
  - Ground mat - Insulation from ground. Roll, fold or self inflate
  - Basha sheet - Camouflage or green waterproof sheet
  - Bungees x 4 - 6 or green string
  - Tent pegs x 6 - 8
- **Camouflage cream**
- **Carrying and load bearing**
  - Bergan or rucksack
  - Assault vest or webbing
- **Feeding**
  - Rations - food to last for the duration of event
  - Burner/cooker - for heating rations
  - Mess tins - for cooking
- **Waterproof jacket & trousers**
- **Compass**
- **Water bottle & mug**

CHAPTER FIVE: KIT & EQUIPMENT

FULL KIT LIST: EXPEDITION

There is a lot of choice when it comes to expedition clothing and equipment and getting it right will make the experience a lot more enjoyable. Safety and comfort should be the main factors when choosing items but weight, pack size and price are also major considerations.

DON'T BUY EVERYTHING

Before heading out to buy lots of new things, work out if you already own items that can be used such as ACF issue T-shirts which are moisture wicking and are ideal base layers. Also ask what items are loaned to you from your expedition organisers, as items such as tents and cookers are normally issued. If you do need to buy items, shop around and make sure to prioritise essentials over luxury items and, if you are still growing, avoid expensive items as you will probably need to renew them again at a later date.

THE FULL KIT LIST

You will be given a kit list of what to pack before any expedition and, for cadets taking part in the Duke of Edinburgh Award Scheme (DofE - see page 70),there is a specific kit list available through their website.

This also has more advice on what to buy along with a list of recommended shops which stock all required items and offer face to face advice.

Download the DofE kit list here:

https://www.dofe.org/shopping/dofe-expedition-kit-list/

The lists over the following pages give a good overview of what you will need. Some of the items listed and the quantities required will depend on the length of the expedition, the area being covered and the time of year, so plan ahead and make sure to pack all that you need without taking too much and adding unnecessary weight.

Be mindful of weather forecasts too, as weather can be unpredictable, especially in mountainous or hilly areas.

CHAPTER FIVE: KIT & EQUIPMENT

ESSENTIALS

The following items are required for almost any expedition.

- **Clothing**
  - Walking boots
  - Walking socks (for each day)
  - Underwear (for each day)
  - Base layer/T-shirts (for each day)
  - Walking trousers/shorts
  - Mid layer/fleece
  - Camp shoes or flip flops
  - Camp/bed clothes
  - Outer layer/jacket
- **Cold weather kit**
  - Hat
  - Gloves
  - Scarf
- **Warm weather kit**
  - Sun hat
  - Sun glasses
  - Sun cream & aftersun
- **Dry bags (waterproof bags)**
  - To keep all kit dry
- **Small, personal first aid kit**
  - See page 56
- **Medication**
  - Handed into staff by parent or guardian
- **Watch**
- **Mobile Phone (safety only)**
- **Emergency whistle**
- **Notebook & pens**
- **Head torch & spare batteries**
- **Boot cleaning & repair kit**
  - See page 57
- **Wash kit**
  - Small wash kit - see page 55
- **Food - To last trip**
  - Breakfasts
  - Lunches
  - Dinners
  - Snacks to last trip
  - Water bottle & mug
  - Emergency rations
  - Matches or lighter (for cooking)
  - Plastic bowl, plate & cup
  - Plastic cutlery - Known as KFS (Knife, Fork & Spoon).
- **Shared with group**
  - Washing up liquid
  - Cloth/scourer
  - Tea towel
  - Rubbish bag(s)
  - Toilet paper (& trowel)

CHAPTER FIVE: KIT & EQUIPMENT

OPTIONAL
The following items are based on personal preference.

- **Sleeping bag liner**
- **Walking sock liners**
- **Gaiters**
- **Head or neck scarf**
- **Water bladder**
- **Walking poles**
- **Personal survival bag**
- **Mosquito net**
- **Small amount of money**
- **Games or cards**

ISSUED
The following items are normally issued to cadets for the duration of the event but it is a good idea to double check this.

- **Personal items**
  - Rucksack
  - Sleeping bag
  - Sleeping mat
  - Waterproof trousers
  - Waterproof jacket
- **Group (shared) items**
  - Tent
  - Emergency/survival shelter
  - Map, map case & compass
  - Camping stove & fuel
  - Cooking pots & pans

CHAPTER SIX
PROGRESSION

CONTENTS:
- Overview
- Cadet Star Levels
- Cadet Rank Structure
- Cadet Qualifications
- Cadet Badges
- Advanced Cadet Roles
- Adult Rank Structure
- Adult Qualifications

REFERENCES:
- *Army Cadet Force regulations - AC14233 (Version 3.2.0 - November 2022)*
- *Army Cadet Syllabus - AC71101 (Version 1.2 - July 2022)*
- *Army Cadets Military Knowledge Training Manual - AC72158 (Version 1 - 2021)*
- *Westminster course search*

CHAPTER SIX: PROGRESSION

OVERVIEW

There are several ways that Army Cadets can progress in their time as a cadet, some of which show development in maturity and leadership as an Army Cadet, while others can carry over to the civilian world and help with further education or future employment.

CFAVs can also progress in lots of different ways too. The initial training given and subsequent experience of dealing with young people, delivering lessons and working in teams can develop some really important life skills that can help in the work place but there are lots of other opportunities to do courses and gain Army Cadet and civilian qualifications.

This chapter gives an overview of the progression routes and training opportunities for cadets and CFAVs but obviously cannot cover everything so make sure to do your own research and talk to your DC or chain of command.

CHAPTER SIX: PROGRESSION

CADET STAR LEVELS

By completing lessons and assessments in the Army Cadet Syllabus (ACS), cadets work towards passing star levels.

New cadets join as recruits that complete basic training. Once basic training has been completed, they are 'basic passed' cadets that then work towards passing one star training.

There are seven levels in total which are as follows:

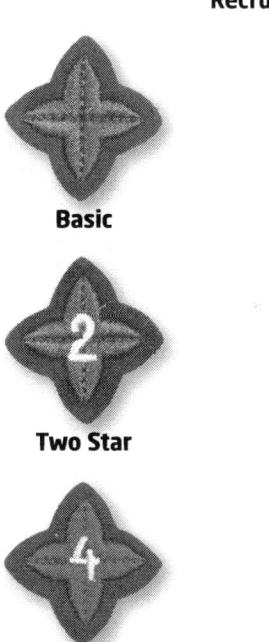

NO BADGE
Recruit

Basic

One Star

Two Star

Three Star

Four Star

Master Cadet

CHAPTER SIX: PROGRESSION

CADET RANK STRUCTURE

The British Army uses a rank structure to identify individuals that display leadership skills. The rank badge they wear shows their level of responsibility. Army Cadets use the same system which helps develop qualities of leadership and responsibility.

Although cadets need to be at certain star level to be eligible for different levels of promotion, ranks are awarded based on the individual's leadership potential and attitude. Cadets are not guaranteed promotion just for passing a star level.

Cadets that have a rank of Lance Corporal or above are referred to as 'Cadet NCOs' (Cadet Non-Commissioned Officers) and take responsibility and look after lower ranks. They can also assist with teaching and other detachment or area tasks.

Cadet
No rank

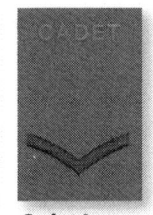

Cadet Lance Corporal
One star or above

Cadet Corporal
Two star or above

Cadet Sergeant
Three star or above

Cadet Staff Sergeant
Four star or above

Cadet Drum Major
Music units only

Cadet Sergeant Major
Four star or above

Cadet Regimental Sergeant Major
Highest rank

CHAPTER SIX: PROGRESSION

CADET QUALIFICATIONS

Being an Army Cadet will develop confidence and self discipline, but there are a few ways to get nationally recognised qualifications. These qualifications are open to everyone and where there is a cost involved, it is normally heavily subsidised or it is free to do.

FIRST AID

Cadets that complete First Aid training up to 3 or 4 star level can achieve qualifications through Voluntary Aid Societies such as St John Ambulance, St Andrew's Ambulance or the British Red Cross.

FIRST AID

NAVIGATION

Qualifications at a higher level can be achieved through the National Navigation Award Scheme (NNAS) and the British Orienteering Federation.

NNAS
a step in the right direction

SHOOTING

Awards from National shooting competitions can be achieved as well as recognition from the National Small-bore Rifle Association (NSRA).

NSRA
NATIONAL SMALLBORE RIFLE ASSOCIATION

COMMUNICATION & INFORMATION SYSTEMS (CIS)

Courses such as Cyber first, Cyber Defender and Cyber advanced teach CIS to a high standard that can carry over as qualifications to real life jobs in the industry.

CHAPTER SIX: PROGRESSION

BTEC (BUSINESS AND TECHNOLOGY EDUCATION COUNCIL)

BTECs are high-quality, career-focused qualifications grounded in the real world of work. This means BTEC learners develop and apply the knowledge, skills and behaviours that employers and universities are looking for. A large portion of the work required for these qualifications is covered within the Army Cadet Syllabus, meaning that very little additional work is required to complete them.

BTEC

CVQO (CADET VOCATIONAL QUALIFICATIONS ORGANISATION)

Cadets can complete achieve levels of CVQO awards which utilise key areas of standard cadet training with a small amount of top up work. These awards are nationally recognised and develop areas such as planning, teamwork and leadership.

CVQO

D OF E (DUKE OF EDINBURGH AWARD)

DofE is a youth awards programme that teaches the core subjects in life, team building, resilience and confidence. Using elements of the Army Cadet Syllabus, such as Expeditions and Community Engagement, a lot of what is done can go towards completing Bronze, Silver and Gold DofE awards. These awards are also greatly valued in the world of higher education and work.

AT (ADVENTUROUS TRAINING)

The Cadet Centre for Adventurous Training (CCAT) is the ACF & CCF Centre of Excellence for all AT training and offers beginner and intermediate courses as well as full qualification course. There is a list of activities available, a diary of events and course application forms.

Visit the website to find out more:

www.armycadetadventure.co.uk

CHAPTER SIX: PROGRESSION

CADET BADGES

When a cadet passes a full star level, they get a badge to go onto their right hand side uniform blanking plate to show what level they are at. There are other badges available for special achievements in certain subjects as well as for attendance at unique Army Cadet events.

SKILL AT ARMS (SAA) BADGES

Badges are issued for completing training on different weapon systems and then passing the subsequent 'Weapon Handling test' (WHT). Only the most advanced badge achieved can be worn.

| AIR RIFLE | .22 RIFLE | GP RIFLE | TGT RIFLE |

SHOOTING (SH) BADGES

Badges are issued for particularly good shooting. Requirements vary for each star level and the most recently achieved badge must be the only one worn.

Trained Shot
Achievable at basic level & above

Marksman
Achievable at one star level & above

Advanced Marksman
Achievable at four star level only

Badge backing colours
- **Olive backing:** Core shooting syllabus.
- **Red backing:** Elective (optional) target rifle programme.

FIRST AID (FA) BADGE

Badges are issued for completing two star First Aid training.

CHAPTER SIX: PROGRESSION

DUKE OF EDINBURGH (DOFE) BADGES

Badges are issued for fully completing Bronze, Silver or Gold DofE.

Fabric embroidered badges are issued to sew onto blanking plates.

The colour of the cotton on the embroidery shows what level (bronze, silver or gold) has been passed. Only the most advanced can be worn.

A metal pin badge is normally also issued for wear on civilian clothing.

COMMUNICATION & INFORMATION SYSTEMS (CIS) BADGES

There are three badges available for CIS training.

Radio
Achievable at two star level

NEW BADGE AVAILABLE SOON

Line
Achievable at three star level

Crossed Flags
Achievable at four star level

OTHER BADGES

Other badges available include the following:

- **Instructor qualifications:** For completing Junior or Senior Cadet Instructor Cadres (JCIC and SCIC)
- **County colours:** For representing a county in an activity or competition.
- **Expeditions or foreign trips:** Including the Royal Canadian Army Cadet (RCAC) exchange trip.
- **Specialist activities:** Including parachuting and large sports events.
- **Qualifications:** Including BTEC and CVQO awards.
- **Affiliations**: Including close links to the Royal British Legion (RBL).

CHAPTER SIX: PROGRESSION

ADVANCED CADET ROLES

As cadets progress through the star levels and achieve promotions, they are given more responsibility at their home detachment and are then expected to also assist more on area and county training events. For the most senior cadets there are specific roles available.

DUTY NCO

On standard detachment parade nights, it is common for one of the cadet NCOs to act as 'Duty NCO' for the evening. Duties can include calling all other cadets onto parade, carrying out a uniform inspection and monitoring timings for breaks and parades.

DETACHMENT SENIOR CADET

The most senior cadet(s) in each detachment tend to be given extra responsibility and is/are a point of contact for junior cadets. They can act as a go between for cadets and staff, can deliver lessons and will normally oversee the duty NCO each night.

AREA CADET SERGEANT MAJOR

One cadet per area is normally promoted to the rank of Area Sergeant Major. This is a prestigious role that shows how well a cadet has done. On area and County training events the Cadet Area Sergeant Major is responsible for tasks such as getting cadets on parade, moving large bodies of cadets around camp and ensuring discipline and dress standards are at the required level.

COUNTY CADET REGIMENTAL SERGEANT MAJOR

This is the pinnacle role for a cadet to achieve and very few can make it this far. One senior cadet from an entire County is given the role of Cadet Regimental Sergeant Major (Cadet RSM). They have extra duties above that of an Area Sergeant Major and may also be required for ceremonial events and visits. They are also quite often responsible for meeting and greeting important visitors and dignitaries.

STAFF CADET

When a cadet reaches 18 years old they have to end their time as a cadet. Cadets are allowed to re-join the organisation as an instructor, or, between the ages of 18 and 21, they can stay on as a Staff Cadet which allows them to continue certain cadet activities.

CHAPTER SIX: PROGRESSION

ADULT RANK STRUCTURE

CFAVs have a similar rank structure to that of cadets, but there is no Lance Corporal or Corporal rank so, after initial training, they become a Sergeant Instructor (SI) straight away.

PROBATIONARY INSTRUCTORS

After joining the Army Cadets and completing all relevant documentation and checks a new CFAV completes a familiarisation weekend and then becomes a Probationary Instructor and works towards becoming a Sergeant Instructor (SI).

(More info on this process is in Chapter One).

Probationary Instructor (PI)
Phase one

Probationary Instructor (PI)
Phase two
(After IIC)

CFAV PROMOTIONS

After passing PI training, CFAVs are promoted to Sergeant Instructor and become Non-Commissioned Officers (NCOs).

Beyond this, there are lots of opportunities to gain more qualifications, specialise in subjects and take on more responsibility which can all result in promotion.

CHAPTER SIX: PROGRESSION

NON-COMMISSIONED OFFICERS (NCOS)

Just as with Lance Corporals and Corporals, Sergeant Instructors are 'Non-Commissioned Officers' (NCOs) meaning they have obtained their rank through internal promotion rather than being 'Commissioned' by the Sovereign (the King).

- Sergeant Instructors are referred to as 'Sergeant' or 'Sarnt'.
- Staff Sergeants are referred to as 'Staff'.

Sergeant Instructor (SI)

Staff Sergeant

WARRANT OFFICERS (WO)

The next level of promotion for NCOs is to that of a Warrant Officer class one or class two. Warrant officers are also not Commissioned by the Sovereign to do their job, but do receive a Warrant from an official source such as the Secretary of State for Defence. They are referred to as 'Sir' or 'Ma'am' but are not saluted.

Sergeant Major
Warrant officer class two (WO2)

Quarter Master Sergeant Major
Warrant Officer class two (WO2)

Regimental Sergeant Major
Warrant Officer class one (WO1)

CHAPTER SIX: PROGRESSION

COMMISSIONED OFFICER TRAINING

Anyone wanting to become an officer starts of as an Adult Under Officer (AUO) and works through a series of interviews and assessments to become a 'Second Lieutenant'. This is a probationary rank where the officer will then have around two years to complete Initial Officer Training (IOT) to gain the full officer rank of Lieutenant.

Officers receive a scroll signed by the King, Commissioning them to carry out their job. This is why they are known as 'Commissioned Officers'. They are referred to as 'Sir' or Ma'am' and are saluted.

Adult Under Officer (AUO)

Second Lieutenant

Lieutenant Full officer

COMMISSIONED OFFICER PROMOTIONS

From the rank of Lieutenant, there are several promotion opportunities that go with more senior jobs within the organisation. There is normally a two year period required between ranks and there is a possibility of going back down a rank if stepping down from a specific job.

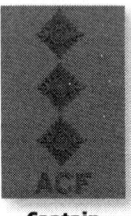

Captain

Major

Lieutenant Colonel

Colonel

CHAPTER SIX: PROGRESSION

ADULT QUALIFICATIONS

Having passed all initial training and qualified as a Sergeant Instructor, CFAVs are allowed to teach most basic, one and two star subjects. There are exceptions though and some subjects need to be taught by instructors who have attended and passed specialist courses.

Passing specialist courses allow CFAVs to do the following:

- Teach specialist subjects such as Skill At Arms.
- Run activities such as ranges or obstacle courses.
- Lead events such as Adventurous Training or Expeditions.
- Be eligible for promotion.
- Take on specialist Area or County roles (see chapter two - 'structure & organisation' for more details on other roles).

The next few pages give a brief overview of what is available:

FIRST AID

To act as a first aider for an event, CFAVS need to have passed and be in date with either the 'Emergency First Aid At Work' (EFAAW) or the full 'First Aid At Work' (FAAW) qualification. The full FAAW qualification also allows CFAVs to teach First Aid up to two star level.

Other courses are available to allow CFAVs to teach three and four star First Aid and/or to allow progression to become the Area or County First Aid Training Advisor (CFATA) or the County Medical Support Officer' (MSO).

ADVENTUROUS TRAINING

Lots of courses are available through cadet counties or the 'Cadet Centre for Adventurous Training (CCAT). Courses vary in activity and level and include things such as kayaking, climbing, mountain biking archery and mountain walking.

OBSTACLE COURSE SUPERVISOR (OCS)

Allows CFAVs to plan and run standard obstacle courses. Participants need to be fit and healthy as the course is fairly demanding.

CHAPTER SIX: PROGRESSION

SKILL AT ARMS INSTRUCTOR (SAAI) COURSE

CFAVs are not permitted to teach any lessons on any weapon system without having first attended and passed the week long SAAI course at Frimley Park. This is a tough course so a good knowledge and understanding of the weapons used in the ACF is a requirement. Some areas insist on a locally run 'pre-SAAI' course to make sure candidates are at the required level before booking them onto an official course.

SHOOTING (SH) COURSES

There are several courses available for CFAVs wanting to get involved in shooting activities. Involvement starts with assisting with range duties, being a safety supervisor and coaching firers. Training can ultimately lead to becoming a Range Conducting Officer (RCO) being fully qualified to plan and run anything from an air rifle range to running full military short or long ranges.

- **Shooting & coaching:** Sometimes done as part of PI training, this course teaches how to effectively coach someone shooting and be able to give them advice on how to improve.
- **Dangerous Goods Awareness - DGA:** Allows handling and movement of all types of ammunition.
- **Range duties - SA (K) (07) Cadet:** Allows CFAVs to act as safety supervisors and carry out other duties on a range of any size.
- **Short Range qualification - SA (SR) (07) Cadet:** Allows CFAVs to run short (25m) and air rifle ranges.
- **Long range qualification - SA (LR) (07) Cadet:** Allows those with a SR qualification to run long (100m+) ranges.
- **Dismounted Close Combat Trainer (DCCT) Basic Operator:** Allows CFAVs to run an indoor, live firing simulator.

CHAPTER SIX: PROGRESSION

FIELDCRAFT 'ECO' QUALIFICATION - SA (M) (07) CADET

Fieldcraft is a great activity for all CFAVs to teach, but for those that want to plan and run blank firing exercises they will need to complete a week-long 'Event Co-ordinating Officer' (ECO) course at Frimley Park. This teaches CFAVs all of the safety and planning requirements to safely run blank firing exercises. The course is great fun and is mostly practical and gives CFAVs the extra confidence to run their own events.

NAVIGATION - NNAS

Navigation qualifications are available to cadets and CFAVs through the National Navigation Award Scheme (NNAS) and the British Orienteering Federation. NNAS awards offer bronze, silver and gold navigator awards as well as a tutor award. Each course develops confidence and allows CFAVs to teach and assess to a higher level.

EXPEDITION - ACS & DOFE

CFAVs should complete the DofE induction course as part of their PI training which allows them to assist on Expeditions. Most counties run training course that allow CFAVs to teach and assess syllabus Expedition. Further specific DofE training will also qualify them to plan and run DofE expeditions and assess at various levels.

CHAPTER SIX: PROGRESSION

COMMUNICATION & INFORMATION SYSTEMS (CIS)

Basic, Intermediate and Advanced CIS instructor courses are available to allow CFAVs to teach and assess cadets and adults using the various radio systems used by the Army Cadets.

MANAGEMENT & LEADERSHIP

There are several courses designed to develop CFAVs leadership skills which are invaluable as more senior roles are taken on. From Becoming a 2IC or Commander of a detachment through to Area HQ roles and then County roles, these skills become more and more important.

- **Adult Leadership & Management (ALM):** This is the first level of Army Cadet leadership and is ideal for those taking on leadership roles at detachment level or when starting to plan and run events.
- **Initial Officer Training (IOT):** For new officers learning the skills required to take on more demanding leadership roles.
- **King George the Sixth Leadership course (KGVI):** This course helps to prepare Officers and Warrant Officers for more senior roles such as Area Sergeant Major, Training Officers and Staff Officers.
- **Area Commanders course:** Prepares more senior officers to take on the role of area commander.
- **Commandant & Senior officer course:** Prepares officers moving into the highest levels of Army Cadet leadership.
- **Cadet Vocational Qualifications Organisation (CVQO):** All Army Cadet leadership courses tie in with CVQO qualifications. CFAVs can earn various levels in qualification that are all nationally recognised in the workplace and can be a real asset when applying for jobs.

CHAPTER SEVEN
ARMY CADET SYLLABUS (ACS)

CONTENTS:
- Introduction
- Recruit Cadet (Basic Training)
- Basic Cadet (One Star Training)
- One Star Cadet (Two Star Training)
- Two Star Cadet (Three Star Training)
- Three Star Cadet (Four Star Training)
- Four Star Cadet (Master Cadet Eligible)

REFERENCES:
- *Army Cadet Force regulations - AC14233*
  (Version 3.2.0 - November 2022)
- *Army Cadet Syllabus - AC71101*
  (Version 1.2 - July 2022)
- *Army Cadets Military Knowledge Training Manual - AC72158*
  (Version 1 - 2021)
- *Army Cadet Resource Centre*

CHAPTER SEVEN: ARMY CADET SYLLABUS (ACS)

INTRODUCTION

The backbone of the Army Cadet experience is the Army Cadet Syllabus (ACS) which covers an array of military and non-military subjects in a progressive manner. Cadets start as recruits working on basic training before then working through training at star levels one to four. For those cadets that do well and stick with the ACF long enough, they can then complete Master Cadet training.

Here are the main subjects of the ACS along with their abbreviation:

- **MK:** Military Knowledge
- **DT:** Drill & Turnout
- **FC:** Fieldcraft & tactics
- **NAV:** Navigation
- **EXP:** Expedition
- **SAA:** Skill At Arms
- **SH:** Shooting
- **FA:** First Aid
- **CE:** Community Engagement
- **KA:** Keeping Active
- **AT:** Adventurous Training
- **CIS:** Communication & Information Systems

Cadets do lessons and assessments in these subjects at each star level that develop in complexity as the cadet progresses. Certain subjects become elective (optional) at higher star levels and four star training cadets just work on two subjects of their choice.

ARMY PROFICIENCY CERTIFICATE (APC)

The current syllabus (ACS) was launched in 2021 to replace the old Army Proficiency Certificate (APC) Syllabus that had been in place for many years. The roll out of the new syllabus is planned to take until the end of 2023 so some areas around the country may still work to the old APC Syllabus as they make the transition. As cadets and CFAVS, it is important to know which is being used in your area and resources are still available for both.

MUSIC

Some detachments around the Country are designated as Music Detachments that train and develop the Drum Corps, Pipes and Bands of the Army Cadets. Cadets following this route complete basic training the same as all other cadets but then move into a completely different music syllabus that also runs from one to four star. More details on this are in chapter 21.

CHAPTER SEVEN: ARMY CADET SYLLABUS (ACS)

STAR LEVELS

Information about cadet progression through star levels are in Chapter Six, but over the next few pages is a breakdown of what is required at each star level. More detail about each individual subject is contained in the later, lesson specific chapters.

RECRUIT CADET = BASIC TRAINING (Junior Cadet)

All subjects are compulsory for basic training	
Subject	Specialist qualifications beyond AIC to teach/assess
MK:	-
DT:	-
FC:	-
NAV:	-
EXP:	-
SAA:	SAAI
SH:	RCO: SA (SR) (07) Cadet Safety: SA (K) (07) Cadet First Aid: EFAAW or FAAW
FA:	FAAW
CE:	-
KA:	-
AT:	-
CIS:	-

Badges Achievable

AIR RIFLE
OR
.22 RIFLE

CHAPTER SEVEN: ARMY CADET SYLLABUS (ACS)

BASIC CADET = ONE STAR TRAINING (Junior Cadet)

All subjects are compulsory for one star training	
Subject	Specialist qualifications beyond AIC to teach/assess
MK:	-
DT:	-
FC:	ECO required for blank firing: SA (M) (07) Cadet
NAV:	-
EXP:	Stove lesson requires an approved instructor
SAA:	SAAI
SH:	RCO: SA (SR) (07) Cadet Safety: SA (K) (07) Cadet First Aid: EFAAW or FAAW
FA:	FAAW
CE:	-
KA:	-
AT:	AT trained staff or approved external company
CIS:	CIS basic instructor for radio lessons

Badges Achievable

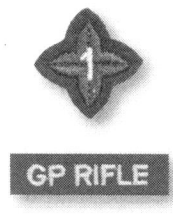

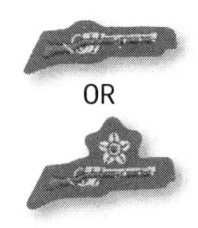

GP RIFLE

OR

CHAPTER SEVEN: ARMY CADET SYLLABUS (ACS)

ONE STAR CADET = TWO STAR TRAINING (Junior Cadet)

Compulsory subjects	
Subject	Specialist qualifications beyond AIC to teach/assess
MK:	-
DT:	-
FC:	ECO required for blank firing: SA (M) (07) Cadet
NAV:	-
EXP:	Stove lesson requires an approved instructor Exped supervisor to assess
SAA:	SAAI
SH:	RCO: SA (SR) (07) Cadet Safety: SA (K) (07) Cadet First Aid: EFAAW or FAAW
FA:	FAAW
CE:	-
KA:	-
Optional (elective) subjects	
AT:	AT trained staff or approved external company
CIS:	CIS basic instructor

Badges Achievable

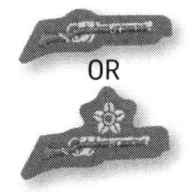

OR

CHAPTER SEVEN: ARMY CADET SYLLABUS (ACS)

TWO STAR CADET = THREE STAR TRAINING (Senior Cadet)

Compulsory subjects	
Subject	Specialist qualifications beyond AIC to teach/assess
DT:	-
FC:	ECO required for blank firing: SA (M) (07) Cadet
NAV:	NNAS Silver
SAA:	SAAI
SH:	RCO: SA (LR) (07) Cadet Safety: SA (K) (07) Cadet First Aid: EFAAW or FAAW
JCIC	-

Plus two of the following (cadet choice)	
MK:	-
EXP:	Stove lesson requires an approved instructor Exped supervisor to assess
FA:	Army Cadet registered trainer/assessor
CE:	-
KA:	-
AT:	AT trained staff or approved external company
CIS:	CIS intermediate instructor

Badges Achievable

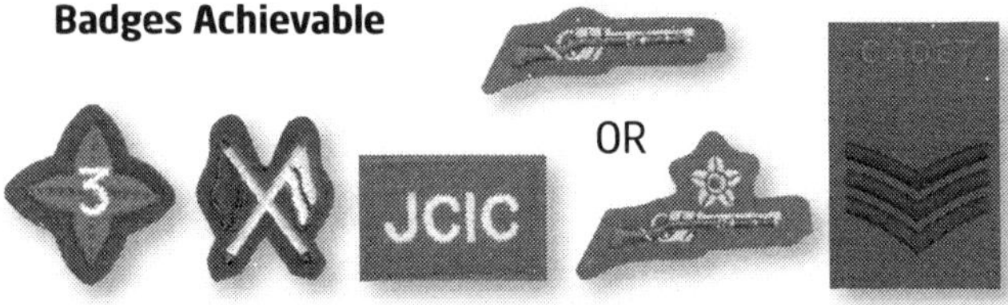

OR

CHAPTER SEVEN: ARMY CADET SYLLABUS (ACS)

THREE STAR CADET = FOUR STAR TRAINING (Senior Cadet)

Any two subjects/activities	
Subject	Specialist qualifications beyond AIC to teach/assess
DT:	County RSM
FC:	ECO required for blank firing: SA (M) (07) Cadet
NAV:	NNAS Silver
EXP:	Stove lesson requires an approved instructor Exped supervisor to assess
SAA:	SAAI
SH:	RCO: SA (LR) (07) Cadet Safety: SA (K) (07) Cadet First Aid: EFAAW/FAAW
FA:	ACCT UK trainer/assessor
CE:	-
AT:	At trained staff or approved external company
CIS	CIS intermediate instructor to teach CIS advanced instructor to assess
SCIC	Cadet Training Team only
The following activities also count towards the requirement	
Royal Canadian Army Cadet (RCAC) Leadership Challenge Course	
RCAC Expedition Instructor Course	
Canadian National Army Cadet Full Bore Marksmanship Course	
Fitness & Sport Instructor course	
CVQO Level 3 ILM	

CHAPTER SEVEN: ARMY CADET SYLLABUS (ACS)

Badges Achievable

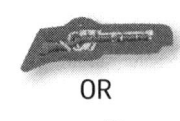

OR

OR

FOUR STAR CADET = MASTER CADET ELIGIBLE (Senior Cadet)

Fully four star passed cadets that hold the rank of sergeant or above are eligible to take part in a week long Master Cadet course held at Frimley Park. All training and assessments are included in the course.

Badges Achievable

CHAPTER EIGHT
INSTRUCTIONAL TECHNIQUES

CONTENTS:
- Cadet Force Instructional Techniques (CFIT) - Introduction
- Overview Of CFIT Lessons
- Stage 1: Identify The Need For Training
- Stage 2: Plan & Prepare The Training
- Stage 3: Deliver The Training
- Stage 4: Assess The Cadets
- Stage 5: Evaluate Training & Implement Improvement

REFERENCES:
- *Army Cadet Syllabus - AC71101 (Version 1.2 - July 2022)*
- *CFIT Handbook & Accompanying Presentations/Lesson plans*
- *Army Cadet Resource Centre via Westminster*

CHAPTER EIGHT: INSTRUCTIONAL TECHNIQUES

CADET FORCE INSTRUCTIONAL TECHNIQUES

All CFAVs and senior cadets receive training in Cadet Force Instructional Techniques (CFIT). The CFIT package is a combination of the CFIT Handbook and a series of ten lessons.

The aim of the CFIT package is to provide the adult instructor and senior cadet instructor with the knowledge, skills and attitudes to deliver the best training possible to cadets.

CFIT LESSONS

The following ten lessons are delivered at different levels of CFAV or cadet training.

CFAVs during BIC & IIC training and three star training cadets during JCIC training:

1. Introduction to Cadet Forces Instructional Techniques.
2. Introduction to planning and preparing training.
3. Introduction to delivering training and assessing cadets performance.
4. Introduction to evaluating training and identifying improvements.
5. Introduction to and planning & preparing a skills lesson.
6. Delivery, assessment & evaluation of skills lessons.

CFAVs during AIC training and four star cadets during SCIC training:

7. Instructional techniques.
8. Planning & preparing training.
9. Delivering effective training.
10. Assessment & evaluation of training.

CFIT LESSONS + CFIT HANDBOOK = CFIT PACKAGE

CADET FORCES INSTRUCTIONAL TECHNIQUES (CFIT)

INSTRUCTOR HANDBOOK

FOR THE ACF AND CCF (ARMY SECTION)

CHAPTER EIGHT: INSTRUCTIONAL TECHNIQUES

OVERVIEW OF CFIT LESSONS

IMPORTANT: The rest of this chapter contains some key points from the CFIT lessons but DOES NOT cover all material in depth so is for revision or interest only.

PRINCIPLES FOR EFFECTIVE CADET INSTRUCTION

The underpinning ideal for all Army Cadet lessons is based on three simple principles referred to as SEA:

S: Safety: All training must, above all, be safe for all involved.

E: Enjoyment: All training must be enjoyable to be successful.

A: Achievement: All training must result in achievement.

The idea is that if all training is safe and enjoyable, cadets will achieve results and develop.

INSTRUCTOR STANDARDS

A good instructor needs to:

- Know their subject matter.
- Know about good training and instructional techniques.
- Be able to perform skills they are instructing.
- Be able to plan and deliver training.
- Have a positive attitude to material and audience.

CHAPTER EIGHT: INSTRUCTIONAL TECHNIQUES

SOURCE MATERIAL

When planning lessons, it is important to research properly using the official source documents provided in the Army Cadet Resource Centre.

For all lessons there are two documents to refer to:

1. **The Army Cadet Syllabus - AC71101**
   This outlines the lessons required for each subject at every star level along with qualifications required to teach, any pre-requisites and the assessment criteria.

2. **Subject training manual - (various codes)**
   Every subject within the ACS has its own training manual (ACS Drill Manual, ACS Fieldcraft Manual etc). These have all the required information for every lesson within their specific subject.

Information within this pocketbook and other cadet handbooks are for reference and should be used as an 'aide memoir' only. Always refer to the official manuals.

FIVE STEPS TO EFFECTIVE INSTRUCTION

The following diagram shows the 5 steps for effective training:

1. Identify the need for training
2. Plan & prepare the training
3. Deliver the training
4. Assess the trainees
5. Evaluate the training & implement improvements

These five steps are explained in a bit more detail over the next few pages.

CHAPTER EIGHT: INSTRUCTIONAL TECHNIQUES

1. IDENTIFY THE NEED FOR TRAINING

To find out what lessons to teach cadets there are a few options:

- Looking on Westminster to view cadets progress.
- Keeping records at detachment on what lessons have been delivered to what cadets.
- Asking cadets what they have covered already.
- Observing cadets carrying out certain activities.

When deciding what lessons to prepare, don't teach your trainees a subject or part of subject that they have been taught before, or something which is above their level of understanding.

2. PLAN AND PREPARE THE TRAINING

THE SIX PS

Prior Planning & Preparation Prevents Poor Performance

Planning and preparing lessons is an extremely important part of the process and time spent on this will ensure the three principles of Army Cadet instruction are achieved (Safety, Enjoyment, Achievement). Lack of time spent on this will result in poor lessons and results.

AUDIENCE

Think about who you will be teaching and consider the age, star level and previous experience when organising lesson material.

AIM

Have a clear aim for your lesson that is **CRAM:**

C: Clear - Use minimal words to clearly explain your aim.

R: Relevant - The aim should be relevant to the audience and the ACS subject material.

A: Achievable - The aim should be achievable within the time-scale of the lesson by the audience being taught. Don't attempt too much.

M: Measurable - Make sure that what is being taught can be assessed to measure progress and achievement.

CHAPTER EIGHT: INSTRUCTIONAL TECHNIQUES

By The End Of This Lesson You Will Be Able To...

Start all lesson aims with this statement as it is positive and direct and ensures your aim has an measurable goal.

Examples:

By the end of this lesson you will be able to...

... correctly fit a sling onto the L98 A2 Cadet GP rifle.

... identify all badges of rank that Army Cadets wear.

... polish your boots correctly.

LESSON STRUCTURE

All lessons should follow the same simple format.

- **Introduction 10%:** General introduction including safety points and lesson aim.
- **Main Body 80%:** The main delivery of lesson content. The main body can be broken down into different sections.
- **Conclusion 10%:** Summary of the lesson, brief revision and assessment of cadet's understanding.

Lesson times are normally 40 minutes to include setting up and packing away so always try and allocate timings to each part of your lesson to avoid running out of time.

LESSON TYPES

ACS training is designed to be practical rather than classroom-based, whenever possible. The training should be interesting, imaginative and purposeful and include competitions, exercises and games.

There are two main formats that are used to deliver lessons.

- **Theory:** Normally classroom based and delivered in the form of presentations or lectures. Theory lessons can still involve breakout groups and practical tasks and games to keep lessons engaging.
- **Practical:** Can be indoors or outdoors and cover practical skills such as drill and shooting. Skills are explained and demonstrated before cadets get to imitate and then practice.

CHAPTER EIGHT: INSTRUCTIONAL TECHNIQUES

LESSON CONTENT

Identify and organise the content. The content must be from the Army Cadet Syllabus and the relevant training manual. Ensure that you are up to date with the content, as subject matter does change over time.

Decide the following:

- How to deliver (lecture, game, presentation, practical lesson).
- Where to deliver (indoors, outdoors, specific room or location).
- What materials & kit are required (handouts, props, stationary etc.).
- How to assess (quiz, written test, game etc.).

LESSON PREPARATION

Once the lesson has been planned, it is important to spend time preparing and setting up for the lesson. Carry out tasks such as setting up a projector and laying out chairs and tables before any cadets arrive. Also take time to rehearse and practice your lesson.

LESSON PLANS

On the next page is an example of a lesson plan. These are essential tools for planning and delivering lessons. They are simple template documents that are laid out in a logical order to help instructors structure their lessons correctly and cover all elements of the lesson.

Lesson plans should be used for every lesson and can be printed out and then filled in by hand or can be edited on a computer and then printed out. It is not necessary to have too much information written as the lesson plan is there as a guide and not an in depth script.

- **Section 1:** This is where you make notes on introductory information such as lesson title, aim, revision, safety points etc.
- **Section 2:** This is for bullet points and brief notes on the main lesson content. This can be broken down into sections (a, b, c etc.) and does not need to be too in depth.
- **Section 3:** This is for the conclusion of the lesson and includes a summary and notes on how to assess cadets.

Example blank lesson plan over page

CHAPTER EIGHT: INSTRUCTIONAL TECHNIQUES

BASIC LESSON PLAN

LESSON TOPIC:	Badges of Rank
DESCRIPTION OF GROUP TO BE INSTRUCTED:	Six basic cadets at detachment
NEED FOR TRAINING:	To understand the ACF rank structure and to progress through basic Military Knowledge training

Ser	Content	Time (mins)	Remarks
1	INTRODUCTION		
	Revision: Values & standards of the Army Cadets Aim of lesson/session: By the end of this lesson you will be able to identify the different ranks of the ACF Safety points: Fire exits	4	Include personal intro, question policy, note taking and ground rules
2	MAIN BODY - DEVELOPMENT		
a.	Rank structure - Army & Cadet Force	2	Use Powerpoint for lesson delivery
b.	Officer ranks	5	
c.	NCO ranks	5	
d.	Compliments & history of rank	4	
3	CONCLUSION		
	Summary: You now understand the ACF rank structure and know who to salute. Assessing cadets: Group exercise arranging rank slides in order. Look forward: Structure of the ACF area and detachment.	10	Packs of rank slides in groups to assess. Arrange in order and then name all ranks.

CHAPTER EIGHT: INSTRUCTIONAL TECHNIQUES

3. DELIVERY OF THE TRAINING

The following 'CRAVED' can help with effective delivery of lessons:

C: Confidence - Research your lesson content so you know it well. Talk in a clear and positive manner and stay in control.

R: Rapport - Engage with your audience and relate to the group you are instructing. Be friendly and develop a good relationship.

A: Attitude - Develop mutual respect and remember you are a role model to the group you are instructing.

V: Voice - Speak slowly and clearly and adjust the tone of your voice to create interest and avoid sounding flat and uninteresting.

E: Enthusiasm - Be enthusiastic about the subject you are teaching even if you do not find it interesting yourself.

D: Distractions - Make sure your teaching area is free of any physical distractions and avoid any mannerisms that could be distracting (constantly saying a particular word such as 'right', 'ok', 'er' or 'so' can become distracting to the people you are teaching).

PRACTICAL LESSON TECHNIQUE

Practical lesson are taught using the **EDIP** method:

E: Explanation: A verbal description of a movement or skill. Instructor should not gesture or demonstrate while talking.

D: Demonstration: A clear demonstration of the movement or skill. Instructor should not talk or add explanation while demonstrating.

I: Imitation: Under direction of the instructor, the trainee should imitate exactly the process that has been demonstrated. Whilst the imitation is being carried out, observation should be made by the instructor(s) to ensure appropriate feedback is given.

P: Practice: Trainees then have a period to practice the movement or skill. This can be done individually or in small groups or pairs. Trainees can help each other and instructors can observe to give constructive feedback and correction as needed.

CHAPTER EIGHT: INSTRUCTIONAL TECHNIQUES

4. ASSESSING CADETS

At the end of a lesson it is important to assess the cadets to make sure they have achieved the aim set out at the start.

The following techniques can be used to assess cadets learning:

- Verbally asking questions.
- Playing games based on the lesson content.
- Carrying out a short quiz.
- Completing a short written test.

All will confirm if the lesson aim has been met.

THE FOUR Ps (not to be confused with the six ps)

This is a verbal questioning technique for confirming understanding.

Explain to cadets at the start of a lesson during the introduction that when questions are asked, cadets are to simply think of an answer. They should not shout out or put their hands up to answer. A cadet will then be picked at random to answer the question.

The technique then works as follows:

P: Pose - Pose the question to the group

P: Pause - Pause for a few moments to allow all cadets to think

P: Pick - Pick a cadet at random to answer the question

P: Praise - If the answer is correct, praise the cadet for a correct response and move on to the next question. If the answer is incorrect, praise the cadet for attempting to answer and pick another cadet to answer.

This technique makes all cadets think of an answer just in case they are picked and avoids a situation where some cadets actively take part while others stay quiet and don't engage.

5. EVALUATE THE TRAINING & IMPLEMENT IMPROVEMENTS

After every lesson it is important to take the time to evaluate how it has gone. Your own thoughts along with feedback from cadets or other instructors can give development opportunities to ensure your lessons continually improve as you gain experience.

CHAPTER NINE
MILITARY KNOWLEDGE (MK) OVERVIEW

CONTENTS:
- Introduction
- Basic MK Training Overview
- One Star MK Training Overview
- Two Star MK Training Overview
- Three Star MK Training Overview
- Four Star MK Training Overview

REFERENCES:
- *Army Cadet Syllabus - AC71101*
  (Version 1.2 - July 2022)
- *Army Cadets Military Knowledge Training Manual - AC72158*
  (Version 1 - 2021)
- *Army Cadet Resource Centre via Westminster*

CHAPTER NINE: MILITARY KNOWLEDGE (MK) OVERVIEW

INTRODUCTION

Military Knowledge (MK) covers the basics around being an Army Cadet and links to the British Army. Lessons cover topics such as the History of the Army Cadets, badges of rank and structure of the British Army.

- **Badges available:** None.
- **Specialist qualifications required to teach:** AIC passed.
- **Further progression beyond the syllabus:** Battlefield tours and military museum visits etc.

BASIC MK TRAINING OVERVIEW

Basic Military Knowledge (MK) consists of five lessons and a theory based assessment. Here is a brief overview of lessons covered:

01. THE ARMY CADET EXPERIENCE *(basic training)*

Covers an introduction to the Army Cadets including the following:

- The ACS syllabus (see chapter seven).
- Broader development opportunities (see Chapter Six).
- Nationally recognised qualifications (see Chapter Six).

02. THE VALUES & STANDARDS OF THE ARMY CADETS *(basic training)*

How cadets and CFAVs should act and behave (see Chapter One).

03. RANK & BADGES OF RANK *(basic training)*

Promotion opportunities for cadets and CFAVs (see Chapter Six).

04. STRUCTURE OF THE ACF AREA & DETACHMENT (OR CCF CONTINGENT & SECTION *(basic training)*

How do cadets and CFAVs fit into the bigger picture. Also covers key roles that staff play at a local level (see chapter two).

05. HISTORY OF THE ARMY CADETS *(basic training)*

An overview of the long history of the Army Cadets (Summary opposite).

BASIC TRAINING MK ASSESSMENT

Conducted in written or verbal from and contains ten questions on the subjects covered (two on each subject). Pass mark is 50%.

CHAPTER NINE: MILITARY KNOWLEDGE (MK) OVERVIEW

- **1859:** The ACF can trace its beginnings back to this date when there was a threat of invasion by the French.
- **1860:** At least 8 schools had formed 'Volunteer Companies' and some had started their own 'Cadet Companies'. (Seen as the start of the Army Cadet Force).
- **1889:** Southwark Cadet Company was formed by Cadet Forces pioneer, Octavia Hill who introduced some of the standards seen today.
- **1899:** At the start of the Boer War there were around 50 schools with cadets.
- **1908:** The term 'Cadet Force' was first used.
- **1914:** During the First World War there was a big expansion of the Cadet Force.
- **1923:** Funding for the Cadet Force stopped.
- **1930:** The War Office withdrew recognition of the Cadet Forces and the British National Cadet Association (BNCA) was formed to get recognition back again.
- **1942:** During the Second World War, there was another big expansion of the Cadet Force and the War Office resumed funding and providing uniforms.
- **1945:** The BNCA became the Army Cadet Force Association (ACFA).
- **1948:** The CCF (Combined Cadet Force) was introduced which combines Army, Air and Sea Cadet units in schools.
- **1959:** The Cadet Training Centre at Frimley Park was opened.
- **1960:** The centenary (100 year anniversary) of the ACF. HRH the Duke of Edinburgh presented the force with a special banner.
- **1980:** In the mid 1980s girls were first allowed in the ACF.
- **1988:** Introduction of the Army Proficiency Certificate (APC): a syllabus that changed how a lot of lessons were taught.
- **2010:** The 150th anniversary of the Army Cadets with events running all over the country.
- **2012:** A cadet expansion program was launched by the UK government to create more units in schools.
- **2021:** The Army Cadet Syllabus (ACS) was released to replace the APC syllabus.

CHAPTER NINE: MILITARY KNOWLEDGE (MK) OVERVIEW

The National Banner of the ACF

The Banner of the ACF was first presented on 9th February 1960 at the Tower of London, by his Royal Highness the Duke of Edinburgh as Colonel in Chief, on the occasion of the Centenary of the Army Cadet Force.

A new banner was presented by His Royal Highness the Duke of Edinburgh at the Chapel of the Royal Hospital, Chelsea on 27th March 1982. The original Banner was laid up in St. Peter's Church, Frimley, Surrey in July 1982 where it may be seen to this day.

THE CADET PRAYER

O God our Heavenly Father, who hast brought us together as members of the Army Cadet Force; help us to do our duty at all times, and be loyal to each other.

May all that is good and true prosper among us; strengthen us to defend the right; and bless our work that it may be acceptable to thee.

CHAPTER NINE: MILITARY KNOWLEDGE (MK) OVERVIEW

ONE STAR MK TRAINING OVERVIEW

One star Military Knowledge (MK) consists of two lessons and a theory based assessment. Here is a brief overview of lessons covered:

01. STRUCTURE OF THE ACF COUNTY *(one star training)*

A more in depth look at the structure of the ACF and the people involved at county level (see chapter two).

02. STRUCTURE OF THE BRITISH ARMY - ARMS & SERVICES
(one star training)

How the British Army is structured and organised (see Chapter Two).

ONE STAR TRAINING MK ASSESSMENT

The one star MK assessment is conducted in written or verbal from and contains eight questions on the subjects covered (four on each subject). Pass mark is 50%.

TWO STAR MK TRAINING OVERVIEW

Two Star Military Knowledge (MK) consists of one lesson and a theory based assessment. Here is a brief overview of lessons covered:

01. AFFILIATED REGIMENTAL HISTORY *(two star training)*

A lesson specific to the affiliated regiment of each unit. There is lots of material on the Army Cadet Resource Centre and several good videos on YouTube.

The lesson should include the following basics:

- History and formation of the regiment or corps.
- Origins of cap badge.
- Battle honours.
- Traditions and customs.

How the British Army is structured and organised (see Chapter Two).

TWO STAR TRAINING MK ASSESSMENT

The two star assessment is conducted in written or verbal from and contains six questions covering the formation, traditions & customs and battle honours (two questions on each). Pass mark is 50%.

CHAPTER NINE: MILITARY KNOWLEDGE (MK) OVERVIEW

THREE STAR MK TRAINING OVERVIEW (optional)

Three Star Military Knowledge (MK) is optional and consists of one lesson, a briefing and an assessment on cadet's presentations.

Here is a brief overview of lessons covered:

01. FAMOUS BATTLE PRESENTATION *(three star training - optional)*

Cadets are to research a famous battle (ideally linked to their affiliated regiment/corp) and spend a minimum of two hours preparing a presentation.

The presentation should include the following:

- Reasons for the battle.
- Significant locations.
- Start date of the battle.
- End date of the battle.
- Who were the parties involved.
- Significant commanders.
- Result (did anyone win, who was it etc?).
- After effects of the battle (effect on the area and on history etc.).

THREE STAR TRAINING MK ASSESSMENT

The presentation needs to be delivered to a minimum of two people including an assessor and should last between 15 - 20 minutes.

The assessor scores the presentation out of ten points (based on eight different criteria). Pass mark is 50%

FOUR STAR MK TRAINING OVERVIEW (none)

There are no lessons or assessments in MK at this level.

CHAPTER TEN
DRILL & TURNOUT (DT) OVERVIEW

CONTENTS:
- Introduction
- Drill Timing
- Basic DT Training Overview
- One Star DT Training Overview
- Two Star DT Training Overview
- Three Star DT Training Overview
- Four Star DT Training Overview

REFERENCES:
- *Army Cadet Syllabus - AC71101*
  (Version 1.2 - July 2022)
- *Army Cadets Drill & Turnout Training Manual - AC72147*
  (Version 1 - 2021)
- *Army Cadet Resource Centre via Westminster*

CHAPTER TEN: DRILL & TURNOUT (DT) OVERVIEW

INTRODUCTION

Drill and Turnout (DT) covers everything from basic foot drill and how to wear uniform through to rifle and cane drill. Senior Cadets will also take parades and teach drill lessons.

- **Badges available:** None.
- **Specialist qualifications required to teach:** AIC passed.
- **Further progression beyond the syllabus:** Carrying out of ceremonial duties such as standard bearer at local events.

Lessons are mainly practical and can be taught indoors or outdoors where there is enough space.

HISTORY

Through history, British Army drill has been the foundation upon which discipline, teamwork, pride and pageant have all been built.

Many years ago, when in battle, the infantry formed a square in their three ranks in order to give effective firepower. This action was carried out as a drill, taught and practiced on the barrack square. The discipline required to 'hold the line' was the difference between defeat and victory. Drill parades were hard and rigorous, with harsh violence dished out by the instructors.

Times have changed but the Regular Army still rely on drill to build team spirit and train soldiers to respond quickly to orders given.

When first introduced to Drill Commands, you may find that your reactions are slow and mistakes are easily made. Fortunately, initial lessons are all completed at the 'Halt' (stood still). Once you have mastered the initial movements and been taught how to march you will suddenly find it all comes together and your squad starts to move as a team.

It will probably feel even better when you take part in a Public Parade. You will be with the rest of your Detachment, smartly turned out and marching behind a band. Taking part in such parades can be quite exciting and gives pride in your detachment and the Army Cadet Force (particularly if your family and friends are watching!).

CHAPTER TEN: DRILL & TURNOUT (DT) OVERVIEW

DRILL TIMING

When practicing drill movements, it is normal practice for the squad to call out the timings as they do so.

TIMING FOR DRILL MOVEMENTS (BY NUMBERS)

When breaking drill movements into separate parts, unless instructed otherwise, repeat the number of the part you are carrying out as you move. For example:

- Instructor "Turnings by numbers, right turn, one".
- Squad calls out "one" as the move is performed.

In some cases, the instructor will call out a number but the squad calls out a different response such as "in" or "forward". This will be explained by the instructor though.

TIMING FOR DRILL MOVEMENTS (FULL MOVEMENTS)

When practicing full movements as a squad, it is important that everyone moves at the same time and at the same speed to create a smart and uniformed display. To aid with this, timings are called out using the numbers one, two and three.

When called out, movements are made on the number one with the other numbers there to assist with timing. For example:

Salute to the front at the halt: One - two three one

- On the first 'one', the right hand comes up to the salute position and there is a slight pause before continuing with the count.
- The salute is then held for the counts of 'two' and 'three'
- The right hand returns to the position of attention on the final count of 'one'.

Different movements have different applications of this counting system that will be covered as each is taught.

Drill timing

ONE - TWO THREE ONE

CHAPTER TEN: DRILL & TURNOUT (DT) OVERVIEW

BASIC DT TRAINING OVERVIEW

Basic Drill and Turnout (DT) consists of nine lessons and an assessment in three parts. Here is a brief overview:

01. CLOTHING & APPEARANCE *(basic training)*

Covers an introduction to wearing and maintaining Army Cadet uniform. For more detail see Chapter Three.

02. AIM & PURPOSE OF DRILL *(basic training)*

Foot drill is made up of a series of standard moves that all cadets need to learn for use on parade at detachment, external events or when away training.

Aim of Drill

- To produce a cadet who is proud, alert and obedient.
- Provide the basis of teamwork.

Purpose of Drill

- Enable bodies of cadets to be moved easily and quickly from point to point in an orderly manner.
- Improves posture.
- Develops lungs and muscles.

03. ATTENTION, STAND AT EASE & STAND EASY *(basic training)*

The first static drill movements which are most commonly used.

04. TURNINGS AT THE HALT - LEFT & RIGHT TURN *(basic training)*

Starting from the position of attention, turn 90 degrees to the left or right and end in the position of attention facing a new direction.

05. TURNINGS AT THE HALT - ABOUT TURN *(basic training)*

Starting from the position of attention, turn 180 degrees to the right and end in the position of attention facing the opposite direction.

06. TURNINGS AT THE HALT - LEFT & RIGHT INCLINES *(basic training)*

Starting from the position of attention, turn 45 degrees to the left or right and end in the position of attention facing a new direction.

CHAPTER TEN: DRILL & TURNOUT (DT) OVERVIEW

Attention

At ease (front)

At ease (rear)

Right turn (first move)

About turn (first move)

Second move for right turn, about turn or right incline

CHAPTER TEN: DRILL & TURNOUT (DT) OVERVIEW

07. COMPLIMENTS: REASONS, ORIGIN & INFORMATION
(basic training)

A compliment is a gesture made to show respect, that also shows loyalty and trust. There are three main types of compliments paid in the military:

- Salute with the hand.
- Salute with the sword.
- Present arms with a rifle.

Compliment are paid to all officers. If not wearing head dress, do not salute, simply brace up into the attention position.

All compliments derive their origin from the Sovereign (the King), to whom the highest compliment, the Royal Salute, is paid.

The following are also paid compliments:

Members of the Royal Family, governors and ministers to whom the Sovereign delegates authority. Formed bodies of troops on the Sovereign's business. All standards, guidons and colours of the Army, Royal Navy, Royal Marines and Royal Air Force

Compliments are also paid on the following occasions:

National Anthem
- On an organised parade, officers and warrant officers salute. NCOs will only salute if they are in charge of the group.
- When in uniform, but not on parade, all ranks will salute. When not on parade or in uniform, simply stand to attention.

Military Funerals
- Salute the bier (coffin).

Passing standards, guidons and colours
- Entitled to the highest compliments.
- Formed bodies on the march give eyes left/right. Individuals will halt, and salute in the correct direction, or salute as passing.

When boarding His Majesty's ships
- Salute the quarterdeck.

CHAPTER TEN: DRILL & TURNOUT (DT) OVERVIEW

08. SALUTING TO THE FRONT *(basic training)*

The most common form of paying compliments.

Start in the 'Attention' position:

1. Raise the right arm sideways until it is horizontal. Straighten the fingers and thumb keeping them together, with palm facing the front.
2. Bend the elbow, keeping the hand and wrist straight until the tip of the forefinger is 25 mm (1 inch) above the right eye.
3. Return to the position of attention by dropping the elbow forward to the side of the body, then straighten the arm and close the hand.

Stage 1　　　　**Stage 2**

CHAPTER TEN: DRILL & TURNOUT (DT) OVERVIEW

09. MARCHING AND HALTING *(basic training)*

Marching is a smart and uniformed way of walking. When moving around as a group, cadets will nearly always be required to march.

Start by simply walking in time with other cadets, with an instructor or a senior cadet calling your left and right foot fall. As you gain confidence, start to move your arms more until your hands swing as high as your shoulder to the front and level with your waist to the rear.

- When marching in a group, you will be given the words of command "quick march". Immediately after this command you set off with your left foot while swinging your right arm to the front and pushing your left arm to the rear.

BASIC TRAINING DT ASSESSMENT

The basic training DT assessment is done as part of a squad in three parts:

1. Inspection (clothing & appearance).
2. Two questions on the aim & purpose of drill and the origin of compliments.
3. Practical assessment of all drill moves learnt at basic level using a set sequence outlined in the ACS syllabus.

All assessments must be passed in full to pass basic DT. If a cadet fails any section they can retake straight away. If a cadet fails after a second attempt, re-training is required before attempting again.

CHAPTER TEN: DRILL & TURNOUT (DT) OVERVIEW

Marching - points to note

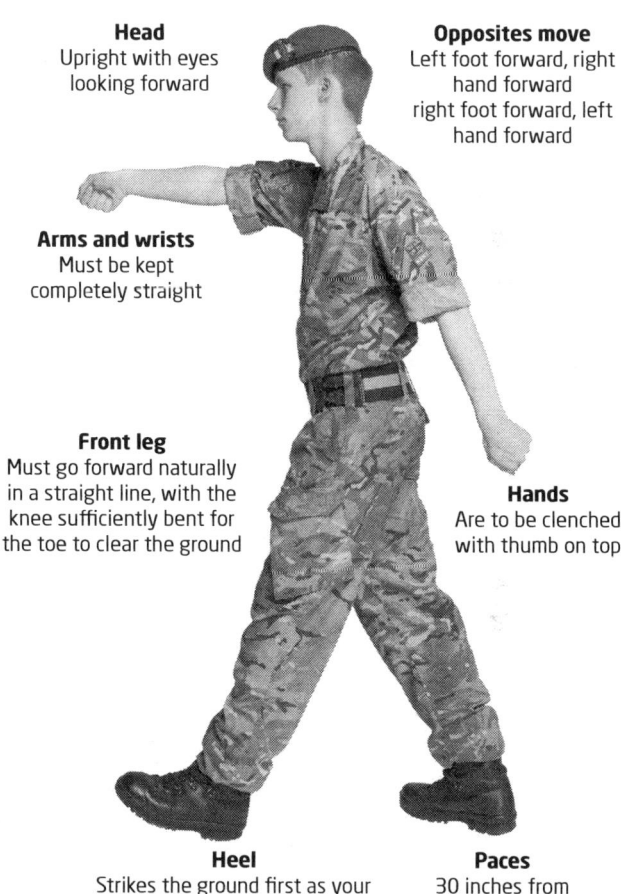

Head
Upright with eyes looking forward

Opposites move
Left foot forward, right hand forward
right foot forward, left hand forward

Arms and wrists
Must be kept completely straight

Front leg
Must go forward naturally in a straight line, with the knee sufficiently bent for the toe to clear the ground

Hands
Are to be clenched with thumb on top

Heel
Strikes the ground first as your hands reach their furthest points

Paces
30 inches from heel to heel

CHAPTER TEN: DRILL & TURNOUT (DT) OVERVIEW

ONE STAR DT TRAINING OVERVIEW

One star Drill and Turnout (DT) consists of seven lessons and a practical assessment. Here is a brief overview:

01. DRESSING IN THREE RANKS *(one star training)*

When on parade with enough cadets, you will most likely form up in three ranks. When formed up in this manner, cadets must be in neat lines and correctly spaced, which is called dressing. With the right marker (cadet front, right of the squad) as the reference point, cadets line up with those to their right and their front, which is called covering.

02. OPEN ORDER AT THE HALT FRONT RANK AND CLOSE ORDER AT THE HALT REAR RANK *(one star training)*

When in two or three ranks, the space between ranks is known as 'open order' or 'close order' depending on the distance between them. Close order is an arms distance apart and open order is an extra step away from that.

Close order is the standard way to form up, but open order creates more space which is good for when inspecting a squad or making presentations.

To get the movements correct to allow us to move between open and close order, we need to learn two movements:

1. Step forward - Front rank moving to the open order or the rear rank moving to the close order.
2. Step backwards - Front rank moving to the close order or the rear rank moving to the open order.

This lesson deals with the first movement, stepping forward.

03. CLOSE ORDER AT THE HALT FRONT RANK AND OPEN ORDER AT THE HALT REAR RANK *(one star training)*

This lesson deals with the second movement mentioned above, stepping backwards.

Once both lessons have been mastered, they are put together to allow a squad to move smartly from close to open order and open order back to close order. Note: If there are only two ranks, only the rear rank moves.

CHAPTER TEN: DRILL & TURNOUT (DT) OVERVIEW

Close order in three ranks

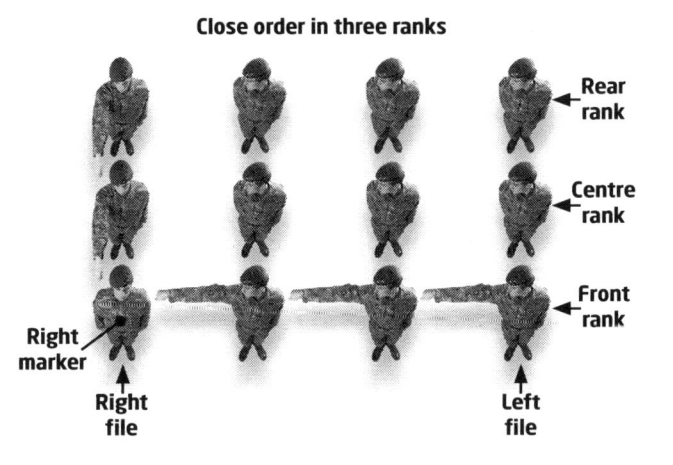

- Rear rank
- Centre rank
- Front rank
- Right marker
- Right file
- Left file

Open order in three ranks

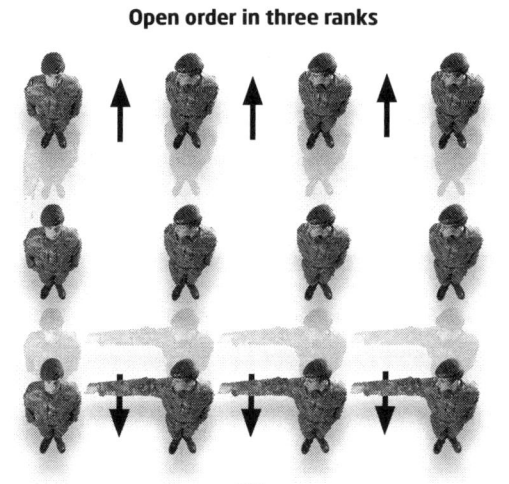

CHAPTER TEN: DRILL & TURNOUT (DT) OVERVIEW

04. SALUTING TO THE RIGHT & LEFT FLANKS ON THE MARCH
(one star training)

Moving on from saluting at the halt, this lesson now looks at saluting while marching.

Saluting to the front: It is also sometimes required for an individual cadet to approach an officer to deliver a message or receive an award etc. In this instance, march up to the officer, halt and then salute. After delivering a message or receiving an award etc. salute again and then turn to the left or right and march off.

Eyes right or left: Sometimes when a compliment is needed while marching, only the NCO or officer in charge of the squad will be the person to salute, with everyone else just turning their heads in the required direction.

The sequence for this is the same as for saluting on the march except the head turns with no salute and both arms continue to swing.

The compliment is held until the words of command "EYES FRONT" are called. This will be called as the left heel strikes the ground. Heads turn to the front as the left heel next hits the ground.

05. DISMISSING & FALLING OUT *(one star training)*

At the end of a parade, cadets will be given the words of command 'Dismiss' or 'Fall out', depending on what is happening after the parade.

Fall out: Leave the parade but you will be returning at some point (e.g. at the end of the first parade at detachment).

Dismiss: Leave the parade and you will not be required again (e.g. at the end of the final parade at detachment).

06. ABOUT TURN IN QUICK TIME *(one star training)*

When a marching squad needs to turn 180 degrees in a smaller area without halting first, the squad will need to perform an about turn on the march.

07. WHEELING TO THE LEFT & RIGHT IN QUICK TIME
(one star training)

Basic training cadets learn how to march and halt over a short distance. There will however be times when you will march over longer distances such as when on official parades or when moving around a camp, where you may need to change direction.

CHAPTER TEN: DRILL & TURNOUT (DT) OVERVIEW

To negotiate bends in roads, or to march around the perimeter of a parade square, you will need to be able to 'wheel' left or right.

Right wheel: On hearing the word of command 'wheel', the cadet on the front right of the squad will change direction and shorten their pace. All other cadets on the right hand side will also shorten their pace and follow.

Cadets in the centre will maintain a normal pace, but will follow the change of direction while maintaining formation.

Cadets on the left hand side will have to widen their pace slightly to follow the change of direction and maintain formation.

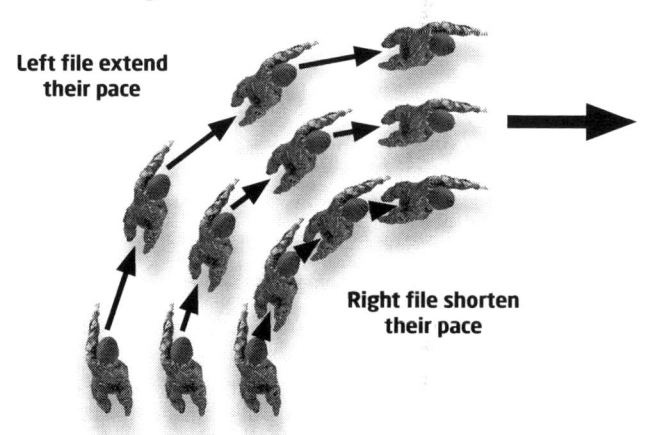

Left file extend their pace

Right file shorten their pace

Left wheel: Carry out the same sequence as above but with the left side shortening their pace and the right side widening their pace.

ONE STAR TRAINING DT ASSESSMENT

To pass one star DT cadets need to take part in a practical assessment of all drill moves learnt at one star level using a set sequence outlined in the ACS syllabus. The squad should be of a minimum of nine cadets.

All assessments must be passed in full to pass one star DT. If a cadet fails any section they can retake straight away. If a cadet fails after a second attempt, re-training is required before attempting again.

CHAPTER TEN: DRILL & TURNOUT (DT) OVERVIEW

TWO STAR DT TRAINING OVERVIEW

Two star Drill and Turnout (DT) consists of five foot drill lessons and 12 rifle drill lessons along with two practical assessments.
Here is a brief overview:

01. TURNING TO THE LEFT & RIGHT FLANK IN QUICK TIME
(two star training)

This is a similar to movement to the 'about turn in quick time' covered at one star level but allows a complete change of direction by 90 degrees while marching.

02. CHANGE STEP IN QUICK TIME *(two star training)*

This is a movement that allows an individual or squad to change step while marching, useful when getting out of step on a parade. Take a half step with the right foot to bring it into the left and then quickly step off with the left again to achieve two left foot paces in a row.

03. MARK TIME AND HALT FROM MARKING TIME *(two star training)*

Marking time is basically marching on the spot. It is used to hold position when marching without actually stopping. It is also used when faced with an obstacle that cannot be marched through. In this instance, either an about turn on the march or a halt will be given.

04. FORWARD FROM MARK TIME *(two star training)*

After a period of marking time (marching on the spot), this allows the continuation of marching with everyone stepping off together.

05. CHANGE STEP WHILE MARKING TIME *(two star training)*

This movement combines both the 'change step in quick time' lesson and the 'mark time' lesson and allows the change of step while marking time.

01. RIFLE DRILL - ATTENTION, STAND AT EASE, STAND EASY WITH THE RIFLE AT THE SHOULDER *(two star training)*

The first stage of rifle drill is to be able to carry out simple drill movements but with the rifle being carried.

Stand easy: Feet are a shoulder width apart as in the standard position of 'at ease'. With the butt of the rifle in the right hand, both hands are in front with the left hand over the right.

CHAPTER TEN: DRILL & TURNOUT (DT) OVERVIEW

Stand at ease: Feet stay as they are, but both hands move to the sides leaving the hands in a similar position to the 'attention' position but with the butt of the rifle in the right hand and the rifle pulled tight into the side and shoulder.

Attention: Hands now stay where they are but the left leg is lifted and then stepped sharply down into the position of attention. This is the 'shoulder' position for the rifle.

02. RIFLE DRILL - CHANGE ARMS AT THE SHOULDER
(two star training)

This movement allows the rifle to switch from being held in the right shoulder to the left or the left shoulder to right.

03. RIFLE DRILL - SLOPE ARMS FROM THE SHOULDER
(two star training)

This position is used for a lot of rifle drill movements and is the correct way for carrying a rifle while marching. Rather than the rifle being held upright along the left or right side, the supporting arm is bent at the elbow to the front at 90 degrees to the body supporting the rifle butt which then leans at approximately 45 degrees to rest at an angle (slope) on the shoulder.

Stand easy	Stand at ease	Shoulder arms (attention)	Slope arms

CHAPTER TEN: DRILL & TURNOUT (DT) OVERVIEW

04. RIFLE DRILL - SHOULDER ARMS FROM THE SLOPE
(two star training)

This movement returns the rifle to the side so that the rifle is shouldered. This needs to happen before a squad can be stood at ease.

05. RIFLE DRILL - CHANGE ARMS AT THE SLOPE
(two star training)

This is a similar movement to change arms at the shoulder but keeps the rifle in the slope position. Allows movement from the left shoulder to the right and the right shoulder to the left.

06. RIFLE DRILL - PRESENT ARMS FROM THE SLOPE
(two star training)

'Present arms' is the highest compliment that can be paid with a rifle and involves bringing the rifle out to the front and 'presenting' it. This can only be done from a static position.

07. RIFLE DRILL - SLOPE ARMS FROM THE PRESENT
(two star training)

Return to the slope arms position after presenting arms.

08. RIFLE DRILL - GROUND ARMS FROM THE SHOULDER
(two star training)

This allows an individual or squad to place the rifle on the ground in front of them from the shoulder arms position in unison. It involves holding the rifle with the right hand, stepping forward with the left foot and crouching down to place the rifle on the floor before stepping back up into a standard position of attention.

09. RIFLE DRILL - TAKE UP ARMS FROM THE GROUND
(two star training)

With the rifle placed on the ground in front, this movement allows the rifle to be picked up again and returned to the position of shoulder arms individually or as a squad in unison.

10. RIFLE DRILL - SALUTING TO THE FRONT AT THE HALT
(two star training)

This is a standard compliment paid with the rifle . When in the slope arms position with the rifle being supported by the left arm, the right hand is then placed over the stock of the rifle to the front.

CHAPTER TEN: DRILL & TURNOUT (DT) OVERVIEW

11. RIFLE DRILL - SALUTING TO A FLANK AT THE HALT
(two star training)

Hands do exactly the same as when saluting to the front but the head is turned in the desired direction in the same way as eyes left or right.

12. RIFLE DRILL - SALUTING TO A FLANK ON THE MARCH
(two star training)

The hand and head movements for saluting to a flank on the march are the same as above and the timing is the same as for a standard salute with the hand to the left or right on the march.

| Present arms | Ground arms | Saluting to the front | Saluting to the right |

TWO STAR TRAINING DT ASSESSMENT

To pass two star DT cadets need to take part in two practical assessments that cover all foot drill movements and all rifle drill movements that have been learnt at two star level using set sequences outlined in the ACS Syllabus. The squad should be of a minimum of nine cadets.

All assessments must be passed in full to pass two star DT. If a cadet fails any section they can retake straight away. If a cadet fails after a second attempt, re-training is required before attempting again.

CHAPTER TEN: DRILL & TURNOUT (DT) OVERVIEW

THREE STAR DT TRAINING OVERVIEW

Three star Drill and Turnout (DT) consists of three lessons along with two practical assessments.

Here is a brief overview:

01. CANE DRILL PART ONE *(three star training)*
The basic of cane drill for use on parade. As with rifle drill there are certain movements such as Attention and At Ease etc. that need to conducted correctly whilst carrying a cane.

02. CANE DRILL PART TWO *(three star training)*
The second part of cane drill for use on parade and continues into elements such as saluting with a cane.

Attention with cane
(When talking to NCOs or WOs)

At ease with cane
(When talking to NCOs or WOs)

Saluting with cane

CHAPTER TEN: DRILL & TURNOUT (DT) OVERVIEW

03. WORDS OF COMMAND *(three star training)*

When on parade 'words of command' are given in a specific way to ensure everyone reacts with the same movement at exactly the same time. Commands are given in a loud, clear manner and can be broken down into parts.

1. Introductory: (Not given on all commands):
- Normal paced command.
- Gives an indication of what drill movement is coming.
- E.G. "TURNINGS AT THE HALT".

2. Cautionary:
- Drawn out (stretched) command.
- Allows time to think and prepare to react correctly.
- E.G. "RIGHT".

3. Executive:
- Short sharp command.
- Gets immediate reaction from the entire squad.
- E.G. "TURN".

The cautionary word of command should be consistently drawn out over about the equivalent of four paces in quick time. There should be a pause between that and the executive word of command.

Good Technique

Many drill instructors end up with sore throats after a prolonged drill practice. To avoid this, the lungs are used to help project the voice rather than trying to shout.

When delivering words of command stand to attention with your head up, looking forward. Breathe deeply and push the air out aiming your voice straight over the squad.

Commands

Over the next few pages are the words of command for all foot drill carried out by cadets along with a few pointers on when to call.

CHAPTER TEN: DRILL & TURNOUT (DT) OVERVIEW

FOOT DRILL - STATIC (AT THE HALT)

Movement	Introductory	Cautionary	Executive
Attention	-	Squad	Shun
Stand at ease (from attention)	-	Stand at	Ease
Stand at ease (from stand easy)	-	-	Squad
Stand easy	-	Stand	Easy
Left/right turn	Turnings	Left/right	Turn
About turn	Turnings	About	Turn
Left/right incline	Inclines	Left/right	Incline
Salute to the front	Saluting	Salute to the front	Salute

FOOT DRILL - PARADE

Movement	Introductory	Cautionary	Executive
Right dress (2 parts)	Dressing	Right	Dress
	-	Eyes	Front
Open order (2 parts)	Dressing in open order	Right	Dress
	-	Eyes	Front
Close order (2 parts)	Dressing in close order	Right	Dress
	-	Eyes	Front

CHAPTER TEN: DRILL & TURNOUT (DT) OVERVIEW

FOOT DRILL - PARADE			
Movement	**Introductory**	**Cautionary**	**Executive**
Numbering	-	From the right	Number
Proving (2 parts)	-	Number	(Number)
	Left of right half		Squad
Sizing (5 parts)	Tallest on the right, shortest on the left	In single rank	Size
	-	From the right	Number
	Odd numbers one pace forward, even numbers one pace backwards		March
	Stand still the right-hand cadet, front rank to the right, rear rank to the left	Ranks right and left	Turn
	Form three ranks	Quick	March
Get on parade (2 parts)		Right	Marker
	-	Get on	Parade
Dismiss	-	Dis	Miss
Fall out	-	Fall	Out

CHAPTER TEN: DRILL & TURNOUT (DT) OVERVIEW

FOOT DRILL - ON THE MARCH (IN QUICKTIME)			
Movement	Introductory	Cautionary	Executive & which foot called on
Marching	-	Quick	March	-
Halting	-	Squad	Halt	Left
Salute to the left/right	Saluting	Salute to the left/right	Salute	Left
Eyes left/right (2 parts)	By the right	Eyes	Left/right	Left
	-	Eyes	Front	Left
Left/right wheel	-	Left/right	Wheel	Left
About turn	Turnings	About	Turn	Left foot passes right
Left/Right turn	Turnings	Left/right	Turn	Right/Left
Change step	Changing step	Change	Step	Right
Mark Time	-	Quick mark	Time	Right
Halt from mark time	-	Squad	Halt	Right
Forward from mark time	-	-	Forward	Right
Change step while marking time	-	Change	Step	Right

CHAPTER TEN: DRILL & TURNOUT (DT) OVERVIEW

INTRODUCTORY WORDS OF COMMAND

When a squad is formed and performing drill, the person giving the words of command give extra direction.

1. Squad facing front, left or right

SQUAD WILL ADVANCE

MOVE TO THE LEFT IN THREES

MOVE TO THE RIGHT IN THREES

SQUAD WILL RETIRE

2. Squad facing the rear only

SQUAD WILL ADVANCE

SQUAD WILL MOVE TO THE RIGHT

SQUAD WILL MOVE TO THE LEFT

SQUAD WILL RETIRE

CHAPTER TEN: DRILL & TURNOUT (DT) OVERVIEW

THREE STAR TRAINING DT ASSESSMENT

To pass three star DT cadets need to take part in two practical assessments:

1. Cane drill: All cane drill movements learnt at three star level using a set sequence outlined in the ACS syllabus.
2. Taking a squad & performing correct drill movements: Cadets take a squad through a drill sequence outlined in the ACS syllabus.

All assessments must be passed in full to pass three star DT (a score of nine or above is acceptable for the words of command section). If a cadet fails any section they can retake it straight away. If a cadet fails after a second attempt, re-training is required before attempting again.

FOUR STAR DT TRAINING OVERVIEW (optional)

Four star Drill and Turnout (DT) is optional and consists of one lesson and a practical assessment. Here is a brief overview:

01. DRILL INSTRUCTION & DELIVERY *(four star training)*

Four star Drill and Turnout is not compulsory but can be chosen as one of the two subjects to specialise in. Lessons are delivered by the County RSM (or someone delegated in their place) on how to effectively deliver drill lessons before assessing them on their practical drill teaching skills.

FOUR STAR TRAINING DT ASSESSMENT

To pass four star DT cadets need to complete a practical assessment where they prepare four teaching practices (two movements at the halt & two on the march). They are then assessed on two of them.

All assessments must be passed in full to pass four star DT. If a cadet fails any section they can retake straight away. If a cadet fails after a second attempt, re-training is required before attempting again.

CHAPTER ELEVEN
FIELDCRAFT (FC) OVERVIEW

CONTENTS:
- Introduction
- Basic FC Training Overview
- One Star FC Training Overview
- Two Star FC Training Overview
- Three Star FC Training Overview
- Four Star FC Training Overview

REFERENCES:
- *Army Cadet Syllabus - AC71101 (Version 1.2 - July 2022)*
- *Army Cadets Fieldcraft Training Manual - AC71966 (Version 1 - 2021)*
- *Army Cadet Resource Centre via Westminster*

CHAPTER ELEVEN: FIELDCRAFT (FC) OVERVIEW

INTRODUCTION

Fieldcraft (FC) covers everything to do with military life outdoors. Being 'out in the field' means that you are away from modern facilities and have to operate and survive with just whatever you can carry and take with you. This can be in woodland, fields or even mountainous areas.

- **Badges available:** None.
- **Specialist qualifications required to teach:** AIC passed to teach but an ECO (Exercise Co-ordinating Officer) is required for all blank firing.
- **Further progression beyond the syllabus:** Four star cadets develop leadership skills and Master Cadet teaches advanced FC.

Lessons are mainly practical and can be taught outdoors.

ELEMENTS OF FIELDCRAFT

Fieldcraft covers the following:

- Looking after yourself and your equipment.
- Providing your own food and shelter.
- How to move and observe without being seen.
- Observing, and judging distances.
- Moving around in a section and patrolling.
- Operating outside at night.
- Reacting to enemy fire and contact with an enemy.
- Defending against attack and using sentries.

There are many lessons covering different aspects of fieldcraft, but most are hands on and are lots of fun. As you progress through the Army Cadet syllabus, fieldcraft training is about practical application of skills learnt as well as the development of leadership skills.

Skills learnt in other subjects are all relevant in Fieldcraft and transfer over. Skills such as Navigation or First Aid can all be built into Fieldcraft exercises.

CHAPTER ELEVEN: FIELDCRAFT (FC) OVERVIEW

BASIC FC TRAINING OVERVIEW

Basic FC training has seven lessons and a practical assessment.

01. INTRODUCTION TO FIELDCRAFT & TACTICS *(basic training)*

An introduction and overview of the subject along with what lessons are covered at what star level.

02. PREP AND PACKING OF PERSONAL EQUIPMENT *(basic training)*

A suggested kit list for Fieldcraft exercises is in Chapter Five but this lesson teaches you a bit more along with how to pack.

- **CEFO - Complete Equipment Fighting Order:** This is the minimum requirement used when on patrol or on short training activities. It consists of an assault vest (or webbing set), rifle and cadet helmet.
- **CEMO: Complete equipment Marching Order:** This consists of everything within the CEFO load out but with all other equipment required for staying out overnight including shelter, sleep system and cooking kit etc.

03. WHY THINGS ARE SEEN *(basic training)*

Fieldcraft is tactical which means you need to be able to move and observe without being detected by the enemy. Being able to blend in with your surroundings so you are not seen is a big part of that. To blend in though, you need to understand why things are seen.

The main things to be aware of are as follows:

- **Shape:** Obvious shapes such as the outline of a person or a rifle are easy to spot so need breaking up.
- **Silhouette:** Being in front of a contrasting background makes you stand out. E.g. Walking along a hill with a clear sky behind you.
- **Texture:** Shiny or reflective surfaces such as skin or mess tins within an area of foliage will stand out and be easy to spot.
- **Shadow:** The sun casts shadows. Hiding in the shadows is good but allowing the sun to cast your shadow onto the ground is not.
- **Spacing:** Objects in nature are not evenly spaced out so things that are stand out. Avoid regular spacing when patrolling.
- **Movement:** Fast movement attracts the eye so keep movement slow. Knocking foliage or branches also attracts attention.

CHAPTER ELEVEN: FIELDCRAFT (FC) OVERVIEW

04. MOVING WITH OR WITHOUT PERSONAL WEAPONS
(basic training)

Different types of movement are required depending on the environment, light available and enemy threat level.

Monkey run
Possible enemy threat, fair visibility, low cover

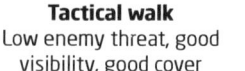

Tactical walk
Low enemy threat, good visibility, good cover

Leopard crawl
Higher enemy threat, fair visibility, minimal cover

05. ELEMENTARY NIGHT MOVEMENT *(basic training)*

When moving at night or in close proximity to the enemy, more cautious movement is required.

Cat walk
Possible enemy threat, poor visibility, low cover

Kitten crawl
High enemy threat, poor visibility, minimal cover

Ghost walk
Low enemy threat, poor visibility, good cover

CHAPTER ELEVEN: FIELDCRAFT (FC) OVERVIEW

06. FIELD SIGNALS *(basic training)*

Field (hand) signals play a major part of communication when out in the field, either to avoid speaking or shouting when attempting to remain undetected, or when it is too noisy to shout over the volume of a fire fight.

Basic movement signals: These signals give basic commands around movement. When received, pass on to the next person.

Ready to move	Advance	Halt	Slow down
Space out	Go back	Close on me	Double
Move up	Freeze & listen	Lie down	As you were

CHAPTER ELEVEN: FIELDCRAFT (FC) OVERVIEW

07. ORGANISATION OF A RIFLE SECTION *(basic training)*

The section: (8 cadets):
A section is a small group that can carry out various tasks and objectives. Made up ideally of around eight cadets, there are several roles to be fulfilled.

- **Section commander (IC) x 1:** This will normally be an instructor or senior cadet and is In Command (IC) of the section.
- **Section second in command (2IC) x 1:** This will also be an instructor or Senior Cadet.
- **Riflemen x 6:** Takes direction from the IC or 2IC.
- **Specialists:** Riflemen can also fill other roles such as 'scout' who is the lead person on a patrol. Other specialist roles may include support gunner, medic or radio operator.

Fire teams: (4 cadets):
A section is broken down into two fire teams, Charlie and Delta. This allows a section to split into two halves for achieving objectives.

- **Charlie Fire team:** Section commander (IC), scout and two riflemen.
- **Delta Fire team:** Section second in command (2IC) and three riflemen.

Battle buddies: (2 cadets):
Within each fire team there are two pairs. These pairs work together throughout any exercise. It is good to stick together for setting up shelter, cooking and eating, checking kit together and patrolling.

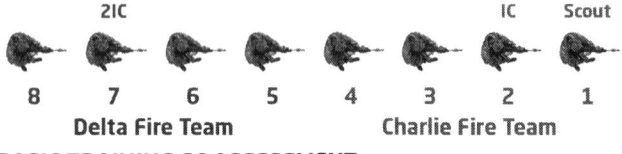

2IC					IC	Scout
8	7	6	5	4	3	2	1
Delta Fire Team				Charlie Fire Team		

BASIC TRAINING FC ASSESSMENT
The basic training FC assessment is a practical assessment of all elements of basic training backed up with confirmation questions.

Cadets must score 50% to pass basic FC. If a cadet fails any section they can retake straight away. If a cadet fails after a second attempt, re-training is required before attempting again.

CHAPTER ELEVEN: FIELDCRAFT (FC) OVERVIEW

ONE STAR FC TRAINING OVERVIEW

One star FC training has thirteen lessons and a practical assessment broken into three parts.

01. ADMINISTRATION IN THE FIELD *(one star training)*

Looking after your kit and equipment along with your own health and hygiene is extremely important. This lesson is broken into three parts.

A: Maintaining Clothing & Equipment

This lesson looks at how to check your kit and equipment before setting off and how to make minor repairs of you have problems when away from camp. A small sewing kit along with items such as paracord or string and some good tape are essential. Looking after your rifle and keeping that clean are looked at as part of Skill At Arms training.

B: Maintaining standards of personal hygiene

Keeping your hair, face, teeth and body clean is extremely important to prevent poor health and risk of infection. Details on what to pack for a fieldcraft wash kit are on page 55.

C: Feeding in the Field

When on exercise in the field you will be provided with 24 hour Operational Ration Packs (ORP) along with cooking equipment and fuel. Full training is given on how to heat meals and what is included.

02. THE TWO PERSON SHELTER *(one star training)*

When staying out overnight, you will create a shelter out of a basha sheet held between two trees with bungee cords or string/paracord and held down with a few tent pegs. It is a simple structure but quick and easy to put up and take down and will keep you sheltered from the elements. There are several versions including 'A-frame', 'Lean-to' and 'Open'.

A-frame basha

Lean-to basha

CHAPTER ELEVEN: FIELDCRAFT (FC) OVERVIEW

03. PERSONAL CAMOUFLAGE & CONCEALMENT *(one star training)*

Understanding why things are seen will allow you to blend in with your surroundings and observe without being observed.

Camouflage: Disguising yourself using camouflage (MTP) clothing, camouflage cream for your skin and local foliage to blend in with your surroundings and hide regular shapes and shiny surfaces.

Applying Camouflage (Cam) Cream

1. Texture: Evenly apply brown camouflage cream to any exposed skin (hands, face, neck) to remove shine.

2. Shape: Apply random lines of darker brown and green to disguise the recognisable shape of your features.

3. Shape: Use foliage from your immediate surroundings to disguise the shape of your body and equipment.

Apply enough to do the job, without adding too much. Apply more cam cream at night than during the day as skin can be more visible in dim light. Use string, elastic or natural loops in clothing and equipment to affix just the right amount of foliage and change it if your environment changes.

Concealment: Using the environment to blend in through the use of cover, shadows and correct movement.

- Cover: Look through or around cover, not over it.
- Isolated cover: Avoid isolated cover such as a lone tree.
- Avoid contrasting backgrounds such as a skyline.
- Hide in shadows, avoid making shadows.

04. OBSERVATION *(one star training)*

Observation is a key skill that cadets must acquire when operating out in the field. It is the ability to systematically scan an area to search for enemy positions or potential threats. This is useful when patrolling, observing enemy positions or when on sentry duty.

CHAPTER ELEVEN: FIELDCRAFT (FC) OVERVIEW

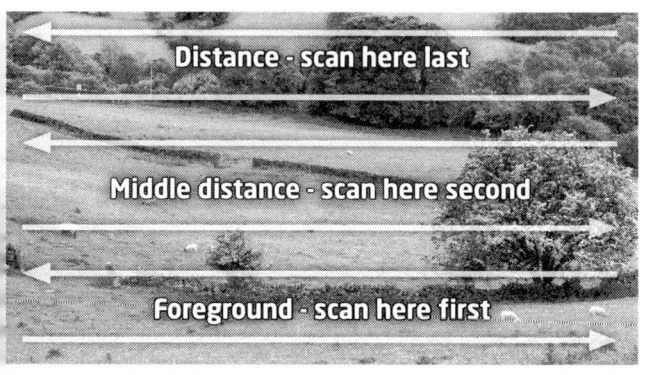

Distance - scan here last

Middle distance - scan here second

Foreground - scan here first

Start bottom left. Scan with your eyes along, up, along, up etc. until you have scanned the whole scene. Make sure to overlap your scan to avoid missing areas. When finished scanning horizontally, scan again along any feature lines (hill slopes, walls, hedge lines etc.).

When scanning, identify areas that may have a potential threat, or that look unusual. Remember why things are seen!

05. JUDGING DISTANCE *(one star training)*

When observing an area, or when under attack from an enemy, it may be necessary for you to let others know what you have seen. To do this you need to be able to give an estimated distance away from where you are situated.

This lesson is broken into three sections:

1. Judging Distance by Unit of Measure

The most common form of measurement for this is the metric system which uses centimetres, metres and kilometres.

- 1 centimetre (cm) is made up of 10 millimetres (mm).
- 1 metre (m) is made up of 100 centimetres (cm), or 1000 millimetres (mm).
- 1 kilometre (km) is made up of 1000 metres (m).

CHAPTER ELEVEN: FIELDCRAFT (FC) OVERVIEW

When judging how far away something is, it is useful to remember how large certain common items are so that you can imagine how many of those items would fit into the distance you are trying to estimate. (E.g. • Football pitch = approx 100m • Aeroplane = approx 50m • Coach = approx 30m • Car = approx 5m).

2. Judging Distance by Appearance

Understanding how things appear as they get further away can also help you estimate distance. Here is a guide to how a person looks at different intervals:

- **100m:** Clear.
- **200m:** Fairly clear with skin colour and equipment easily identifiable.
- **300m:** Clear body outline and skin colour, but other details blurred.
- **400m:** Body outline clear, but everything else is blurred.
- **500m:** Body begins to taper and the head becomes indistinct.
- **600m:** Body now looks wedge shaped and head cannot be identified.

Things can seem closer or further away depending on light and other things around them.

3. Aids to Judging Distance

- **Key ranges:** Knowing how far away certain key locations are.
- **Bracketing:** Midway point between your highest and lowest estimate.
- **Halving:** With longer distances, estimate the distance to the half way point and then double it to get your full estimate.
- **Group average:** Take an average of everyone's estimate within a group to get a final estimate.

06. INDICATION OF TARGETS *(one star training)*

There may be instances when someone sees something no-one else does and they need to indicate a location to others. This may be when under attack and you are the only person that has seen the enemy.

To indicate a target to others, you must be clear, loud and precise and the order of delivery is always the same.

1. **Range** - (distance away) in metres: e.g. "100".
2. **Indication** - (direction/where to look). e.g. " Left of Farm".

CHAPTER ELEVEN: FIELDCRAFT (FC) OVERVIEW

There are several methods of identifying a target:

Arc of fire: You can break your view in front of you into 'arcs'.

- **The Axis:** The centre of the arc, directly in front of you.
- **Left & right of arc:** The extent of the arc to the left and right.
- **Reference points**: Obvious locations in your view such as a building or lone tree.

Methods of Indication

Direct method: The elements above can be used alone or combined to easily identify a target. The arc can also be further broken down into smaller sections such as 'half left' or 'slightly right'.

Examples:

- "300" (range) "Axis of arc" (arc)
- "200" (range) "Left of barn" (reference point)
- "350" (range) "Slightly right" (arc) "Lone tree" (reference point)

Clock ray: Placing an imaginary clock face over a reference point is another way to identify a target. E.g: "250" (range) "Barn" (reference point) " 3 o'clock" (clock ray) "Hay bales" (exact location).

Hand angles: Holding your hand out at arm length, you can see how many fingers or knuckles fit between two locations. This can be given using the words 'fingers' or 'knuckles' or can be converted into angles.

Binoculars: These have angles marked in the view which also allows you to indicate degrees difference between locations.

07. RANGE CARDS

A range card is a small sketch map of an area you are observing. This is useful when carrying out the role of a sentry, when in an observation post, or when doing any sort of reconnaissance.

Drawn onto a half circle or full circle template you should place yourself in the middle and mark key reference points either to your front or all around. Record distances to those reference points from where you are and mark one key location as a 'setting ray' to help orientate your range card.

Circles (or half circles) on the range card represent distances which can be set by the person writing the range card (10m or 100m etc.).

CHAPTER ELEVEN: FIELDCRAFT (FC) OVERVIEW

Range card - Semi-circle (area to the front) in 20 metre increments.

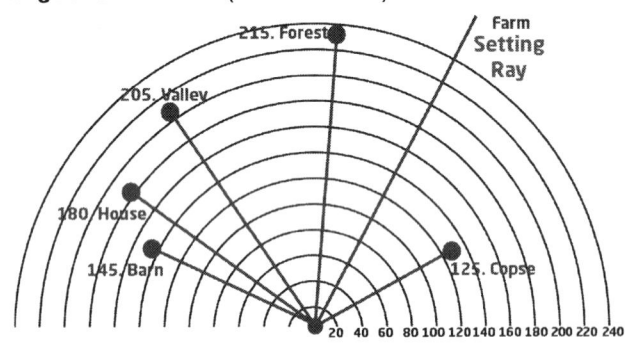

```
                    215. Forest      Farm
                                    Setting
       205. Valley                    Ray

   180/House

  145. Barn                      125. Copse

              20 40 60 80 100 120 140 160 180 200 220 240
```

08. DUTIES OF A SENTRY *(one star training)*

Sentries provide security while the others attend to personal admin, eat meals or catch up on sleep. Around the outside of a patrol harbour, there may be up to three sentry positions watching for enemy movement and check returning patrols are friendly (not an enemy patrol). The sentry post needs to be camouflaged, but must have a good field of vision. A range card is normally drawn up to show key features in front of the position.

Staggered (Stag) Duty

Cadets take turns to be sentries for periods of around one hour each. The section 2IC (second in command) draws up a 'Stag List' of names with timings, but arranges it so that changeovers are staggered (both cadets don't change at the same time). This means that as one cadet hands over to a new sentry, the other maintains observation. It also means that one cadet is always fresher and more awake than the other.

Password

A password is set every 24 hours at 1200. The password is normally a four letter word spelt out in two halves using the phonetic alphabet.

Example: **STAR = Sierra - Tango - Alpha - Romeo**

- **Challenge:** Sentry states **"Sierra, Tango"**.
- **Reply:** Approaching troops or patrol leader states **"Alpha, Romeo"**.

CHAPTER ELEVEN: FIELDCRAFT (FC) OVERVIEW

Sentry procedure for challenging approaching troops

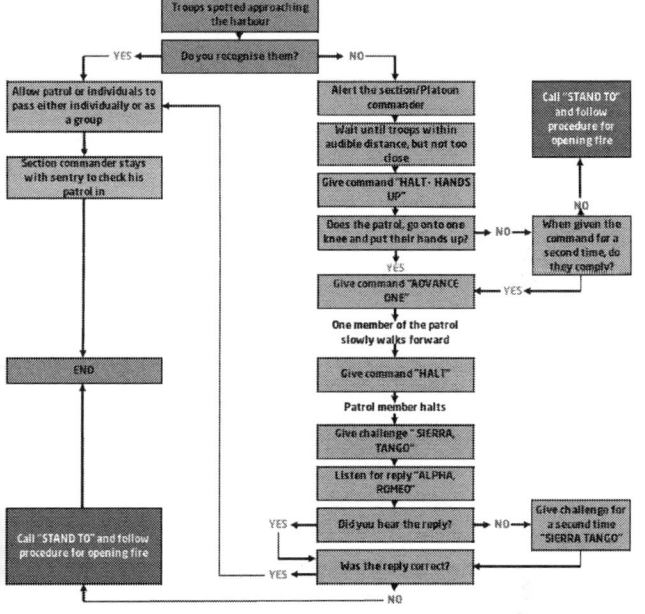

```
Troops spotted approaching the harbour
        │
   Do you recognise them?
   ├── YES ──► Allow patrol or individuals to pass either individually or as a group
   │              │
   │          Section commander stays with sentry to check his patrol in
   │              │
   │             END
   │
   └── NO ──► Alert the section/Platoon commander
                  │
              Wait until troops within audible distance, but not too close
                  │
              Give command "HALT - HANDS UP"
                  │
              Does the patrol, go onto one knee and put their hands up?
                  ├── NO ──► When given the command for a second time, do they comply?
                  │              ├── NO ──► Call "STAND TO" and follow procedure for opening fire
                  │              └── YES ──┐
                  └── YES ─────────────────┤
                                           ▼
                              Give command "ADVANCE ONE"
                                           │
                              One member of the patrol slowly walks forward
                                           │
                              Give command "HALT"
                                           │
                              Patrol member halts
                                           │
                              Give challenge "SIERRA, TANGO"
                                           │
                              Listen for reply "ALPHA, ROMEO"
                                           │
                              Did you hear the reply?
                                  ├── YES ──┐
                                  └── NO ──► Give challenge for a second time "SIERRA TANGO"
                                                     │
                                  Was the reply correct?
                                     ├── YES ──► (back to Allow patrol pass)
                                     └── NO ──► Call "STAND TO" and follow procedure for opening fire
```

09. ELEMENTARY OBSTACLE CROSSING *(one star training)*

An obstacle is anything that will slow a patrol down or make it vulnerable. It is important to get the balance right between getting past the obstacle quickly to avoid being targeted, but not so quickly that attention is drawn to the patrol.

- **Gates & fences:** If possible go under gates and fences, if not go over but try to keep your body as low as possible.
- **Walls:** Assist each other over walls, again keeping as flat as possible over the top.
- **Ditches, streams, hedges & gaps:** Obstacles that force you into a small area are ideal places for an enemy position to observe.

CHAPTER ELEVEN: FIELDCRAFT (FC) OVERVIEW

- **Open ground, roads & junctions:** These may also be covered by enemy fire, and may have several different areas of threat to watch for. Use more of the section to watch and observe different arcs before sending anyone across. Once across, everyone should provide cover and watch ahead as well as behind them.
- **When under fire:** If you are in close contact with an enemy, covering fire is needed while crossing an obstacle.

Tactical Approach

However you cross an obstacle, make sure to have cadets allocated to cover and watch for enemy threat while others move.

Obstacle — **Enemy seen** — **No enemy**

10. SELECTING A ROUTE ACROSS COUNTRY *(one star training)*

When moving from one location to another, it is important to choose our route carefully. The ideal scenario is to have an easy route that has good cover from enemy observation and fire, and allows us to observe without being seen. This is not always possible though.

- **Dead ground:** Enemy cannot see anything in dead ground so it provides good cover. It also means you can't see them though.
- **Streams & ditches:** Provides good cover, but are obvious routes so are quite likely to be watched by enemy.
- **Hedges & bushes:** Good cover from view, but not enemy fire.
- **Woods:** Good cover from ground and air, but easy to get lost in.
- **Buildings & walls:** Good cover from view and enemy fire.
- **Farmland:** Buildings and hedges may provide good cover, but animals are inquisitive and may give away your position.

CHAPTER ELEVEN: FIELDCRAFT (FC) OVERVIEW

11. INTRODUCTION TO NIGHT TRAINING *(one star training)*

One of the best ways to avoid being seen is to work at night under the cover of darkness. Working in the dark can be confusing and your mind can play tricks on you as it attempts to interpret what it is seeing. Special techniques are required for observing at night and special care is required around making noise as sound travels further at night.

Night Vision

Our eyes work differently in the dark and are not as effective as during the day. The full changeover from day to night vision can take over 30 minutes but going back to day vision can take just a few moments and any exposure to bright light can make that happen.

Red Light

Torches that have a red filter do not effect our night vision as much and are harder to spot from a distance, so are ideal to use.

Red light is not good for map reading though so instead, you should use a normal white light torch with just a pin prick of light showing. Green light is good for map reading and preserving night vision.

12. STALKING *(one star training)*

Stalking is moving into an area occupied by an enemy force and observing it without being seen. This brings together a lot of lessons covered so far including camouflage & concealment, why things are seen, observation, types of movement etc.

To carry out a stalk, you need the following information:

- **Stalk location:** Where you will be observing and where the best observation points are located.
- **Routes in and out:** How to get in and out of the stalk location.
- **Rendezvous locations:** Where to meet after the stalk or if there are problems.
- **Aim of stalk:** Who you are observing and why. What info are you trying to obtain?

Quite often a sketch map or full range card is also required when doing a stalk.

CHAPTER ELEVEN: FIELDCRAFT (FC) OVERVIEW

13. REACTION TO FIRE CONTROL ORDERS *(one star training)*

A fire control order gives the location of a target, but also tells a particular group or individual to open fire in a certain manner.

To help remember the sequence of information, we use the word **GRIT**:

G: Group: The group or individual required to fire (section, fire team or individual).

R: Range: The distance away from the target in metres.

I: Indication: Location of target (reference point, arcs of fire etc.).

T: Type of Fire: Speed that you will be firing (part of SAA lessons).
- Deliberate fire: Around 10 rounds per minute.
- Watch and shoot (snap shooting): Fire only when you see a target.
- Rapid fire: Up to around 30 shots per minute.

Type of Fire Control Orders

1. **Full:** Given when there is enough time to give all information.
2. **Brief:** When there is not as much time, but the target is obvious.
3. **Individual:** When the commander passes on the responsibility of when to open fire to the individuals concerned.
4. **Delayed:** Given early to prepare group for firing, but with a delay.

ONE STAR TRAINING FC ASSESSMENT

The one star training FC assessment is broken into three parts carried out over a 24 hour period:

1. Harbour routine (sentry duty & inspection).
2. Stalk.
3. Defence of a harbour area (ideally with blank firing).

Cadets must pass all elements to pass one star FC. If a cadet fails any section they can retake straight away. If a cadet fails after a second attempt, re-training is required before attempting again.

CHAPTER ELEVEN: FIELDCRAFT (FC) OVERVIEW

TWO STAR FC TRAINING OVERVIEW

Two star FC training has eight lessons and a practical assessment.

Most of the lessons are from the 'tactics' section of the FC manual which go into a lot of detail.

01. KEEPING DIRECTION AT NIGHT *(two star training)*

Navigating at night provides more challenges than during the day so specific skills need to be practiced. The following are covered as part of your navigation training:

- **Compass bearings:** Following a bearing on a compass can keep you heading in the correct direction.
- **Pacings:** Knowing how many paces you take over 100 metres can help you to estimate distances better when you can't see any features.
- **Visible landmarks:** Seeing a visible landmark in the distance when following a bearing can keep you going in the correct direction.

Stars

Getting to know star formations can also help with navigation although this relies on a clear night where you can actually see the stars.

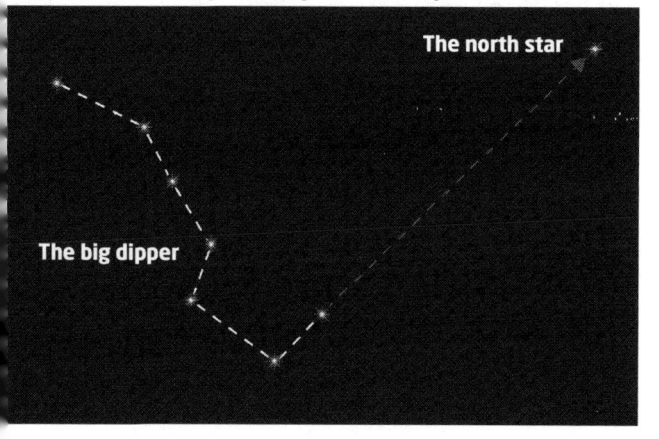

CHAPTER ELEVEN: FIELDCRAFT (FC) OVERVIEW

02. INDIVIDUAL FIRE & MOVEMENT (F&M) *(two star training)*

When a patrol comes under enemy fire (contact), there is a sequence that must happen instinctively to avoid becoming a casualty.

"Contact front/rear/left/right"

This can be called out by anyone in the squad and will be the first person to see/hear the enemy. On hearing this, everyone repeats it so that the message gets passed along.

RTR (Return fire, Take cover, Return appropriate fire)

- **Return fire:** Fire immediately in the general direction of where the fire is coming from. This suppresses the enemy (keeps them down).
- **Take cover:** This must be close to where they are and may even mean just getting down into the prone position.
- **Return appropriate fire:** Once in cover, fire more accurately at the enemy position.

From here, the enemy location needs to be identified and indicated to the rest of the section and then a fire control order needs to be issued. The section commander then makes the decision to advance to contact to beat the enemy or withdraw and regroup.

Fire and Movement

When moving under fire, it is essential that covering fire is provided. Accurate fire on an enemy position is called suppression and ensures that the enemy cannot return accurate fire.

This can be achieved with just two cadets (battle buddies). The idea is that one cadet provides covering fire, while the other cadet moves. They then alternate this process to allow them to either get closer to the enemy or to withdraw.

CHAPTER ELEVEN: FIELDCRAFT (FC) OVERVIEW

Fire & movement example

Phase 1: On hearing 'CONTACT" Both cadets return fire, take cover and then return appropriate fire. (RTR).

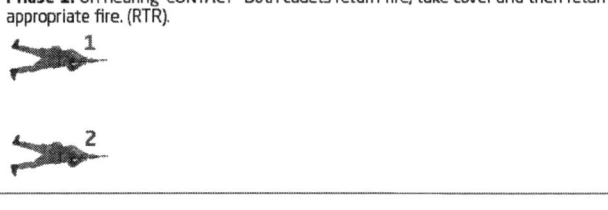

Phase 2: Cadet 1 provides covering fire and calls out 'MOVE NOW".
Cadet 2 on hearing this, gets up, runs forward a few metres and then takes cover again and resumes firing. (Called a tactical bound).

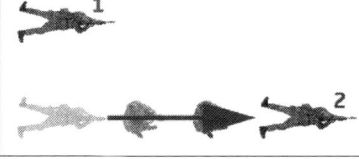

Phase 3: Cadet 2 now provides covering fire and calls out "MOVE NOW".
Cadet 1 on hearing this, gets up, runs level, takes cover and resumes firing.

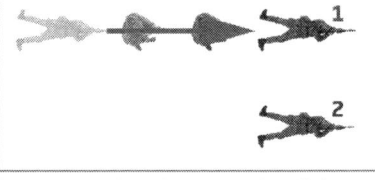

The process above is repeated until the required amount of distance is covered.

Caterpillar or Leap Frog

The example above shows the cadets moving in a caterpillar formation which is where the cadets end up level with each other after both have made their tactical bounds. Leap frog is similar but the cadets run past each other to cover more ground and end up staggered.

CHAPTER ELEVEN: FIELDCRAFT (FC) OVERVIEW

03. OPERATING AS A MEMBER OF A FIRE TEAM AND SECTION
(two star training)

This lesson continues from the previous lesson on fire and movement. Once practiced, the same principle can be applied to a fire team with two cadets providing covering fire while the other two move. For a full section it is the same again but with one full fire team providing covering fire while the other moves.

Peeling

Another form of fire and movement is peeling. This is particularly useful when a section needs to withdraw left or right and involves one cadet moving at a time. Under the protection of covering fire, the first cadet gets up and runs left (or right) behind the other cadets and joins on the opposite end and continues firing. The next cadet does the same and the next until all are out of harms way.

04. ORGANISATION & GROUPING *(two star training)*

This looks in more detail at how a rifle section works with the roles and responsibilities for all members. It also looks at how the section fits into a platoon (see page 31).

05. PATROLLING *(two star training)*

A patrol is a tactical walk carried out in small groups. There are three main types of patrol:

1. **Standing patrol:** Sent out to check or maintain security of an area.
2. **Reconnaissance patrol:** Sent out to observe an area or an enemy position.
3. **Fighting patrol:** Sent out to engage with the enemy.

The lessons go into how to plan and prepare for a patrol along with how they are to be conducted. Elements such as patrol formations (single file, file, arrow head & extended line), patrol rehearsals and 'action on' certain events are all covered.

CHAPTER ELEVEN: FIELDCRAFT (FC) OVERVIEW

06. BATTLE PROCEDURE, FUNCTIONAL GROUPING AND ORDERS *(two star training)*

This looks at how the maximum amount of preparation can be done in the minimum amount of time and how a full company is divided into functional groups (Recce/R group, Orders/O group, harbour and reconnaissance parties and the main body). It also covers the processes around receiving, interpreting and delivering orders (Warning orders, formal orders, quick battle orders/QBO, radio orders and operation orders).

07. PATROL HARBOURS *(two star training)*

Having spent time in patrol harbours and acted as sentries during previous training, this section now looks at the correct procedures for occupying a harbour area and goes into more depth on topics such as harbour routines and variations on patrol harbour set ups.

08. OBSERVATION POSTS (OPS) *(two star training)*

This involves establishing a single temporary position, set up covertly to observe from. The position must be close enough to the target to be able to observe, but not so close that there is a risk of being discovered. It needs to be concealed and allow the observers to see without being seen. It can be made using natural cover, or can be dug into the ground and camouflaged. All evidence must be removed on leaving the OP.

TWO STAR TRAINING FC ASSESSMENT

The two star training FC assessment is broken into four parts carried out over a 24 hour period:

1. Occupation of harbour & harbour routine.
2. Reconnaissance Patrol.
3. Observation Post.
4. Break Contact Drills (reaction to enemy contact).

Cadets must pass all elements to pass two star FC. If a cadet fails any section they can retake straight away. If a cadet fails after a second attempt, re-training is required before attempting again.

CHAPTER ELEVEN: FIELDCRAFT (FC) OVERVIEW

Triangular Patrol Harbour

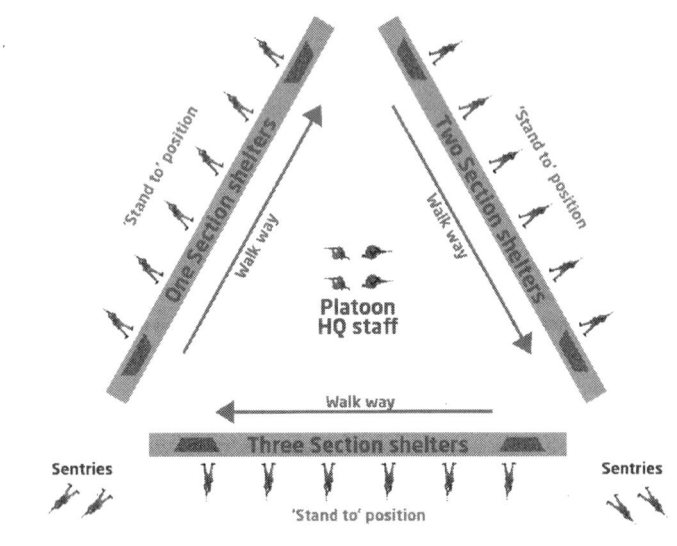

Sentries

'Stand to position
One Section shelters
Walk way

Two Section shelters
'Stand to' position
Walk way

Platoon HQ staff

Walk way
Three Section shelters
'Stand to' position

Sentries   Sentries

CHAPTER ELEVEN: FIELDCRAFT (FC) OVERVIEW

THREE STAR FC TRAINING OVERVIEW

Three star FC training has three lessons and a practical assessment.

Lessons are from the 'tactics' section of the FC manual which go into a lot more detail.

01. DEFENCE & DELAY EXERCISES *(three star training)*

By predicting what an enemy might do when attacking a position, it is possible to create defensive positions that are effective from all directions and confuses the enemy. Understanding what ground and cover is desirable to the enemy highlights what needs to be denied to them. The key principles for defence is as follows:

- **Depth:** Leaving enough space for an enemy to get close.
- **Mutual support:** Support for all defensive positions through direct fire cover.
- **All-round defence:** The ability to defend an attack from any direction even if attack is expected from a specific location.
- **Deception & concealment:** Confusing and delaying the enemy by confusing them. Camouflage, fake positions and radio silence helps.
- **Striking forces/reserves:** Holding a unit back allows them to be deployed to back up a struggling position or launch a counter attack.
- **Offensive spirit:** Attack is the best form of defence, so an aggressive defence can gain and hold the initiative.

02. AMBUSHES *(three star training)*

An ambush is a tactical 'trap' set to eliminate an enemy force before they can react. It is aimed at an enemy that is moving through an area or temporarily halting. They can be very quick and are not normally designed to take and hold an area.

The lesson is broken into three sections:

1. **Organisation:** Types of ambush, organisation of those involved and procedures for moving in and out of ambush locations.
2. **Planning & preparation:** Using the available intelligence to plan ambush type, location, timings, procedures, organisation etc.
3. **Conduct:** The sequence of events that leads up to the ambush and the following withdrawal.

CHAPTER ELEVEN: FIELDCRAFT (FC) OVERVIEW

03. THE ATTACK *(three star training)*

An attack can be a planned, deliberate attack or a hasty attack on the move. Either way the procedure is the same:

- Planning & preparation.
- Suppressing the enemy.
- The assault.
- Exploitation.
- Reorganisation.

The lesson is broken into six sections:

1. Principles.
2. Fire & movement.
3. Hasty attack - section battle drills.
4. Hasty attack - platoon battle drills.
5. The deliberate attack.
6. Advance to contact.

THREE STAR TRAINING FC ASSESSMENT

The three star training FC assessment is broken into two parts carried out over a 24 hour period:

1. The ambush.
2. The attack.

Cadets must pass all elements to pass three star FC. If a cadet fails any section they can retake straight away. If a cadet fails after a second attempt, re-training is required before attempting again.

CHAPTER ELEVEN: FIELDCRAFT (FC) OVERVIEW

FOUR STAR FC TRAINING OVERVIEW (optional)

Four star FC training is optional and focusses on leadership which allows cadets to act as section commanders and 2ICs. Previous material is looked at again from a leadership and planning perspective.

Lessons are from the 'tactics' section of the FC manual which go into a lot more detail.

01. TACTICAL PRINCIPLES AND LEADERSHIP *(four star training)*

This is the first lesson for four star training cadets which then leads onto revisiting all of the two and three star lessons but from a section commander or 2IC perspective.

1. **Organisation & grouping.**
2. **Issuing fire control orders** (FCO).
3. **Battle procedure, functional grouping and orders.**
4. **Patrolling** (planning & preparation + conduct).
5. **Patrol harbours.**
6. **Defence & delay exercises.**
7. **Observation posts** (OPs).
8. **Ambushes** (Organisation + planning & prep + conduct).
9. **The attack** (Principles + Fire & movement + Hasty attack - section battle drills + hasty attack - platoon battle drills + the deliberate attack + advance to contact).

Note: Issuing fire control orders *(four star training)*

Taking the information from the lesson on reacting to fire control orders, this now looks at issuing the orders and how they should be delivered by a section commander or 2IC to a section.

As with any orders given to a group, they need to be heard and understood so we use the acronym **CLAP** for their delivery:

C: Clearly, calmly and concisely.

L: Loud enough for the cadet(s) to hear.

A: As an order.

P: Pauses to allow for target acquisition and sights to be set etc.

CHAPTER ELEVEN: FIELDCRAFT (FC) OVERVIEW

FOUR STAR TRAINING FC ASSESSMENT

The four star training FC assessment is broken into four parts:

1. **Recce Patrol.**
2. **Standing Patrol.**
3. **Fighting Patrol.**
4. **The attack.**

Cadets must pass all elements to pass four star FC. If a cadet fails any section they can retake straight away. If a cadet fails after a second attempt, re-training is required before attempting again.

CHAPTER TWELVE
NAVIGATION (NAV) OVERVIEW

CONTENTS:
- Introduction
- Basic Nav Training Overview
- One Star Nav Training Overview
- Two Star Nav Training Overview
- Three Star Nav Training Overview
- Four Star Nav Training Overview

REFERENCES:
- *Army Cadet Syllabus - AC71101 (Version 1.2 - July 2022)*
- *Army Cadets Navigation Instructor Guide (Version 1 - Oct 2021)*
- *NNAS Outdoor Navigation - Handbook for Tutors*
- *Army Cadet Resource Centre via Westminster*

CHAPTER TWELVE: NAVIGATION (NAV) OVERVIEW

INTRODUCTION

Navigation training teaches how to read, understand and use maps to aid navigation. Starting with the basics such as how to look after maps and read basic information, right through to using maps to estimate distances and times for specific routes, navigation is a lot simpler than people initially think and the progressive delivery of lessons ensures that each element is understood before moving on.

Navigation is an essential skill for Army Cadets as it is used extensively in fieldcraft training and on expeditions. It is also used in certain AT activities such as orienteering, mountain biking, hill walking and inland canoeing.

Away from the Army Cadets, Navigation is a great skill to learn as it is used in everyday life all the time and can be useful in emergency situations.

- **Badges available:** None.
- **Specialist qualifications required to teach:** AIC passed or NNAS bronze at basic, one and two star level. NNAS silver at three and four star level.
- **Further progression beyond the syllabus:** NNAS navigation awards are available as well as opportunities for UK and foreign walking trips and expeditions.

Lessons are mainly practical and most can be taught outdoors.

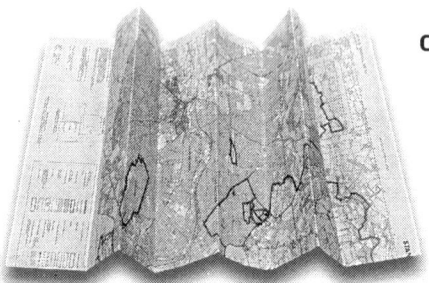

Correctly folded map

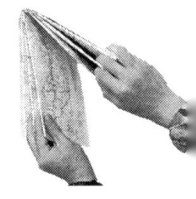

CHAPTER TWELVE: NAVIGATION (NAV) OVERVIEW

BASIC NAV TRAINING OVERVIEW

Basic Navigation looks at the very basics of reading maps and navigating. There are three lessons followed by a practice period and a short practical assessment.

01. IDENTIFY MAPS, DEMONSTRATE HOW TO CARE FOR AND USE MAPS *(basic training)*

A map is a birds-eye view of an area, scaled down to a manageable size. They are only 100% accurate at the time of manufacture and can be extremely accurate or just give a general guide. The information shown and scale varies dependant on the type of map.

Types of maps include:
- Street maps
- Road maps
- Town/shopping centre maps
- Local attraction maps
- Ordnance Survey (OS) maps
- Military maps
- Sketch maps
- Atlas/world maps
- Google maps

Looking After Maps

Maps can be expensive to replace if they are damaged and you can be in actual danger if you get lost and are unable to read your map. It is therefore essential to look after your maps and fold them properly.

Maps can be waterproofed by laminating, placing into a waterproof bag or keeping in a map case. You can also write onto a waterproof cover with non-permanent marker pens. Never write directly onto a map with pen.

Folding Maps

Maps should be folded into a 'concertina' so that any small area of the map can be viewed without having to unfold the whole map. This also makes them a manageable size that can easily fit in a pocket or bag.

CHAPTER TWELVE: NAVIGATION (NAV) OVERVIEW

Map Information

Maps contain lots of information that can help us navigate and explore. Information includes roads, footpaths, rivers, train lines, hills, lakes and towns.

Marginal Information

Maps usually have some extra information about the map to make it easier to read. This is normally in one place, to the side, above or below the main map and is called 'marginal information'.

Marginal information has some or all of the following:

- Map scale (common scales are 1:25,000 and 1:50,000 - The smaller the number, the more detail there is).
- Date of creation.
- Area covered.
- Key to map symbols (called a 'legend').
- Magnetic north.

02. HANDRAILS AND MAP ORIENTATION *(basic training)*

A handrail is a linear feature that appears on the ground and on a map. It can be followed to assist navigation. Examples of handrails are:

- Roads
- Paths
- Tracks
- Hedges
- Tree lines
- Railway lines
- Field edges
- Power cables
- Rivers
- Streams
- Lake edges
- Coastlines

Map Orientation

To follow a map, it has to be orientated (positioned) so that it matches up with the ground around it. To do this, identify some key features on the map and then find them on the ground. Rotate the map until the features on the ground and the map line up.

While navigating, the map should then never need to be turned as you will move around the map instead.

CHAPTER TWELVE: NAVIGATION (NAV) OVERVIEW

Rivers, roads and tracks are all examples of handrails.

03. DEMONSTRATE HANDRAILS AND THEIR USE TO MAINTAIN POSITION ON AN ORIENTATED MAP *(basic training)*

Maintain Position
When following a map, keep your thumb on your last known position to easily find where you are whenever looking at it.

Collecting Features
When following a route it is important to look for features along your route that are on the map and check them off as you walk past them. Any feature can act as a Collecting Feature. For example, seeing a church on the map that you will walk past on your route is a good thing to look for while walking to confirm you are in the correct place.

Catching Features
When navigating, you also need to look for something to let you know if you have gone too far on a route. This is known as a 'Catching Feature'. Any feature on a map that is further along a route than you should be walking can be a good Catching Feature. For example, seeing a lake on a map that is just past a junction you need to turn off at can be a great Catching Feature. If you end up seeing the lake while walking, you know you have gone too far.

BASIC TRAINING NAV ASSESSMENT
This is a practical assessment outdoors. Follow a given route of at least 3 legs with frequent changes in direction that is 1.5 - 2km long.

If a cadet fails they can take the test again but, if they fail after a second attempt, re-training is required before attempting again.

CHAPTER TWELVE: NAVIGATION (NAV) OVERVIEW

ONE STAR NAV TRAINING OVERVIEW

One star nav is made up of four lessons followed by a practice period and a practical assessment.

01. IDENTIFY MAP SYMBOLS AND FEATURES USED TO AID NAVIGATION *(one star training)*

Map Symbols are small pictures or letters that represent various features on a map. These symbols are normally quite easy to recognise and avoid using lots of text. Map Symbols vary for different types and scales of maps, so it's important to check the key within the Marginal Information of any map you use to make sure you understand what they mean. The most common maps you will be using will be 1:25,000 or 1:50,000 scale ordnance survey or military maps.

Map Symbols are used as Handrails, Collecting Features and Catching Features.

Example map symbols on a 1:25,000 scale map

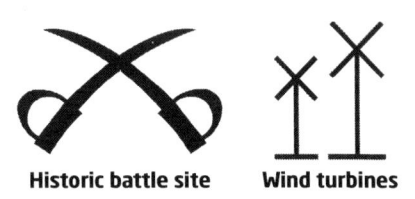

Place of worship with tower

Footbridge

Telephone

Historic battle site

Wind turbines

CHAPTER TWELVE: NAVIGATION (NAV) OVERVIEW

02. ESTIMATE DISTANCE USING GRID SQUARES, SHOW HOW TO USE FOUR FIGURE GRID REFERENCES *(one star training)*

Most maps that you will use have very faint lines on them which break the map into small squares, these are called grid squares and can be extremely helpful.

Estimating Distance

Grid squares on 1:25, 000 and 1:50,000 scale maps represent 1km square on the ground, meaning that if you walked a straight line between two locations that were one grid square apart on a map, you would have walked 1km.

Walking diagonally from corner to corner of a grid square is 1.5km approx.

Map scale: 1:50,000

Printed square size: 2cm x 2cm

Ground area covered: 1km x 1km

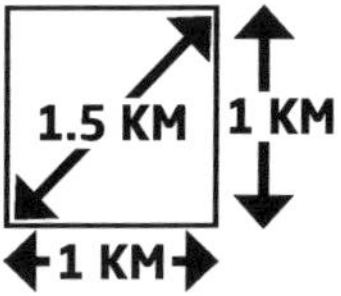

Map scale: 1:25,000

Printed square size: 4cm x 4cm

Ground area covered: 1km x 1km

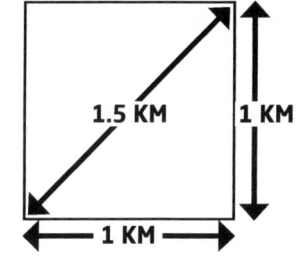

CHAPTER TWELVE: NAVIGATION (NAV) OVERVIEW

Four Figure Grid References

All grid squares are numbered, making it easier to find specific locations.

The image below shows a small section of a full map with numbers along the bottom (called eastings), and up the side (called northings).

The numbers are in line with the grid lines, and cover the square to the right of it (eastings), or above it (northings). To find which square something is in, we work out which number along it is, and then which number up it is. (Along and up).

In the example below, the large 'X' is in the 03 square along and the 01 square up. The four figure grid reference for this is therefore 03 01.

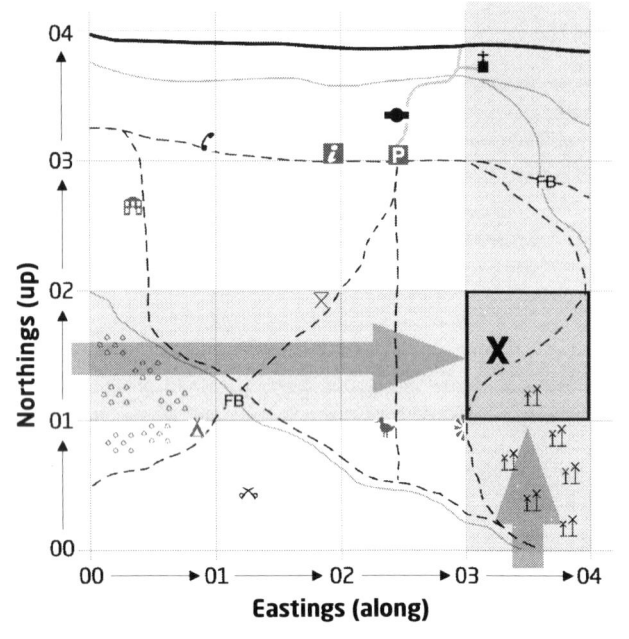

FOUR FIGURE GRID REFERENCE: 03 01

CHAPTER TWELVE: NAVIGATION (NAV) OVERVIEW

03. DEMONSTRATE HOW TO USE A SIX FIGURE GRID REFERENCE *(one star training)*

Four figure grid references are great for finding a general area on a map, but because one grid square is 1km square it is not so good at pinpointing more specific locations. For this we need to use six figure grid references. To work out a six figure grid reference, we simply add one number to the easting and one number to the northing.

In the example below, the large numbers show the original four figure grid reference, 03 01. The smaller numbers show how the square is broken down into smaller squares which allow you to pinpoint more accurately where in the square the 'X' is. Add the extra Easting and extra northing number to get the six figure grid reference 033 015

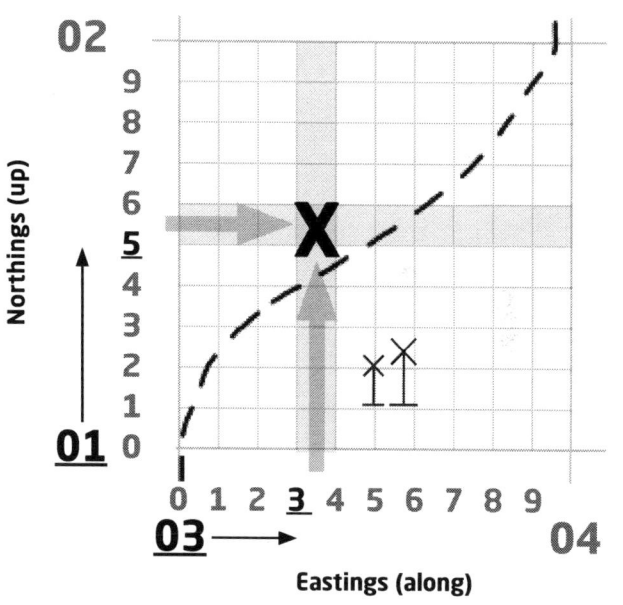

Eastings (along)

SIX GRID REFERENCE: 033 015

CHAPTER TWELVE: NAVIGATION (NAV) OVERVIEW

04. ESTIMATING DISTANCE ON THE GROUND *(one star training)*

Being able to estimate distance when navigating is an important skill to learn. It can really help when finding locations in poor light, or when finding a specific track or path when there are several in the same general area.

Estimate Distance Using the Eye

This is covered during one star fieldcraft. See pages 137 - 138.

Estimate Distance Using Pacing

If we work out how many paces we take when walking 100 metres, we can use that to judge how far we have walked.

Do the following to work out your pacing:

- Measure out 100 metres using a long tape measure and mark the start and end.
- Walk naturally from start to end (100m).
- Step off with your left foot, but just count every time your right foot hits the ground. This is called double pacing. (Say "and" "one" "and" "two" "and" "three" etc.).
- Complete this four times and record how many steps you take each time.
- Add all four totals together and divide by four to get an average. This is your pacing over 100 metres.

Note: Different terrain, weather conditions, hills and weight of equipment carried will all effect your pacing, so make sure to take that into account when navigating.

When navigating, you can use this to help you walk correct distances. For example, if you are walking between two locations that are half a grid square apart on your map (500 metres) you just count your 100 metre pacing out five times to arrive at the correct location.

CHAPTER TWELVE: NAVIGATION (NAV) OVERVIEW

Estimate Distance Using Timing

When working out your pacing over 100 metres, you can also use a stopwatch to time how long it takes for you to walk 100 metres. You will then also know how long it takes you to cover that distance and can use that to work out timings for different distances too. To work out how long it would take to walk 500 metres, multiply your time by five. To work out how long it would take to walk 1km (1000 metres), multiply your time by ten. This method can be used for any distance.

The average walking pace for most people is around 4 - 5km per hour, so those figures can also be used to make good estimates. Here's a timing break down for those two walking speeds. Make a note of them as they will be useful.

	5km	4km	1km	500m	250m	100m
4kmph	75 mins	60 mins	15 mins	7.5 mins	>4 mins	1.5 mins
5kmph	60 mins	48 mins	12 mins	6 mins	3 mins	<1 min

ONE STAR TRAINING NAVIGATION ASSESSMENT

Practical assessment: Follow a given route covering two to three km depending on terrain. The route should have changes of direction, encourage route following decisions, and have adjacent point features or prominent landforms.

If a cadet fails they can take the test again but, if they fail after a second attempt, re-training is required before attempting again.

CHAPTER TWELVE: NAVIGATION (NAV) OVERVIEW

TWO STAR NAV TRAINING OVERVIEW

Two star Nav is made up of seven lessons followed by a practice period and a practical assessment.

01. IDENTIFY THE SHAPE OF THE GROUND ON THE MAP
(two star training)

A less obvious feature seen on maps are 'contour lines'. These are faint brown or orange lines that show hills and slopes. These lines appear every five or ten metres (dependant on steepness) of climb or fall and show the height above sea level in metres.

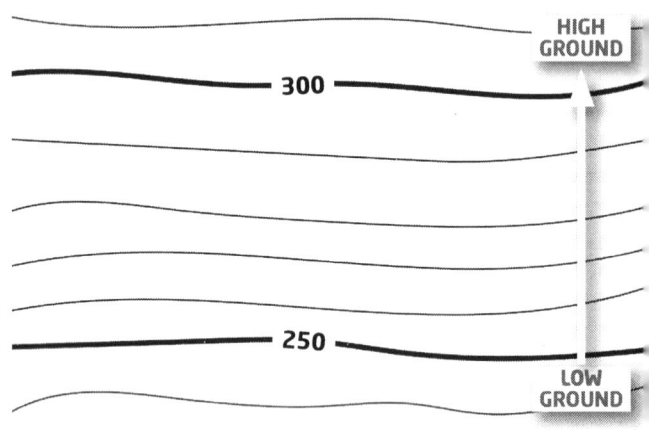

The thicker lines are called Index contours and give the height every 50 or 100 metres of climb or drop. The thinner lines represent the five or ten metre increments in between the index contours.

Uphill or Downhill

If the height numbers appear to be the correct way up when your map is correctly orientated, you will be heading uphill. If they appear upside down, you will be heading downhill. Another way to identify up and downhill is to remember that streams will run downhill.

CHAPTER TWELVE: NAVIGATION (NAV) OVERVIEW

Steep or Shallow

The closeness of the contour lines show how steep a climb or drop is. The closer the contour lines are to each other, the steeper the slope.

Convex or Concave

You can also see the type of slope from the spacing of the contours:
- **Even:** Contours evenly spaced.
- **Convex:** Steep climb to start and then shallow.
- **Concave:** Shallow climb to start and then steep.

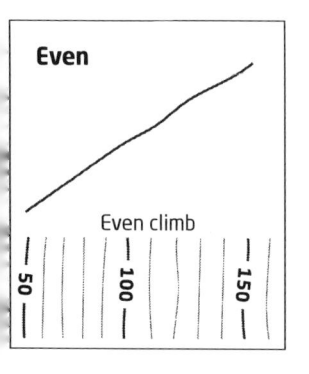

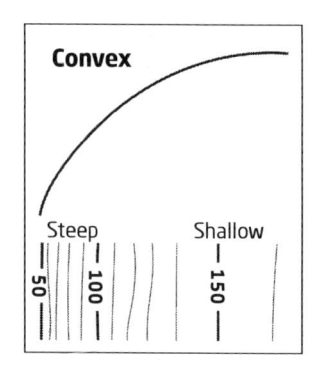

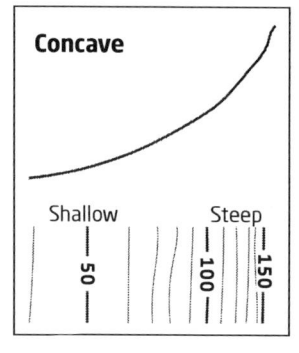

CHAPTER TWELVE: NAVIGATION (NAV) OVERVIEW

Shape of the Ground
The shapes created by contour lines on a map can also tell us what the ground will look like.

Hill
Slope all the way around up to a single peak

LOW GROUND

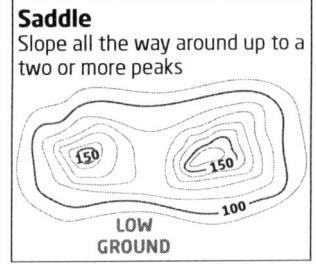

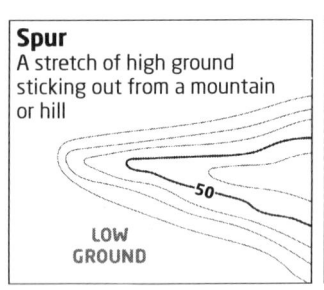

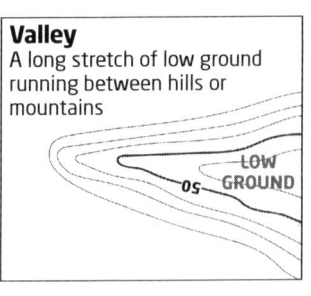

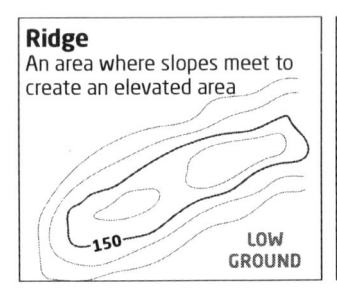

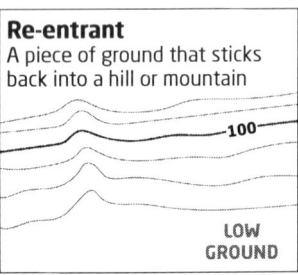

Saddle
Slope all the way around up to a two or more peaks

LOW GROUND

Spur
A stretch of high ground sticking out from a mountain or hill

LOW GROUND

Valley
A long stretch of low ground running between hills or mountains

LOW GROUND

Ridge
An area where slopes meet to create an elevated area

LOW GROUND

Re-entrant
A piece of ground that sticks back into a hill or mountain

LOW GROUND

CHAPTER TWELVE: NAVIGATION (NAV) OVERVIEW

02. IDENTIFY PROMINENT FEATURES ON THE GROUND USING MAPS *(two star training)*

This is a practical lesson that continues on from the previous lesson. Cadets need to get outside and identify the different land formations and compare them to how they look on the map. Get used to identifying them from different heights, angles and distances.

The internet also has a mass of images for quick reference.

03. ORIENTATE A MAP USING PROMINENT FEATURES ON THE GROUND *(two star training)*

Now having an understanding of how the ground looks by looking at the contour lines on a map, these land forms can also now be used to orientate a map. During basic training, cadets were taught to orientate a map using the prominent features that are easily recognised such as handrails and map symbols. Being able to identify the shape of the land now allows more accurate orientation when there are fewer more obvious features.

04. ORIENTATE THE MAP USING A COMPASS *(two star training)*

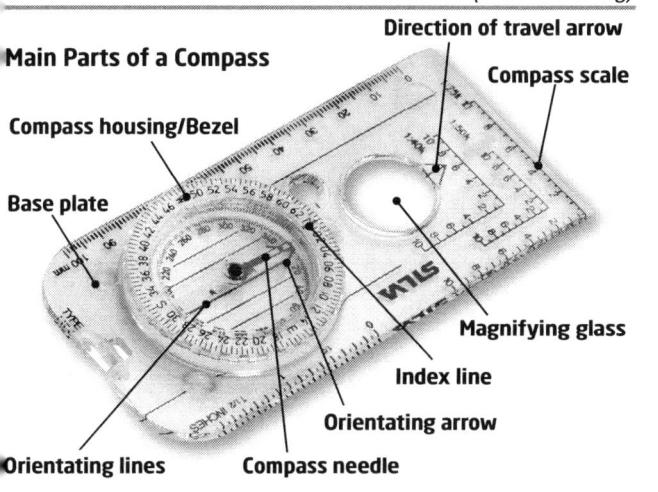

Main Parts of a Compass

- Direction of travel arrow
- Compass scale
- Compass housing/Bezel
- Base plate
- Magnifying glass
- Index line
- Orientating arrow
- Orientating lines
- Compass needle

CHAPTER TWELVE: NAVIGATION (NAV) OVERVIEW

The Compass
Up until this point, navigation training has all been achieved by simply looking at the map and the ground around you. Handrails and key features help to orientate a map correctly and can sometimes be enough to navigate entire routes. There are situations thought where we need some extra help and this is where the compass comes in.

North, East, South and West
Planet Earth has a North Pole and a South Pole which are used to help us navigate. The North Pole has such a strong magnetic pull that wherever we are in the world, the tiny needle of a compass will always point to it as long as there are no other magnetic items near it.

Three Types of North
There are three slight variations on where north is.

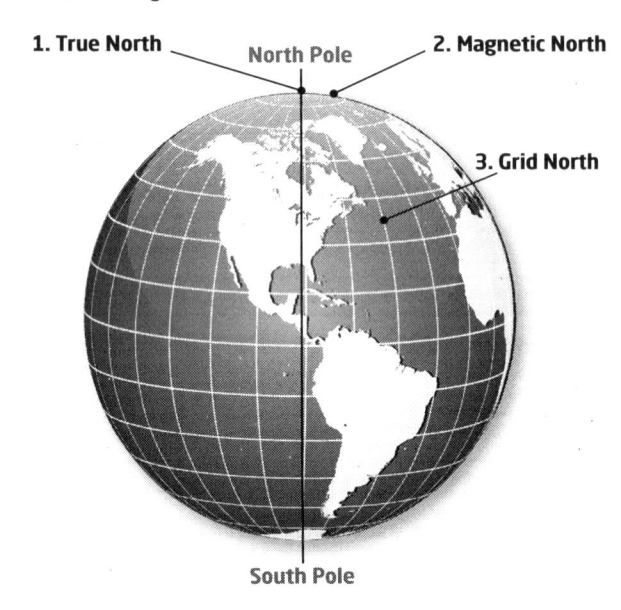

1. **True North**
2. **Magnetic North**
3. **Grid North**

North Pole

South Pole

CHAPTER TWELVE: NAVIGATION (NAV) OVERVIEW

1. **True north:** The most northerly point of the planet.
2. **Magnetic north:** The magnetic pull from the North Pole. This moves around ever so slightly over a period of years so adjustments sometimes need to be made (one degree every six years).
3. **Grid north:** Grid line 'northings' on maps all point towards north. Due to the curved earth being represented on a flat map, these lines are slightly distorted so also don't point exactly to true north.

Orientating a Map Using a Compass

A compass can help with navigating when visibility is poor due to weather, in areas with no major features, at night time and when there are multiple paths heading in different directions to choose from.

Simply place a compass on your map and then rotate yourself, map and compass until the compass needle lines up with the northing lines on the map. This will then tell you which way you are facing and help identify what direction you need to head in to get to your objective.

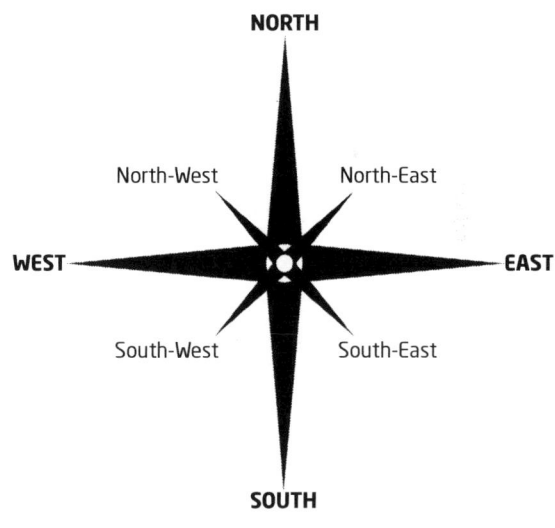

NORTH

North-West   North-East

WEST — **EAST**

South-West   South-East

SOUTH

CHAPTER TWELVE: NAVIGATION (NAV) OVERVIEW

05. CHECKING THE DIRECTION OF HANDRAILS USING A COMPASS AND A MAP *(two star training)*

If the direction you need to travel in to follow a handrail is not clear, it is easy to work out using a compass.

1. Line up the base plate edge with the handrail you intend to follow.
2. Turn the bezel to line up the north/south markings on the compass with the northing grid lines on the map.
3. Turn with the map until the compass needle lines up with the north/south markings on the bezel and the northings on the map.

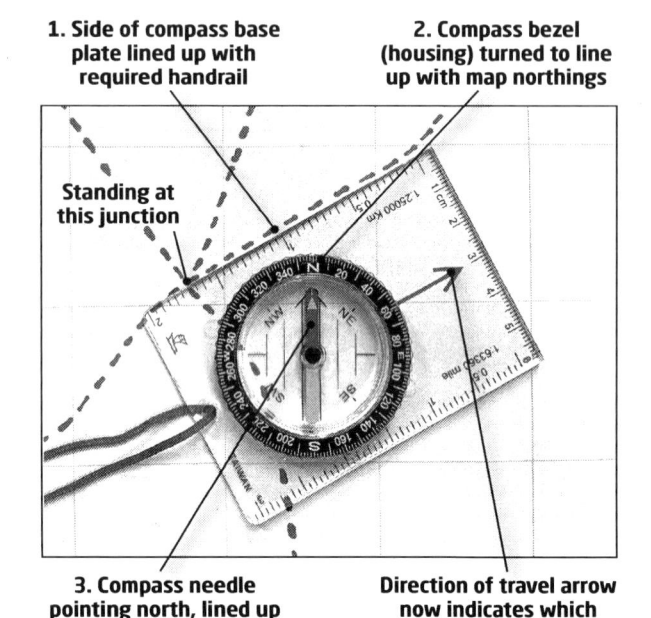

1. Side of compass base plate lined up with required handrail

2. Compass bezel (housing) turned to line up with map northings

Standing at this junction

3. Compass needle pointing north, lined up with map northings

Direction of travel arrow now indicates which way to walk

CHAPTER TWELVE: NAVIGATION (NAV) OVERVIEW

06. ACCESS IN THE OUTDOORS *(two star training)*

This lesson expands on the basic Expedition lesson (see page 190) that covers the Countryside Code, Scottish Outdoor Access Code and Northern Ireland Country Code.

All land in the UK is owned by someone and access to walk across it is granted by the owners. Interaction between different users can cause problems and moving off of any accepted routes may result in trespassing which can be a serious offence. It is therefore important to not just stick to the rules in the various Country Codes, but to be aware of access rights and know where to find out relevant information when planning walks or expeditions.

Source Material:
- The Countryside Code (Countryside Agency).
- Scottish Outdoor Access (Scottish Natural Heritage).
- Northern Ireland Country Code (Countryside Access & Activities Network).
- Tread Lightly (British Mountaineering Council - BMC).
- Access page on the BMC website.
- Walking Group Leader (WGL) and Mountain Leader (ML) award handbooks - Mountain Training England.

Legislation:
- England & Wales: Countryside & Rights of Way Act 2000 (CRoW Act).
- Scotland: Land Reform (Scotland) Act 2003.
- Northern Ireland: Access to the Countryside (Northern Ireland) Order 1983.
- Military: Training on Private Land (TOPL) and issues concerning military groups on private land.

Local Research:
- Access and Conservation Trust (ACT).
- Local tourist and National park offices.
- Websites and local notice boards.
- Local outdoor centres and instructors.
- Route recces.

CHAPTER TWELVE: NAVIGATION (NAV) OVERVIEW

07. PLANNING A ROUTE & IMPLEMENTING A ROUTE-PLAN *(two star training)*

When heading out walking it is important to know as much about the intended route as possible so that you know it is achievable and you already have a clear idea on how to navigate it.

A route plan breaks a larger journey into shorter, more manageable sections (legs) and gives the following information:

- How far the route is.
- How long it will take to walk.
- What the terrain is like.
- What the handrails, collecting features and catching features are for each leg of the journey.
- Potential hazards to avoid or navigate around.
- Potential escape routes in case of emergency (vehicle access etc.).

A route plan can take quite a while to prepare, but the more time spent planning, the easier the navigating will be and, therefore, the more enjoyable the walk will be.

There are various types of route planning.

- **Route trace:** Route marked on tracing paper or acetate placed over the map.
- **Route trace using digital mapping software:** Similar to above, but the route is marked onto the map which can then be printed.
- **Route card:** A written (or printed) set of instructions which lists all information required in a logical order which can be followed like a set of directions alongside the map. This can also be used by someone not walking with the group to know where they will be at certain times.

Tips:

- Estimate distance on a map by using grid squares or trailing a piece of string along paths/roads and then measuring them.
- Estimate time taken using 4kph (or 3kph if carrying weight)
- Estimate height gain and loss using contour lines. Add 1 minute to time taken for every 10m of climb.

CHAPTER TWELVE: NAVIGATION (NAV) OVERVIEW

Route Card

Team name: Walking With Legends
Date: 10 April 2023
Depart Time: 09:15
End time: 12:45
Start Grid Ref: 136 403
Finish Grid Ref: 199 382

Leg	From Location	From Grid Ref	To Location	To Grid Ref	Bearing Degrees	Distance km/m	Climb Metres	Time Mins	Remarks (Landmarks/Hazzards)
1	Start	136 403	Farmhouse	154 393	40	3km	50	50	Follow woodland on the left, pass lake on the right. Do not cross road.
2	Farmhouse	154 393	Cross roads	161 388	98	1km	100	25	Start with farm behind and head towards the church on the hill.
3	Cross roads	161 388	Church	169 391	32	1.4km	-120	21	Cross track and head uphill towards the church.
4	Church	169 391	Car Park	178 393	110	2km	100	40	Turn right at the church and follow the track along past the pub.
5	Car park	178 393	Bridge	184 393	82	0.8km	0	12	Footpath heads out from the far corner of the car park and heads downhill.
6	Bridge	184 393	Finish	199 382	122	2.3km	-80	35	Cross the bridge and follow the path that runs alongside the main road.
						Total	Total	Total	
						10.5km	250	3hrs 5	Add 25 minutes for stops

175

CHAPTER TWELVE: NAVIGATION (NAV) OVERVIEW

TWO STAR TRAINING NAVIGATION ASSESSMENT

The two star Navigation assessment is in two parts.

1. **Preparation of route cards:** Cadets are to be given a start and end point of a route which they then prepare a route card for. The route card must have at least six legs and the route must meet the criteria below.

2. **Practical assessment:** Follow a given route of at least three km with six changes of direction, obvious handrails, several changes of direction and identifiable landmarks visible from the route.

If a cadet fails after a second attempt, re-training is required before attempting again on a different route with a new route card.

CHAPTER TWELVE: NAVIGATION (NAV) OVERVIEW

THREE STAR NAV TRAINING OVERVIEW

Three star Nav is made up of four lessons followed by one daytime and one night time practice period and practical assessments.

01. MEASURING DISTANCES WITH REASONABLE ACCURACY WITH DOUBLE PACING AND TIMING *(three star training)*

One star Navigation training looked at estimating distance on the ground using various techniques. This lesson, re-visits that information in a bit more detail to estimate distances more accurately.

Pacing

Page 164 gives details on how to work out how many paces (double pacing) you take when walking 100 metres. At three star level it is important to understand know this and also understand how it may alter based on different factors.

- **Shorter paces = More paces in 100m:** Carrying a heavy load, wearing bulky clothes, feeling tired, going up or down steep hills and when walking through heavy vegetation or snow will make your paces shorter and therefore there will be more in 100 metres.
- **Longer paces = Less paces in 100m:** Wearing light clothing, carrying little or no weight, swinging your arms and feeling full of energy will make paces slightly longer and therefore there will be less in 100 metres. A good navigator will know what their pacing is for various situations.

Timing

Page 165 gives details on how to work out how long it takes to walk 100 metres and also has a chart to work out how long various distances will take. The different factors above that effect pacing may also effect timing, so bear that in mind as well when planning.

Combine Pacing and Timing

To reduce the risk of errors, it is always good to monitor pacing and timing together when walking.

Example: A distance of 1000 metres (1km) walked at 4km per hour will take approximately 15 minutes. To monitor your pacing, when walking, if you have counted your 100m ten times and walked for about 15 minutes you should be right.

CHAPTER TWELVE: NAVIGATION (NAV) OVERVIEW

02. SET A COMPASS BEARING FROM MAP TO GROUND
(three star training)

A bearing is normally given in degrees of 0 - 359 and can help work out the exact direction of travel over short distances between two locations where the end point is not visible.

1. Line up the base plate edge with the launch (start) point and the attack (finish) point where you are heading with the direction of travel arrow pointing in the direction you need to head.
2. Turn the bezel to line up the north/south markings with the northing grid lines. The orientating arrow must be pointing north.
3. Read the number on the bezel in line with the direction of travel arrow to get a bearing.

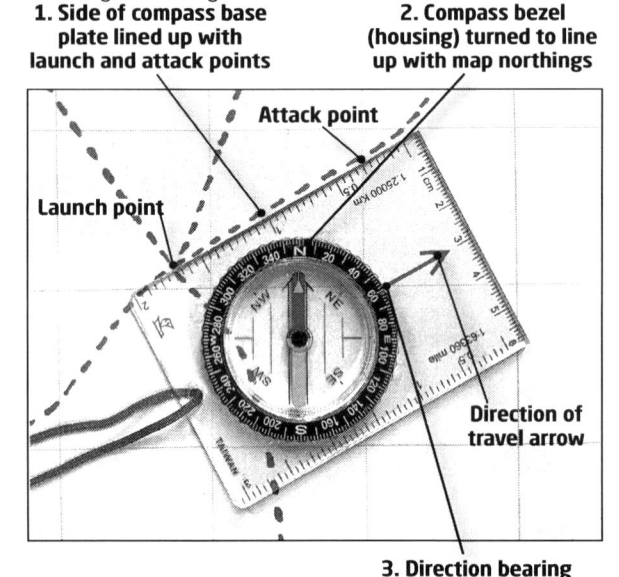

1. Side of compass base plate lined up with launch and attack points

2. Compass bezel (housing) turned to line up with map northings

Attack point

Launch point

Direction of travel arrow

3. Direction bearing given in degrees

CHAPTER TWELVE: NAVIGATION (NAV) OVERVIEW

Magnetic Variation

Due to the variation between magnetic north and grid north (see page 170), it may be necessary to make an adjustment. In the UK, the adjustment is very slight and sometimes not required at all, but in some places in the world, the adjustment is over 20 degrees. In the marginal information of most maps, the adjustment required is noted.

- **West:** Any adjustments west are negative so the degree adjustment is subtracted (turn the bezel right/clockwise).
- **East:** Any adjustments east are positive so the degree adjustment is added (turn the bezel left/anti-clockwise).

03. FOLLOWING A COMPASS BEARING *(three star training)*

Once a bearing has been identified, it can be followed to locate the desired attack point. This technique is only required when the location is not visible due to being a small 'spot feature' or if visibility is poor. Accuracy is essential as any slight error when finding or following the bearing can result in missing your objective completely.

To follow a bearing:

- Hold the compass in front of you.
  - Hold it with both hands.
  - Pull your elbows in tight to your side to keep the compass steady and close to your body.
  - Keep the compass level and parallel to the ground.
  - Have the direction of travel arrow pointing to your front.
- Move your feet in small steps to turn until the north end of the compass needle is in line with the north arrow of the compass bezel.
- Look along the line of the direction arrow to see exactly the direction you need to walk.
- Look for any features near or far that are in line with the direction you need to walk that you could aim for.
- Using pacing and timing, walk along the bearing using visual aids such as features where possible to reach your attack point.

If aiming for a feature in line with your bearing that is between you and the attack point, you can check your bearing again at that feature.

CHAPTER TWELVE: NAVIGATION (NAV) OVERVIEW

04. ESTIMATE TIME FOR HEIGHT GAIN *(three star training)*

Working out distance on a map is only accurate when the ground is flat. When walking up or down hill, the distances are actually greater due to the climb/descent. Walking uphill is also harder work so extra time is required to allow for the extra distance and effort.

As a guide, add one minute for every ten metres of climb.

In this example, the distance between the launch and both attack points (A and B) would look the same on a map but the route going uphill is actually longer.

At 4kph, walking the route on flat ground would only take approximately 1.5 minutes. Walking the route uphill with the climb would add another 10 minutes making the total time 11.5 minutes

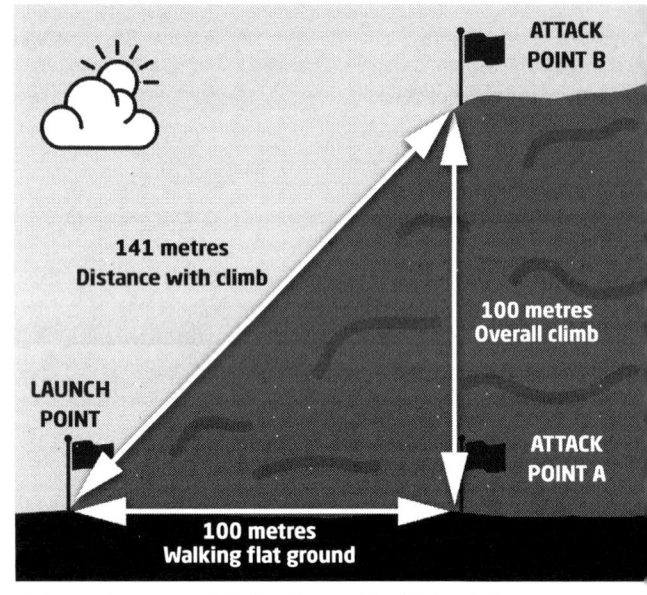

ATTACK POINT B

**141 metres
Distance with climb**

**100 metres
Overall climb**

LAUNCH POINT

ATTACK POINT A

**100 metres
Walking flat ground**

Refer back to page 168 for tips on identifying hills on maps.

CHAPTER TWELVE: NAVIGATION (NAV) OVERVIEW

THREE STAR TRAINING NAVIGATION ASSESSMENT

The three star Navigation assessment is in three parts.

The following must be completed after a two hour day time practice and a two hour night time practice.

1. **Preparation of route cards:** Cadets are given start and end points of the assessment routes which they then prepare route cards for.
2. **Practical assessment 1 - Day navigation:** Follow a given route of at least four km with a minimum of three changes of direction and noticeable elevation changes.
3. **Practical assessment 2 - Night navigation:** The same criteria as the daytime navigation but on a different route.

NOTE: Instructors must be at NNAS silver level (or similar qual) to be permitted to train and assess at three star level.

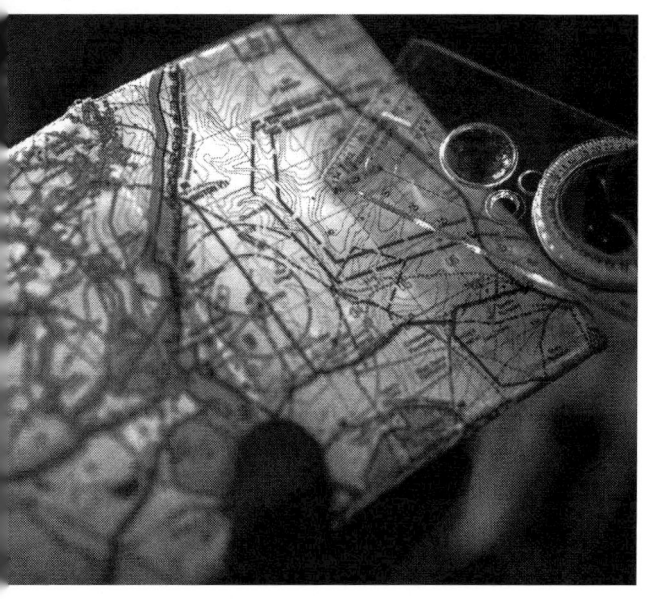

CHAPTER TWELVE: NAVIGATION (NAV) OVERVIEW

FOUR STAR NAV TRAINING OVERVIEW (optional)

Four star navigation is an optional subject which is made up of six lessons and a slightly longer and more detailed day time navigation assessment and night time assessment.

01. USE MAJOR LANDFORMS AS A MEANS OF NAVIGATION
(four star training)

This is a very practical lesson that develops understanding of contour lines and shape of the ground that was covered at two star level.

When viewing a map, it is now important to be able to visualise the ground based on the shape and closeness of contour lines. If you can successfully predict what the ground will look like based on what is printed on a map, the actual landforms around you can act as handrails and/or collecting/catching features.

Revise pages 166 - 168 and practice visualising what the ground will look like by viewing a map and then comparing it to the ground. Look for other features such as rivers and streams flowing down or through these features to help orientate yourself with the ground.

This process will also alert you to any hazards such as extremely steep slopes or cliffs that may be on a planned route.

02. IDENTIFYING SMALLER CONTOUR FEATURES ON MAP AND GROUND *(four star training)*

This lesson continues straight on from the previous lesson and is also very practical.

Identifying large landforms and relating them to the map can be fairly easy with practice, but doing the same with much smaller landforms made up of only two or three contour lines can be a bit trickier. These smaller landforms known as knolls (small hill or ring contour), spurs, re-entrants and cols are quite often part of larger landforms and are useful for navigation checkpoints.

Look at some of these smaller landforms on a map and visualise how they may appear on the ground. Also see how they relate to larger landforms. Try viewing from different viewpoints to see how they look from different angles.

CHAPTER TWELVE: NAVIGATION (NAV) OVERVIEW

03. USING AIMING-OFF TO REACH A TARGET ON A LINEAR FEATURE *(four star training)*

When following a bearing to a very specific attack point, a small error can lead to missing your target and getting lost. If your attack point happens to be on a linear feature, there is a technique called 'aiming-off' that helps guide you directly to the correct location.

Example

In the example below there are two options when following the bearing from the start point to the footbridge that crosses the river.

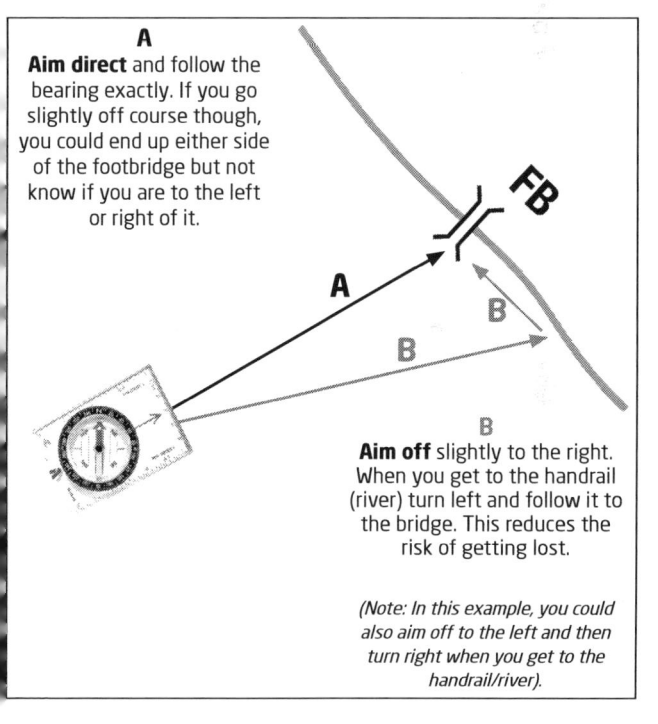

A
Aim direct and follow the bearing exactly. If you go slightly off course though, you could end up either side of the footbridge but not know if you are to the left or right of it.

B
Aim off slightly to the right. When you get to the handrail (river) turn left and follow it to the bridge. This reduces the risk of getting lost.

(Note: In this example, you could also aim off to the left and then turn right when you get to the handrail/river).

CHAPTER TWELVE: NAVIGATION (NAV) OVERVIEW

04. IDENTIFYING THE MOST APPROPRIATE ROUTE WHERE MORE THAN ONE OPTION IS AVAILABLE *(four star training)*

When planning a route, there are sometimes several options available to get to the same location. This lesson looks at route planning (pages 174 - 175) in a bit more detail and how to decide on the most appropriate route.

Here are some things to consider:

- **Direct route:** On the map this may look like the quickest route, but does it have steep hills or cross rivers/hazardous ground etc.?
- **Follow paths and tracks:** These routes may look longer but if they go around steep hills and avoid hazards they may be more suitable.
- **Open ground:** This may enable more direct navigation and have easy to follow handrails and features, but it might also contain hazards or areas with little or no features.

The choice is down to the people planning the route but the main priority is always safety. Other considerations are the ease of walking, duration and enjoyment of the walk.

Relocate if Lost

If you get lost while walking, find a near-by view point and attempt to identify your location using major landforms and contours. Look at handrails and other features around to orientate yourself. If you are still unsure, retrace your steps back to a known location.

05. USING COARSE NAVIGATION AND COLLECTING FEATURES TO LOCATE AN ATTACK POINT *(four star training)*

Basic cadets learn to navigate simple routes using handrails, collecting and catching features and do not use a compass at all. At four star level it is possible to do the same thing, but using major landforms, contour lines and other features to act as handrails, collecting and catching features.

Different Levels of Detail

- **Macro-detail:** This is the overall look at a route or leg using major features and landforms.
- **Micro-detail:** This is the more close up detailed look at smaller landforms, contours and minor features to assist with accuracy.

CHAPTER TWELVE: NAVIGATION (NAV) OVERVIEW

Even separate legs of a journey can be broken down into smaller 'bounds' and this is where micro-detail comes in. Looking at the smaller features and landforms on route to the end of a particular leg can be used as collecting and catching features and help navigate without the need for a compass and bearings.

Traffic Light Navigation

Some sections of a route may be very obvious and easy to follow, whereas others may be quite tricky and can be referred to as follows:

- **Green:** Simple sections with no real need to refer to the map.
- **Amber:** Slightly more complicated sections where slowing down to check position is often required.
- **Red:** Difficult sections where constant monitoring of the map is required to micro-navigate through smaller bounds.

06. FROM AN ATTACK POINT USE FINE NAVIGATION TO LOCATE A TARGET *(four star training)*

This is the final lesson in the Army Cadet Navigation Syllabus and combines all elements covered. White light is allowed for night nav.

Be able to walk accurately on a bearing using pacing and timing to measure distance travelled.

This is 'red traffic light' navigation and is slow, deliberate and cautious to be as accurate as possible. With each stage of navigating, remember the seven 'W' (what) questions.

1. **What direction?** Correct bearing.
2. **What distance?** Estimate on the map then use pacing and timing.
3. **What height gain?** How many contour lines? How many metres?
4. **What time will it take to get there?** Estimate time.
5. **What will you see on the way?** Collecting features/handrails etc.
6. **What will you see when you get there?** Attack point location.
7. **What will you see if you go too far?** Catching feature(s).

Micro-details on contour lines

Use the magnifying glass on the compass to find fine detail on contours and more easily identify smaller features.

1mm on a 1:25,000 scale map is a 25m feature on the ground.

CHAPTER TWELVE: NAVIGATION (NAV) OVERVIEW

FOUR STAR TRAINING NAVIGATION ASSESSMENT

The four star Navigation assessment is in three parts.

1. **Preparation of route cards:** Cadets are given start and end points of the assessment routes which they then prepare route cards for.
2. **Practical assessment 1 - Day navigation:** Follow a given route of at least five km with a minimum of three changes of direction and noticeable elevation changes over suitably challenging terrain.
3. **Practical assessment 2 - Night navigation:** The same criteria as the daytime navigation but on a different route.

NOTE: Instructors must be at NNAS silver level (or similar qual) to be permitted to train and assess at four star level.

CHAPTER THIRTEEN
EXPEDITION (EXP) OVERVIEW

CONTENTS:
- Introduction
- Basic Exp Training Overview
- One Star Exp Training Overview
- Two Star Exp Training Overview
- Three Star Exp Training Overview
- Four Star Exp Training Overview

REFERENCES:
- *Army Cadet Syllabus - AC71101 (Version 1.2 - July 2022)*
- *Expedition Training Guide for Army Cadet Instructors - AC72149 (Version 2 - 2021)*
- *Army Cadets Expeditions (ACS 21 & DofE) and Adventurous Training Manual - AC71849 (Version 2 - 2022)*
- *Army Cadet Resource Centre via Westminster*

CHAPTER THIRTEEN: EXPEDITION (EXP) OVERVIEW

INTRODUCTION

An expedition is journey that has a specific aim or goal. In the ACF, expeditions are normally carried out on foot in teams of up to around seven cadets and combine elements of navigation and first aid with specific expedition skills.

Expeditions are always carried out in civilian clothing, although it is acceptable to wear elements of uniform such as t-shirts and boots.

Duke of Edinburgh Award (DofE)

ACS Expedition training is the same as the Duke of Edinburgh (DofE) Award Expedition element so anyone completing Expedition in the ACF can also sign off sections of their DofE training.

One star passed = Bronze practice
Two star passed = Bronze DofE
Three star passed = Silver practice
Four star passed = Silver DofE

Interested cadets need to talk to their DofE rep at detachment to enrol.

- **Badges available:** DofE Bronze, Silver and Gold if enrolled
- **Specialist qualifications required to teach:** Any competent CFAV or senior cadet can deliver all Expedition lessons with the exception of lessons involving the cooking stove. The Commandant (or designated rep) must approve CFAVs that can teach the stove lessons.
CFAVs must be qualified to the required level to supervise or assess expeditions. The training manual AC72149 has more detail.
- **Further progression beyond the syllabus:** Gold DofE along with other national and international Expedition opportunities.

CHAPTER THIRTEEN: EXPEDITION (EXP) OVERVIEW

BASIC EXP TRAINING OVERVIEW

Basic expedition training provides an introduction and overview only. There are two lessons followed by a written or verbal assessment.

01. INTRODUCTION TO EXPEDITIONS *(basic training)*

Topics covered through Expedition (Exped) training are as follows:

- **Expedition environment:** How to behave in the countryside, what areas you have access to and how the weather effects your planning.
- **Planning:** Setting aims and how to plan an expedition from scratch.
- **Health and safety:** Awareness of risk and dealing with emergencies.
- **Clothing and equipment:** What to wear and how to pack.
- **Camping:** Where to camp and how to set up a tent.
- **Food:** What to pack and how to cook safely.
- **Teamwork:** How to behave in a team and work with others.
- **Leadership:** Taking control and providing leadership.

Benefits

- Physical Fitness
- Mental health
- Respect for outdoors
- Respect for others
- Self confidence
- Perseverance
- Self reliance
- Confidence
- Leadership
- Mental resilience
- Organisation
- Teamwork

The Expedition Sequence

1. **Training:** Correct training before setting out on an expedition.
2. **Planning:** Every expedition needs an aim and a specific location.
3. **Prepare:** Create route cards, buy adequate food and pack.
4. **Check:** Everyone has the correct kit and maps and the weather is going to be acceptable.
5. **Go for it:** Carry out the expedition and have fun.
6. **Debrief:** Make notes of anything that went well or could have gone better and discuss this with your team mates how to make improvements for next time.

CHAPTER THIRTEEN: EXPEDITION (EXP) OVERVIEW

02. EXPEDITION ENVIRONMENT *(basic training)*
The Countryside Code - Respect. Protect. Enjoy

Expeditions take place in public places such as footpaths, woodland, moorland, mountains and wild country so we need to make sure we act in an appropriate way and respect the people and wildlife we may encounter.

To guide us, we follow the Countryside Code which is produced by the Government to help ensure everyone gets along and enjoy the outdoors.

Respect Everyone
- Be considerate to those living in, working in and enjoying the countryside.
- Leave gates and property as you find them.
- Do not block access to gateways or driveways when parking.
- Be nice, say hello, share the space.
- Follow local signs and keep to marked paths unless wider access is available.

Protect the Environment
- Take your litter home - leave no trace of your visit.
- Do not light fires and only have BBQs where signs say you can.
- Always keep dogs under control and in sight.
- Dog poo - bag it and bin it - any public waste bin will do.
- Care for nature - do not cause damage or disturbance.

Enjoy the Outdoors
- Check your route and local conditions.
- Plan your adventure - know what to expect and what you can do.
- Enjoy your visit, have fun, make a memory.

CHAPTER THIRTEEN: EXPEDITION (EXP) OVERVIEW

Follow the Signs

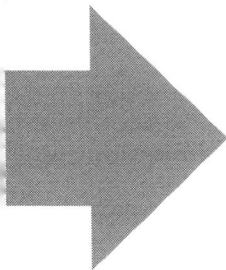

Yellow - Footpath: Walkers (& mobility scooters) only.

Blue - Bridleway: Same as footpath but also open to cyclists and horse riders.

Purple - Restricted Byway: Same as bridleway but also open to other non-motorised vehicles.

Red - Byway Open to All Vehicles: Open to all including cars and motorbikes.

Open Access
Areas where you do not need to stick to the footpaths

National Trail
Well marked routes for walkers and sometimes cyclists and horses

PERMISSIVE PATH

THE PUBLIC MAY WALK THIS ROUTE BY PERMISSION OF THE LANDOWNER. IT IS NOT DEDICATED AS A PUBLIC RIGHT OF WAY

Permissive Path
Access granted by land owner, but can be revoked

UK Variations

The main principles of the Countryside code are based on common sense and decency, there are however a few variations in the code and access in Northern Ireland and Scotland so it is worth researching more if in these areas.

Northern Ireland: There are some differences in the wording of the code and a few points made that are not covered on the previous page. Visit the website for more info: https://www.nidirect.gov.uk/articles/countryside-code

Scotland: Walkers do not have to stick to footpaths on most of the land in Scotland which gives more freedom to explore. There are restrictions however, so it is wise to research more if walking in Scotland. Visit the website for more info: https://www.outdooraccess-scotland.scot

CHAPTER THIRTEEN: EXPEDITION (EXP) OVERVIEW

Progression

Expeditions start off on a small scale to be able to put training into practice in a safe and enjoyable environment. That is why there is progression built into the Army Cadet Syllabus to allow cadets to develop and practice and build up to more adventurous expeditions.

- **Basic training:** Introduction to expeditions and the expedition environment.
- **One star training** (Bronze DofE training): More training around safety, kit and cooking along with an accompanied expedition that lasts at least six hours. Cadets will navigate, set up tents and cook and will ideally stay out over night.
- **Two star training** (Bronze DofE exped): Cadets will further develop skills around planning and teamwork and will then complete a two day unaccompanied (remotely supervised) expedition with two nights sleeping out. They will automatically pass the expedition phase of Bronze DofE.
- **Three star training** (Silver DofE practice): Further training in expedition is followed by another unaccompanied (remotely supervised) expedition over two days and two nights.
- **Four star training** (Silver DofE exped): Further training followed by an unsupervised (remotely supervised) expedition running over three days and two nights.

BASIC TRAINING EXPEDITION ASSESSMENT

The Basic Exped assessment is conducted in written or verbal from and contains two questions on the subjects covered (several responses required).

ONE STAR EXP TRAINING OVERVIEW

One star Exped is made up of a series of eight lessons followed by a one day supervised expedition (minimum of six hours) with cadets ideally camping out for one night.

CHAPTER THIRTEEN: EXPEDITION (EXP) OVERVIEW

01. EXPEDITION AIMS *(one star training)*

Setting an aim for an expedition gives it a purpose which helps motivate the team and can develop skills such as teamwork, communication and leadership.

Aims can be specific to a location such as getting to the peak of a certain mountain or can be very general such as creating a video diary of a two day walking expedition. Whatever the aim it must be decided by the team and needs to appeal to all involved and be achievable.

02. EMERGENCY PROCEDURES *(one star training)*

With the correct training and planning, expeditions should always be safe and enjoyable, but we need to be prepared to deal with any unexpected emergency situations if they arise. Always let your supervisor know if you have any problems or concerns at all and call 999/112 if there are any serious issues.

- **Injury or accident:** Deal with as per your first aid training and if serious call 999 and if possible, get casualty to an access point for easy collection.
- **Ill health:** Same as for injury/accident, but try to maintain good hygiene standards if dealing with something contagious.
- **Team getting lost:** Retrace steps to a last known location and use navigation training to look for landmarks.
- **Losing a team member:** Always stay as a group to avoid this, but if it does happen, stay where you are and contact your supervisor.
- **Access issues on route:** Check maps to find a suitable alternative that does not deviate too far. If in doubt contact your supervisor.
- **Serious weather changes:** Think of safety first and use the equipment you have available. If extreme, notify your supervisor and arrange to be collected.
  - **Too hot:** Take breaks in the shade until cooler, drink fluids and use sun cream.
  - **Too cold:** Add clothing layers and have hot drinks. Use emergency shelter or tents if needed.
  - **Too wet:** Use waterproof clothing and put up tents if extreme. If continuing to walk, check map and avoid rivers, streams and bogs.

CHAPTER THIRTEEN: EXPEDITION (EXP) OVERVIEW

Calling the Emergency Services

In remote areas, you may need to move around to get a phone signal and, if possible, move location to a track or junction that is easy to locate. Get an accurate grid reference (or what 3 words location) and shout/whistle for help every 10 minutes. You can also use a distress marker such as torch or mirror to highlight your location to search teams. Remember to take notes ready to hand over.

DO NOT

- Call any parents as this will cause panic and could hinder recovery.
- Leave a casualty on their own or go alone to get help.
- Use any social media to contact people or share information.

Available to ACF instructors through the Cadet Resource Centre is a template 'safety card' which can be printed, filled in and given to everyone taking part on an expedition. It has spaces to record expedition details and important points of contact.

03. HEALTH & SAFETY: AWARENESS OF RISK *(one star training)*

Lots of ACF activities have an element of risk, but through careful planning and regular 'risk assessments' these risks can be minimised. During expeditions, cadets can be in situations where they are not under direct supervision so it is important for everyone to be aware of risks and how to manage them.

- **Hazard:** Something you may encounter during an activity. E.g. Lake.
- **Risk:** What could potentially happen with that hazard. E.g. Drowning.

Risk Assessment

- **Before activity:** Carrying out a formal risk assessment before an activity can help to minimise all risks by putting processes in place or taking extra equipment or clothing. Hazards can be man made, natural or personal.
- **During activity (dynamic risk assessment):** There may be times when a hazard appears that was not expected such as weather or animals. We need to assess these risks as we encounter them.
- **After activity:** Team discussions after an activity are a good way to revisit risks encountered that had not been planned for and decide on the best ways to deal with them in future.

CHAPTER THIRTEEN: EXPEDITION (EXP) OVERVIEW

04. CLOTHING, FOOTWEAR & EMERGENCY EQUIPMENT
(one star training)

A full kit list for expedition is given on pages 62 - 64, but the following are considered items of safety equipment:
- First Aid kit
- Emergency whistle
- Adequate tent
- Emergency rations
- Hat & gloves
- Map & compass
- Notepad & pen/pencil
- Emergency bag
- Emergency shelter
- Head torch
- Mobile phone
- GPS device

05. PACKING, WATERPROOFING AND MANUAL HANDLING OF A RUCKSACK *(one star training)*

Rucksacks are available in all sizes, shapes, styles and colours so choosing the right one can be a bit confusing. Look for one with a strong and substantial waist belt and wide, padded shoulder straps with an adjustable sternum strap. You will need enough pockets and compartments to be able to separate kit when packing and an adjustable back system to be able to get a good fit.

60 litres = One night   65 - 70 litres = Two - three nights
80 litres = Extra space for kit such as tent

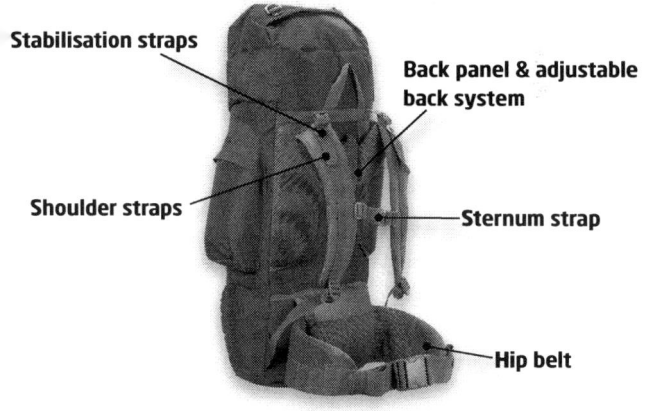

Stabilisation straps

Back panel & adjustable back system

Shoulder straps

Sternum strap

Hip belt

CHAPTER THIRTEEN: EXPEDITION (EXP) OVERVIEW

Packing Your Rucksack

Pack your rucksack so that you can easily get to things you need regularly and the weight is evenly distributed. Ideally pack heavier items closer to your body and distribute smaller items to balance the load. Water and fuels should be stored in bags near the outside of the bag or in outside pouches. Foam ground mats can be attached outside in a waterproof bag.

Pack items you won't need until later in the day such as spare clothes, wash kit, sleeping bag etc lower down. Items you may need to get to during the day or in a hurry nearer the top and in pockets/pouches.

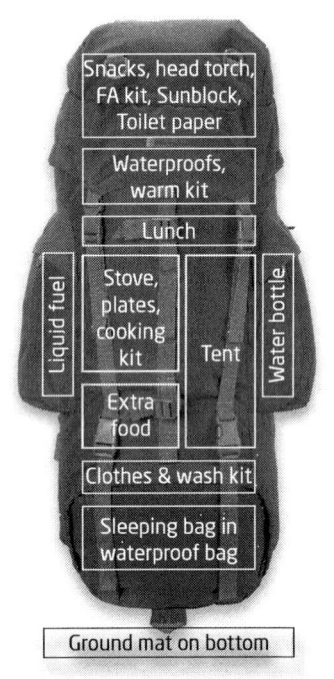

- Snacks, head torch, FA kit, Sunblock, Toilet paper
- Waterproofs, warm kit
- Lunch
- Liquid fuel
- Stove, plates, cooking kit
- Tent
- Water bottle
- Extra food
- Clothes & wash kit
- Sleeping bag in waterproof bag
- Ground mat on bottom

CHAPTER THIRTEEN: EXPEDITION (EXP) OVERVIEW

06. CHOOSING A CAMPSITE, PITCHING & STRIKING TENTS
(one star training)

There are lots of different types of tents available that are suitable for anything from low level camping in your back garden on a nice warm evening right through to extreme expeditions in the mountains. Tents are normally provided for cadets to use on expedition so although you may not need to buy one, you need to know a bit about them.

Pop up tent: Made in one piece they simply 'pop up' when put in place. Normally very cheap but are bulky to carry and are only designed for very light use making them unsuitable for expeditions.

Ridge tent: Made with two end poles and one joining 'ridge' pole, they offer good protection from the elements but are not very suitable for more than one person due to limited headroom and storage space.

Tunnel tent: These have end poles only and are pulled tight using guy ropes and pegs. They have more room but can be bulkier, are not so good in high winds and are harder to put up.

Dome tent: Very simple to put up and are strong due to the two crossed poles. Good for groups but don't always have lots of storage space. They offer good protection from the elements and are light and easy to set up.

Geodesic tent: Similar to dome tents but have more poles and are sturdier. This means they are also more expensive and are harder to put up. They offer great protection from the elements and have a lot of space.

CHAPTER THIRTEEN: EXPEDITION (EXP) OVERVIEW

Camping

Campsites vary from large established sites with lots of facilities to small private sites with minimal facilities. There may even be times when you will need to camp away from an official campsite meaning you will have no facilities.

- Learn how to set your tent up and practice a few times so you can do it quickly and easily when you get to your first camp site.

- Make a note of all of the parts included so you can check you still have everything every time you pack your tent away.

- Check the tent isn't damaged and take items for repairs on the go.

- Split shared items of kit between the group and work out who will do what job when setting up.

- On arrival at the campsite set up tents straight away to immediately have somewhere to store kit and take shelter.

- Set up on the flattest ground you can find with no stones or tree roots. If it's windy, face the door away from the wind. If sunny, look for areas of shade.

- Keep the inside of the tent dry and store damp clothes/kit in the porch. If it is warm, leave the doors and vents open to circulate air.

- Try not to be too far away from facilities such as toilets and showers, but also avoid being in heavy traffic areas where others will be walking constantly.

- Be considerate of other campers. Keep noise down and leave showers and wash facilities clean and tidy.

- When packing your tent away, remove as much moisture and mud as possible.

Wild camping is camping away from official campsites. It may be necessary due to a safety concern and being unable to get to your planned destination or it may be the only option on your expedition due to the remoteness of your location.

As there will be no facilities such as water for washing and cooking or any toilets. Extra preparation, planning and training is required for these situations, but remember that hygiene and safety are the main priorities.

CHAPTER THIRTEEN: EXPEDITION (EXP) OVERVIEW

07. COOKING: SAFE USE OF STOVES AND SAFE HANDLING AND CARRIAGE OF FUELS *(one star training)*

Expeditions involve preparing hot meals and drinks and there are elements of safety involved that need to be taken seriously. Stoves for cooking require fuel and heat which can be dangerous and, if not treated carefully, can lead to burns, scalds or damage to property and the environment. If food is not cooked correctly it can also lead to ill health and food poisoning.

NEVER USE A STOVE WITHOUT ADEQUATE PRIOR TRAINING

Solid fuel stoves: Small, lightweight cookers that use cheap solid fuel blocks or alcohol based gels. These get very hot and produce toxic smoke when used and the flame (heat) cannot be controlled which makes them unsuitable for expedition use.

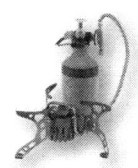

Pressurised liquid fuel stoves: These use petrol or similar branded liquid fuels which need to be carried in a container to be able to fill the stove. Although the flame control is good on these they are not suitable for standard ACF or DofE expeditions. They are good for trips to more remote or high altitude areas though.

3. Gas stoves Portable and easy to use, they have good flame control and run on either Butane or Propane gas. Stoves that have a fitting on top of the gas cylinder can be a bit unstable and the gas may not work so well in very cold temperatures or high altitude. Cannisters must screw on and not be pierced.

Methylated spirit stoves: These run on a liquid fuel that needs to be carried in specific safety bottles that can then be used to re-fill the stove when required. They have good flame control and are portable and reliable.

Trangia stoves are available in gas or methylated spirit versions and are supplied with all the required pots and pans to be able to cook for a whole team.

CHAPTER THIRTEEN: EXPEDITION (EXP) OVERVIEW

Cooking Basics

There are specific ways that each type of stove needs to be handled but there are a few general rules that need to be observed for all.

- Learn how to use your stove before setting off on an expedition.
- Make sure to have enough of the correct fuel for your trip.
- Choose a low, flat, sheltered area to set up, away from dry grass.
- Do not set up on raised areas such as walls or picnic tables.
- Create a windshield from tinfoil or similar if required.
- Don't leave active stoves unattended.
- Have water (or wet tea towel) handy when cooking in case of fire.
- Cook standing up or on one knee so you can move quickly if there is an accident.
- Create a re-fuelling area for stoves that run on liquid fuel that is at least three metres away from tents and the cooking area (take stove to the fuel).
- Make sure flames are completely out and stove has cooled down before re-fuelling.
- Store all fuel types outside or in the porch of your tent in case of fumes.
- Remove gas cannisters and, if possible, burn off excess liquid fuels before packing stoves away for transit.
- When finished cooking, clear away all rubbish and dispose of it in the correct bins or take it away with you. Keep different types of rubbish separate if there are recycling facilities.
- Keep everything within easy reach before starting to cook.
- Know the capacity of your pots.
- Plan cooking times so everything is ready together.
- Cook with lids on pots to speed up cooking times and save fuel.
- Stir cooking food frequently if required to stop sticking or burning.
- Cook thoroughly to improve taste and to avoid food poisoning.

All groups should have adequate cleaning materials and cloths to be able to clean all cooking pots and utensils to maintain hygiene.

CHAPTER THIRTEEN: EXPEDITION (EXP) OVERVIEW

08. PLANNING & COOKING AN APPROPRIATE EXPEDITION MENU *(one star training)*

Cadets need to be self sufficient on expeditions so are expected to plan, purchase, pack and prepare their own meals. They need to make sure they have enough food for the duration of their trip to give energy and boost morale.

Cadets will need around 3500 calories per day on expeditions and food needs to be nutritionally balanced, with a mix of fast and slow release energy sources. (The 'Keeping Active' part of the Army Cadet syllabus covers this in more detail at basic level).

Choosing Food

Fruit & Vegetables: These are good for a healthy digestive system and contain lots of nutrients.

Carbohydrates: These are meal staples such as rice, pasta and potatoes that give the fastest and longest lasting energy release.

Proteins: These come from meat, fish, eggs, nuts, beans and pulses and help to repair damaged and tired muscles.

Dairy & Fats: These have the highest calorie content and include butter, oils, milk, yoghurt and cheese.

Sugars: Sugar is in most processed foods but cakes, sweets and energy bars have a high content which is good for quick release energy and helps boost morale.

As well as looking at the nutritional value of food, there are other considerations.

- Size & weight
- Durability of items and packaging
- Lifespan
- Cooking instructions
- Preparation time
- Flavours

CHAPTER THIRTEEN: EXPEDITION (EXP) OVERVIEW

EXPEDITION MEAL PLANNER

Length of trip	Breakfast	Lunch	Dinner	Snacks	Calories
1 Star 1 day, 1 night	x1	x1	x1		Approx
2 Star 2 days, 1 night	x1	x2	x1		Approx
3 Star 2 days, 2 nights	x2	x2	x2		Approx
4 Star 3 days, 2 nights	x2	x3	x2		Approx
Post 4 Star 4 days, 3 nights	x3	x4	x3		Approx

CHAPTER THIRTEEN: EXPEDITION (EXP) OVERVIEW

ONE STAR TRAINING EXPEDITION ASSESSMENT

There is no theory assessment for lessons received, but all lessons must be delivered and understood by cadets before taking part in a practical supervised expedition assessment.

The expedition must be a minimum of six hours long and should ideally involve camping out for one night. Cadets need to be in teams of four to seven and must plan their own meals and pack their own kit.

Staff are to walk with cadets but should only observe and assess unless it is necessary to intervene.

CHAPTER THIRTEEN: EXPEDITION (EXP) OVERVIEW

TWO STAR EXP TRAINING OVERVIEW

Two star expedition is made up of three revision periods of lessons covered at one star level along with four extra lessons all designed to help cadets plan and prepare for a two day and one night expedition.

01. REVISION PERIOD: EMERGENCY PROCEDURES
(two star training)

Refer back to one star training.

02. REVISION PERIOD: CLOTHING, FOOTWEAR, EMERGENCY EQUIPMENT, PACKING, WATERPROOFING AND MANUAL HANDLING OF A RUCKSACK OR OTHER SUITABLE CONTAINER *(two star training)*

Refer back to one star training

03. REVISION PERIOD: SAFE USE OF STOVES, AND SAFE HANDLING AND CARRIAGE OF FUELS *(two star training)*

Refer back to one star training

04. PLANNING: PRODUCE A PLAN FOR THE AIM OF THE ACTIVITY *(two star training)*

For the two star Exped assessment, cadets must plan an aim and produce a route card for the two day and one night expedition. Briefly looked at during one star training, an aim is an essential part of the planning process and gives more depth than just completing a walk and getting a badge. The aim needs to add purpose and an extra level of enjoyment to an expedition and needs to be decided by the team. When choosing an aim, everyone should get involved in choosing it as all have a role to play in its execution.

When choosing an aim, look at a map of your destination to see if anything on your route inspires any aims. Make a list and then discuss within your group. Here are some ideas:

History: The area being walked across or a specific landmark or building.

Geography: Investigating plants, animals or landforms along a route.

Physical activity: Cover a certain distance or climb a specific summit.

Emotions & feelings: Impact of conditions such as weather and terrain on team morale.

CHAPTER THIRTEEN: EXPEDITION (EXP) OVERVIEW

Aim suggestions
- Investigate the effects of tourism along a national trail.
- Study the physical and mental effects of Expedition on the team.
- Learn about rock formations and types along a route.
- Create a team song or chant.
- Make a team music playlist to represent the expedition.
- Get to a mountain summit and take a team photo.
- Make a video diary to show all aspects of an expedition.
- Take photos to create a montage of the entire expedition.

Post-Expedition Reporting

After all expeditions, it is important to sit down as a team and discuss how the expedition went. This allows everyone to work out what went well and what could be improved on for next time. It is also good to share the experience with others so a talk, presentation or video playback to other cadets, parents or instructors works well.

05. IDENTIFYING HAZARDS & ACCESS ISSUES ON MAPS
(two star training)

This lesson refers back to previous lessons covered during Expedition and Navigation training so should be revisited:

Expedition environment (basic training) pages 190 - 191: This looked at the Countryside code (and other regional variations) as well as basic access rights.

Health & safety - Awareness of risk (one star training) page 194: This covered the basics of identifying hazards and carrying out risk assessments.

Check during the planning stage

Hazards and access issues can be identified before an expedition by referring to maps, aerial photos and local guides. You can also carry out a route 'recce' and talk to others that have done the journey before.

Reacting to changes during the expedition

During the expedition you may come across other hazards such as bad weather or unexpected animals. You may also encounter access issues such as closed or blocked paths. In these instances, think safety first and be prepared to adapt your route or stop the expedition if needed.

CHAPTER THIRTEEN: EXPEDITION (EXP) OVERVIEW

06. ROLES WITHIN AN EXPEDITION TEAM *(two star training)*

Team work on an expedition is essential so it is another thing that needs to be discussed and planned before setting off. Spreading the workload and making sure everyone has some kind of responsibility, brings the team together and creates a much better experience.

Do...
- Discuss as a team what roles need to be fulfilled.
- Allow people to volunteer for roles they are excited to take on.
- Allow people to take turns in more interesting roles.
- Take turns in carrying out less exciting roles.

Do not...
- Allow part of the group to make decisions for everyone.
- Tell people what they will be doing without discussion.
- Stereotype and assume what people are most suited to.
- Set off without a clear plan of how the team will work.

Role suggestions:
- Team leader
- Navigator
- First aider
- Morale booster
- Cook(s)
- Tent builder(s)
- Photographer
- Pacing and/or timing manager

Morale

Morale is the overall mood of the team. Normally in good weather when first setting off on an expedition, morale can be very high. When people get tired and hungry, when the weather changes for the worse or the team gets lost, morale can drop leaving people feeling miserable and possibly angry. It is at these times where the team needs to stick together and help each other through. The real test is be able to keep smiling even when things are not going to plan.

CHAPTER THIRTEEN: EXPEDITION (EXP) OVERVIEW

07. PLANNING THE ROUTE AND PREPARING ROUTE CARDS
(two star training)

Having now decided on the aim for your expedition, identified all of the hazards and allocated roles to everyone in the team, the final stage is to plan your route and prepare a route card.

Route Planning

You will be given a map of the area along with certain key locations such as start point, finish point, campsite location, areas to avoid and locations for official checkpoints. Your team then needs to work out the best route to follow to reach these key locations while also achieving your aim, avoiding hazards and meeting the assessment criteria.

Route Card

Details around completing route cards were covered during two star navigation training and more info is on page 174. There is also an example route card on page 175.

You will need to complete one route card for each day to cover the route to the campsite and the route to the finish point. Aim to fit all details for a whole day onto just one route card but remember to add as much detail as possible. Pick obvious checkpoints and give them a name as well as a grid reference. Be as accurate as possible with distances and bearings and include direction of travel as N, SE etc. even if a bearing is not required.

Be generous with timings to allow time for map reading, achieving expedition aims, taking breaks and having a good lunch stop.

TWO STAR TRAINING EXPEDITION ASSESSMENT

There is no theory assessment for lessons received, but all lessons must be delivered and understood by cadets before taking part in a practical remotely supervised expedition assessment over two days and one night.

Note: Only staff with a relevant National Governing Body expedition qualification can run and assess the expedition.

CHAPTER THIRTEEN: EXPEDITION (EXP) OVERVIEW

THREE STAR EXP TRAINING OVERVIEW (optional)

Three star expedition is made up of three revision periods of lessons covered at one star level along with four extra lessons all designed to help cadets plan and prepare for a two day and two night expedition.

01. REVISION PERIOD: EMERGENCY PROCEDURES
(three star training)

Refer back to one star training.

02. REVISION PERIOD: CLOTHING, FOOTWEAR, EMERGENCY EQUIPMENT, PACKING, WATERPROOFING AND MANUAL HANDLING OF A RUCKSACK OR OTHER SUITABLE CONTAINER *(three star training)*

Refer back to one star training

03. REVISION PERIOD: SAFE USE OF STOVES, AND SAFE HANDLING AND CARRIAGE OF FUELS *(three star training)*

Refer back to one star training

04. PLANNING: PRODUCE A PLAN FOR THE AIM OF THE ACTIVITY *(three star training)*

Refer back to one and two star training.

This is the same process as when preparing for the two star expedition, but cadets are expected to do a bit more research to look at some more varied aims. Talking to instructors, expedition leaders and other more senior cadets as well as using the internet, DofE website, YouTube, blogs etc. is encouraged.

Using the expedition area map, local information and the inspiration from their research, teams can then come up with several aims which can then be narrowed down to just one by group discussion and deciding which is the most appropriate, enjoyable and engaging.

Extra equipment may be needed depending on the aim so that also needs to be factored in when planning for the expedition.

CHAPTER THIRTEEN: EXPEDITION (EXP) OVERVIEW

05. AWARENESS OF LEGISLATION AROUND ACCESS ON LAND & WATER INCLUDING WILD CAMPING & COLLECTING WATER *(three star training)*

Information around access rights on land and looking after the countryside has already been covered in two star navigation (page 173) and basic expedition (pages 190 - 191).

Expeditions at three star level and above are likely to be in more remote areas so understanding access rights is now more important.

CRoW Act 2000

The CRoW (Countryside Right of Way) act 2000 introduced new rights of access on foot to open country and registered land in England and Wales.

- **Public rights of way:** These are footpaths and bridleways etc. that are marked on most common maps. Anyone in England, Wales and Northern Ireland can walk them.
- **Open access land:** This is land such as mountain, moor, heath and down where you can roam without sticking to footpaths. Over 7% of countryside in England and over 20% of countryside in Wales is considered open access.

There is a lot more information on the Government website:

www.gov.uk/right-of-way-open-access-land

Land Reform (Scotland) Act

In Scotland, everyone has access rights to most of the outdoors as long as their countryside rules are strictly followed.

There is a lot more info on the outdoor access Scotland website:

www.outdooraccess-scotland.scot

CHAPTER THIRTEEN: EXPEDITION (EXP) OVERVIEW

Access on Water

Using waterways for expeditions by kayak, canoe etc is allowed but the rules can be more complex.

There is more information on the British Canoeing website:

www.britishcanoeing.org.uk/access-and-environment

Wild camping

Wild camping is camping in the countryside away from official campsites. It is illegal in England, Wales and Northern Ireland without landowner permission but in Scotland it is permitted to wild camp anywhere that doesn't effect businesses, farming or the environment.

Camping away from an official campsite is exciting but causes extra issues such as absence of toilet facilities and running water for washing, drinking and cooking.

Water needs to be bought in by expedition supervisors or it needs to be sourced from local water sources and purified. When washing make sure not to contaminate water sources with chemicals and soaps.

Going to the toilet involves using a trowel to dig a reasonable size hole in an un-walked area, using biodegradable toilet paper and fully filling in holes after use.

When choosing a place to camp, look for level ground that won't hold water if it rains. Avoid areas that may be a common walking route and be careful to leave things exactly as you found them.

CHAPTER THIRTEEN: EXPEDITION (EXP) OVERVIEW

06. WEATHER & ITS IMPACT ON EXPEDITIONS
(three star training)

Weather has a major impact on expeditions and needs to be factored in during the later planning stages. Most people like to check what the weather will be doing in the coming days, but most normal sources such as the Met Office and BBC weather give forecasts for key locations around the country and not remote or mountainous areas.

Forecast

Checking the weather forecast before setting off on an expedition is an important safety check that needs to be done. They are not always 100% accurate, but they do give a good idea of the type of weather you may encounter and will let you know if extreme weather is inbound.

Postponing an expedition due to an extreme weather warning will avoid a potential miserable or even dangerous experience.

Some areas of the country, such as the Lake District, have websites with up to the minute weather forecasts. There are also websites and apps that specialise in mountain weather.

The Mountain Weather Information Service (MWIS) provides great forecasts for most major mountainous areas in the UK:
www.mwis.org.uk

Weather in mountainous and remote areas can change drastically very quickly so it is important to have the right clothing with you and watch for warnings of weather changes. This can be done by monitoring weather forecasts, but can also be done by observing the clouds and wind. Temperature also drops by around 1º for every 100m of climb.

Clouds

If the clouds change then the weather is likely to change too. Wind direction will also change the temperature and can bring in different weather.

Individual, small or extremely high clouds can indicate fair weather, whereas, lots of dark, imposing clouds can indicate bad weather, rain and storms.

CHAPTER THIRTEEN: EXPEDITION (EXP) OVERVIEW

Wind

Wind has a major effect on the weather and how enjoyable an expedition is. Wind is stronger in higher places and valleys and strong wind can make it feel a lot colder than it is, this is called 'wind chill'.

In the UK, wind from the north and north east/west is from Polar or Arctic regions so tends to be colder weather and possibly rain or even snow. Winds from the south, south east/west is tropical air that tends to bring in warmer air.

Wind is recorded in miles per hour (MPH) or gale force.

Gale force one is the equivalent of around two mph. It is easy for walking and adds no wind chill. Gale force ten is the equivalent of around 90 - 100mph and is so extreme you may not be able to walk. The wind chill factor makes it feel around 20 degrees lower than the actual temperature.

Pressure

Air pressure is either high or low and can also change the weather. Low pressure is not very stable and can produce bad weather such as rain, snow and storms etc. High pressure is a lot more stable and can produce good weather. This can be hot in the summer and cold in the winter.

07. PLANNING THE ROUTE AND PREPARING ROUTE CARDS
(three star training)

This is the same as the preparation that was done for the two star assessment (see page 207) but is based on the three star criteria.

THREE STAR TRAINING EXPEDITION ASSESSMENT

There is no theory assessment for lessons received, but all lessons must be delivered and understood by cadets before taking part in a practical remotely supervised expedition assessment over two days and two nights out with a minimum of seven hours activity per day.

Three star expedition assessment can also be used to sign off the silver DofE expedition practice for those enrolled.

CHAPTER THIRTEEN: EXPEDITION (EXP) OVERVIEW

FOUR STAR EXP TRAINING OVERVIEW (optional)

Four star expedition is made up of three revision periods of lessons covered at one star level along with five extra lessons all designed to help you plan and prepare for a two day and one night expedition.

01. REVISION PERIOD: EMERGENCY PROCEDURES
(four star training)

Refer back to one star training.

02. REVISION PERIOD: CLOTHING, FOOTWEAR, EMERGENCY EQUIPMENT, PACKING, WATERPROOFING AND MANUAL HANDLING OF A RUCKSACK OR OTHER SUITABLE CONTAINER *(four star training)*

Refer back to one star training

03. REVISION PERIOD: SAFE USE OF STOVES, AND SAFE HANDLING AND CARRIAGE OF FUELS *(four star training)*

Refer back to one star training

04. PLANNING: PRODUCE A PLAN FOR THE AIM OF THE ACTIVITY *(four star training)*

Refer back to previous training.

This is the same process as when preparing for the two and three star expeditions (P204, 205 & 208). Cadets should reflect back on previous expedition aims to work out what worked and what didn't.

Discuss possible aims and then narrow it down to just one aim that is decided by the group. Plan any extra resources required and plan how to report back after the expedition. The four star expedition takes place over three days and two nights so the aim needs to work over that time scale.

05. WEATHER: SOURCES OF INFORMATION AND READING BASIC WEATHER CHARTS *(four star training)*

This involves revision of the three star lesson 'Weather & its impact on expeditions'. Cadets should also download some recent weather reports to get used to understanding and interpreting the information contained within them.

CHAPTER THIRTEEN: EXPEDITION (EXP) OVERVIEW

06. GROUP MANAGEMENT AND LEADERSHIP; AWARENESS OF NGB AWARDS *(four star training)*

Four star and DofE expeditions are mainly leaderless, but there are times when leadership is required and people with natural leadership qualities soon take control.

A good leader will motivate the team and keep everyone involved, whereas a bad leader will try to take over and dictate to others whilst ignoring the needs of the team.

Leadership Code

The leadership code is a great starting point to become a good leader:

L: Lead by example.

E: Encourage thinking.

A: Apply reward and discipline.

D: Demand high performance.

E: Encourage confidence.

R: Recognise strength and weakness.

S: Strive for team goals.

National Governing Body (NGB) Qualifications

To be permitted to run expeditions for other young people, adults are required to train and gain NGB qualifications. These are national standards that must be achieved to safely run activities and lead young people. There are various qualifications available:

ML: Mountain Leader

TCL: Trail Cycle Leader

BC: British Canoeing

BEL: Basic Expedition Leader (Now LEL: Lowland Expedition Leader)

LLA: Lowland Leader Award

CHAPTER THIRTEEN: EXPEDITION (EXP) OVERVIEW

07. FIRST AID IN THE OUTDOORS *(four star training)*

Through ACS First Aid and expedition training at basic and one star level, cadets will have gained enough First Aid training to be able to deal with most minor incidents themselves and be able to manage a more serious incident safely.

Scenarios

Cadets need to revise their First Aid (pages 247 - 262 and emergency procedures (pages 193 - 194) lessons but then apply them to the outdoor expedition environment. In this four star lesson, cadets are given up to 30 different first aid scenarios to discuss which helps create the correct mindset to deal with lots of different situations.

08. PLANNING THE ROUTE AND PREPARING ROUTE CARDS *(four star training)*

This is the same as the preparation that was done for the two and three star assessments (see page 207) but is based on the four star criteria.

FOUR STAR TRAINING EXPEDITION ASSESSMENT

There is no theory assessment for lessons received, but all lessons must be delivered and understood by cadets before taking part in a practical remotely supervised expedition assessment over three days and two nights out with a minimum of seven hours activity per day.

CHAPTER THIRTEEN: EXPEDITION (EXP) OVERVIEW

CHAPTER FOURTEEN
SKILL AT ARMS (SAA) OVERVIEW

CONTENTS:
- Introduction
- Basic SAA Training Overview
- One Star SAA Training Overview
- Two Star SAA Training Overview
- Three Star SAA Training Overview
- Four Star SAA Training Overview

REFERENCES:
- *Army Cadet Syllabus - AC71101 (Version 1.2 - July 2022)*
- *Cadet Training Skill At Arms - .177" Air Rifles and Associated equipment - AC72195 (2022)*
- *Cadet Training Skill At Arms - The L98A2 Cadet GP rifle (5.56mm) and Associated equipment - AC71807-C (2021)*
- *Cadet Training Skill At Arms - Cadet Small Bore Target Rifle (CSBTR) - AC72027 (2021)*

CHAPTER FOURTEEN: SKILL AT ARMS (SAA) OVERVIEW

INTRODUCTION

LESSONS MUST BE DELIVERED BY A SKILL AT ARMS INSTRUCTOR

Skill At Arms (SAA) lessons look at the safety, handling and operation of various rifles at different star levels.

- **Badges available:** Once training has been delivered and cadets have passed the relevant Weapon Handling Test (WHT), they are entitled to wear the corresponding rifle badge.

| AIR RIFLE | .22 RIFLE | GP RIFLE | TGT RIFLE |

- **Specialist qualifications required to teach:** All lessons must be delivered by a qualified Skill At Arms Instructor (SAAI).
- **Further progression beyond the syllabus:** None.

BASIC SAA TRAINING OVERVIEW

Basic SAA training starts off with the basics of weapon safety. Weapon training is on either an air rifle or a .22 rifle depending on what weapon system is available at the location where training is taking place. The assessment is to complete a Weapon Handling Test (WHT) on whichever weapon system training has been done on.

01. SAFETY WITH WEAPONS *(basic training)*

Handling of weapons within the ACF is completely safe, as long as certain safety procedures are followed. All weapons used can be potentially lethal though and despite being under constant supervision from adult instructors, cadets need to learn, understand and adhere to ALL safety precautions. Failure to do so may result in serious injury.

The Six Rules

1. A weapon must never be pointed at anyone in any circumstances.
2. A weapon must always be handled so that it points in such a direction that there is no danger if a round is accidentally fired.
3. Whenever a weapon is picked up which has not been under an individual's direct supervision, it must be examined to make sure it is not loaded - NSPs (Normal Safety Precautions) must be carried out.

CHAPTER FOURTEEN: SKILL AT ARMS (SAA) OVERVIEW

4. Whenever a weapon is handed to someone else, the recipient must first be shown that it is unloaded (clear). The recipient must insist that he/she is shown that the weapon is unloaded.
5. The muzzle of a weapon must never be rested against any part of the body.
6. A weapon must be in the unloaded state prior to traveling in a vehicle or during non tactical moves on foot.

Normal Safety Precautions (NSPs) are to be carried out on all weapons used in the ACF and in all Armed Forces at the beginning of any lesson, practice period or range period, when picking up a rifle that hasn't been under your direct supervision or when handing over a rifle, or receiving it from someone else.

OPTION 1: AIR RIFLE *(basic training)*

The air rifle is simple to operate and allows cadets to learn and practice the marksmanship principles. There are several air rifles available, all of which are very similar to operate.

Air rifle variants

1. BSA Scorpion Cadet .177" & BSA Scorpion Cadet Sporter .177"
2. Air Arms S200 single shot .177" & Air Arms S200 Multi Shot .177"
3. Break Barrel Air Rifle .177" (single shot)

The BSA Scorpion and the Air Arms S200 are both bolt operated weapons that use air to fire pellets at a range of 5.5 - 10 metres. The air is pumped into a cylinder fixed to the rifle (always done by an adult instructor). They all fire .177 calibre air rifle pellets.

Air Rifle Lessons

Lesson 1: General description, safety, sights, cleaning & maintenance.
Lesson 2: Magazine filling, load & unload.
Lesson 3: Holding & aiming in the prone position.
Lesson 4: Firing in the prone position & stoppage drills.
Lesson 5: Firing from other positions.

This is followed by a practice period before attempting the Weapon Handling Test (WHT) for the relevant air rifle.

CHAPTER FOURTEEN: SKILL AT ARMS (SAA) OVERVIEW

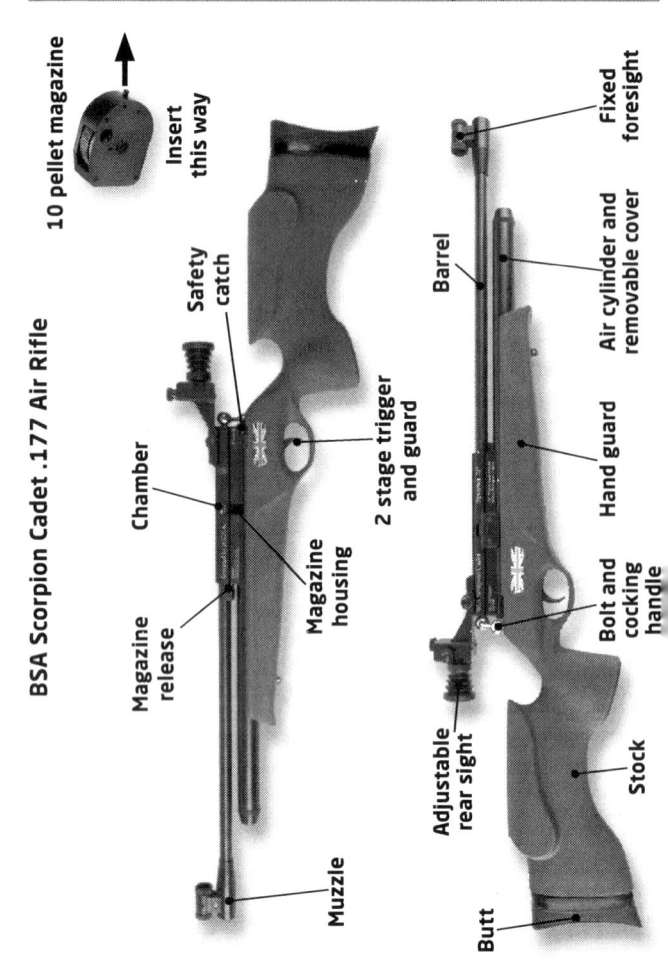

BSA Scorpion Cadet .177 Air Rifle

CHAPTER FOURTEEN: SKILL AT ARMS (SAA) OVERVIEW

OPTION 2: CADET SMALL BORE TARGET RIFLE *(basic training)*

An alternative to the Air Rifle at Basic level, is the L144 A1 Cadet Small Bore Target Rifle (CSBTR) which is a bolt action, manually fed weapon system that needs to be loaded after each round has been fired. It is fitted with iron sights that are accurate up to 25 metres, and can be fired indoors or outdoors on approved purpose built ranges.

CSBTR Lessons

Lesson 1: General description, safety, sights, cleaning & maintenance.

Lesson 2: Stripping, assembling, cleaning, maintenance & preparation for firing.

Lesson 3: Basic handling drills, sight setting, firing & stoppages.

Lesson 4: Zeroing the sight & adjustment for wind.

This is followed by a practice period before attempting the WHT.

BASIC TRAINING SAA ASSESSMENT

The basic SAA assessment is to complete a Weapon Handling Test (WHT) on the weapon system that has been taught. Passing this test also allows the cadet/CFAV to fire that particular weapon on a range for a period of six months. The test needs to be retaken before any firing if a period of six months has passed since the last test pass.

Note: Basic SAA is not required to fully pass basic training. This is because under a National Small-bore Rifle Association (NSRA) Youth Proficiency Scheme (YPS) tutor, a safety assessment is carried out rather than a full WHT. For more details see the shooting manual.

The Weapon Handling Test covers the following areas:

Air Rifle (all variants)	CSBTR
1. Safety	1. Safety
2. Loading	2. Stripping, cleaning & assembly
3. Stoppage drills	3. Loading - prone position
4. Further stoppage drills	4. Stoppages
5. Unloading	5. Stoppages obstruction drill
6. Magazine filling (not applicable for single shot variants)	6. Further stoppages
	7. Unloading

CHAPTER FOURTEEN: SKILL AT ARMS (SAA) OVERVIEW

L144A1 Cadet Small Bore Target Rifle (CSBTR)

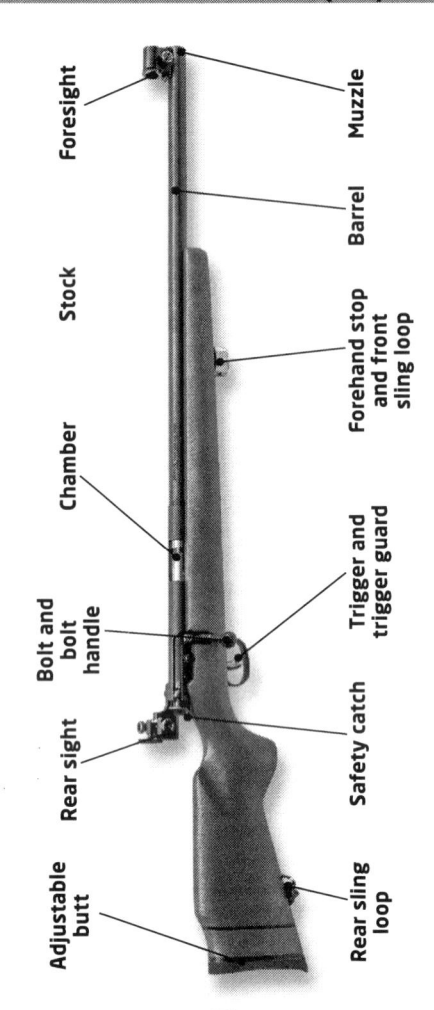

Labels: Foresight, Muzzle, Barrel, Stock, Forehand stop and front sling loop, Chamber, Trigger and trigger guard, Bolt and bolt handle, Safety catch, Rear sight, Adjustable butt, Rear sling loop

CHAPTER FOURTEEN: SKILL AT ARMS (SAA) OVERVIEW

ONE STAR SAA TRAINING OVERVIEW

One star SAA introduces the L98 A2 Cadet GP rifle which is used in Fieldcraft from one star onwards and shooting from two star onwards.

The L98 A2 Cadet GP (General Purpose) Rifle is a single shot, semi-automatic rifle. It is magazine fed and holds up to 30 rounds. The gas created from firing each round is used within the mechanism to force the working parts to the rear and load the next round from the magazine automatically until the magazine is empty.

GP RIFLE LESSONS

Lesson 1: General description, safety and the sights.

Lesson 2: Stripping and assembling.

Lesson 3: Basic handling drills.

Lesson 4: Cleaning and maintenance.

- PRACTICE PERIOD 1

Lesson 5: Holding and aiming in the prone position (1st, 2nd and 3rd marksmanship principle).

Lesson 6: Firing in the prone position (4th marksmanship principle).

Lesson 7: Firing drills.

Lesson 8: Firing from other positions and use of cover.

- PRACTICE PERIOD 2

Lesson 9: Mechanism, immediate action and stoppage drills.

This is followed by a third practice period before attempting the Weapon Handling test (WHT).

THE FOUR MARKSMANSHIP PRINCIPLES

1. **Support & position:** The position and hold must be firm enough to support the weapon.
2. **Pointing (natural alignment):** The weapon must point naturally towards the target without any undue physical effort.
3. **Aiming (sight alignment):** Sight alignment and sight picture must be correct.
4. **Release of shot & follow through:** The shot must be released and followed through without undue disturbance to the position.

CHAPTER FOURTEEN: SKILL AT ARMS (SAA) OVERVIEW

L98 A2 Cadet GP Rifle - Main Parts

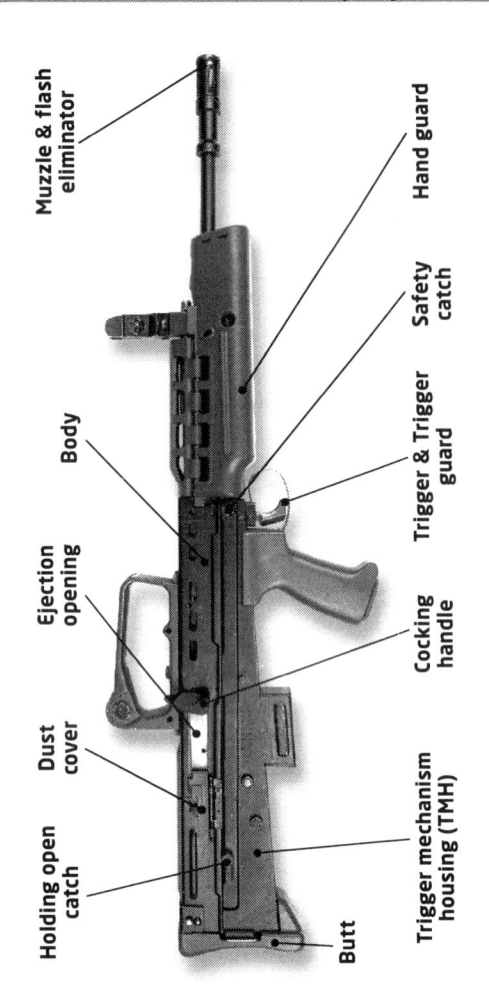

- Muzzle & flash eliminator
- Hand guard
- Safety catch
- Trigger & Trigger guard
- Cocking handle
- Trigger mechanism housing (TMH)
- Butt
- Holding open catch
- Dust cover
- Ejection opening
- Body

CHAPTER FOURTEEN: SKILL AT ARMS (SAA) OVERVIEW

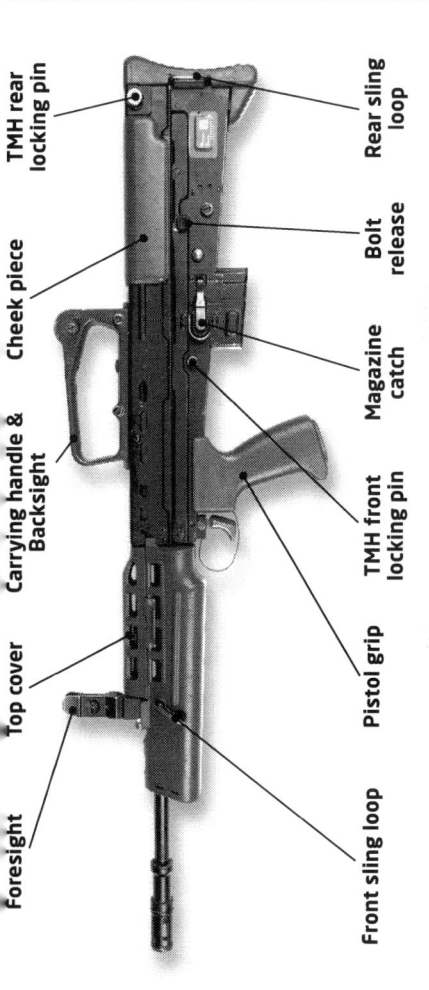

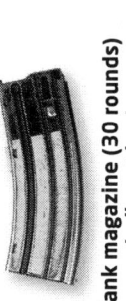

CHAPTER FOURTEEN: SKILL AT ARMS (SAA) OVERVIEW

L98 A2 Cadet GP Rifle - Working Parts

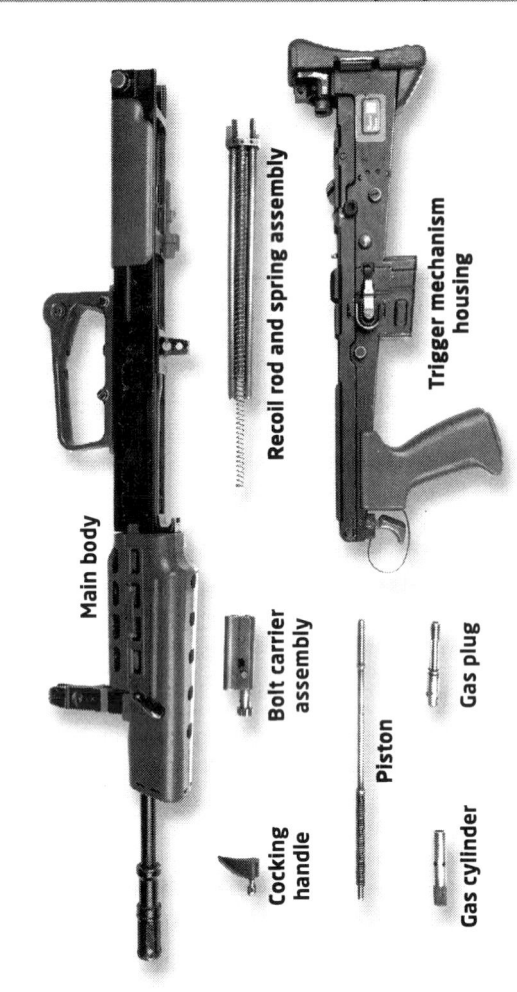

- Main body
- Recoil rod and spring assembly
- Trigger mechanism housing
- Cocking handle
- Bolt carrier assembly
- Piston
- Gas plug
- Gas cylinder

CHAPTER FOURTEEN: SKILL AT ARMS (SAA) OVERVIEW

L98 A2 Cadet GP Rifle - Cleaning Kit Contents

- Muzzle cover
- Oil bottle
- Bore brush
- Chamber barrel extension brush 
- GP soft brush 
- GP wire brush 
- Gas block brush 
- Pull through 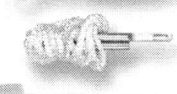
- Barrel extension cleaner
- Cleaning rod handle 
- Two piece cleaning rod 
- Combination tool 

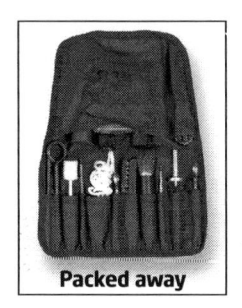

Packed away

CHAPTER FOURTEEN: SKILL AT ARMS (SAA) OVERVIEW

Rifle sling
Attaches via the front and rear sling loops.

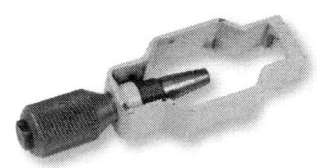

Blank firing adapter (BFA)
Fitted when firing blank ammunition *(yellow)*.

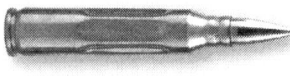

Drill rounds - Silver with dents
For practising loading magazines.

Blank rounds - Bronze, crimped
For blank firing exercises.

Ball (live) rounds - Bronze
For firing on a range only.

L98 A2 - Combi-Tool

- Screwdriver (Iron sight locating stud)
- Screwdriver (iron sight)
- Gas regulator adjustment & Iron sight adjustment
- SUSAT zeroing spanner
- Gas vent reamer point
- Cleaning rod spanner
- Gas cylinder reamer
- Gas plug reamer

CHAPTER FOURTEEN: SKILL AT ARMS (SAA) OVERVIEW

ONE STAR SAA ASSESSMENT

Cadets need to successfully pass all elements of the L98 A2 Weapon Handling Test (WHT). Which must be carried out by a qualified SAA Instructor. Any error which effects safety is an immediate fail.

CHAPTER FOURTEEN: SKILL AT ARMS (SAA) OVERVIEW

TWO STAR SAA TRAINING OVERVIEW

Two star SAA training continues with the L98 A2 by looking at how to react to effective enemy fire during blank firing exercises. There are just two extra lessons at this level.

Lesson 1: Rifle lesson 11 - Carriage of the weapon and reaction to effective enemy fire.

Lesson 2: Blank firing system.

TWO STAR SAA ASSESSMENT

Cadets simply need to receive the two lessons and be able to demonstrate to the SAA Instructor that they understand and are competent with the weapon system.

THREE STAR SAA TRAINING OVERVIEW

Three star SAA training continues with the L98 A2 by looking more in depth at the sighting system. There are just three lessons at this level.

Lesson 1: Rifle lesson 10 - Aiming off and alteration of the sights.

Lesson 2: Rifle lesson 13 - Bore sighting the rifle with iron sight.

Lesson 3: Rifle lesson 14 - Zeroing the rifle with iron sight.

THREE STAR SAA ASSESSMENT

Cadets simply need to receive the three lessons and be able to demonstrate to the SAA Instructor that they understand and are competent with the weapon system.

FOUR STAR SAA TRAINING OVERVIEW (optional)

Four star SAA training is optional and continues with the L98 A2 by looking at firing on the Mechanised Moving Target Trainer Range (MMTTR). There is just one lesson at this level.

Lesson 1: Rifle lesson 12 - Firing at crossing and multiple targets.

FOUR STAR SAA ASSESSMENT

Cadets simply need to receive the lesson and be able to demonstrate to the SAA Instructor that they understand and are competent with the weapon system.

CHAPTER FIFTEEN
SHOOTING (SH) OVERVIEW

CONTENTS:
- Introduction
- Firing Ranges
- Grouping & Zeroing
- The Marksmanship Principles
- Basic SH Training Overview
- One Star SH Training Overview
- Two Star SH Training Overview
- Three Star SH Training Overview
- Four Star SH Training Overview

REFERENCES:
- *Army Cadet Syllabus - AC71101 (Version 1.2 - July 2022)*
- *Cadet Shooting Manual - AC72217 (2022)*
- *Cadet Training - Ranges - AC71855-C (Dec 2022)*

CHAPTER FIFTEEN: SHOOTING (SH) OVERVIEW

INTRODUCTION

This is where you get to fire weapons at targets on a range. Shooting is progressive, and distances fired over and expected standards of shooting is raised in accordance with your training level.

- **Badges available:** Cadets can achieve shooting badges based on performance during shooting practices on all weapons. The most recent weapon system learnt should be the only SAA badge worn and the shooting performance must relate to that rifle.
- **Olive backing:** Core shooting syllabus.
- **Red backing:** Elective (optional) target rifle programme.

Trained Shot
Achievable at Basic level & above

Marksman
Achievable at one star level & above

Advanced Marksman
Achievable at four star level only

- **Further progression beyond the syllabus:** Competitions are available to cadets of any level that display good shooting skills. Competition shoots range from local and regional to national and international.
- **Specialist qualifications required to teach:** Instructors need to hold range qualifications to be able to run any range.

DUKE OF EDINBURGH'S AWARD (DofE)

Shooting in the ACF can also contribute to the Duke of Edinburgh's award scheme which is an award achieved by taking part in several activities. Shooting comes under 'skills'.

SYLLABUS SHOOTING - CADET LIVE FIRING (CLF)

Each rifle has a series of Cadet Live Firing (CLF) practices that must be completed before progressing onto further star levels and different weapon systems.

CHAPTER FIFTEEN: SHOOTING (SH) OVERVIEW

FIRING RANGES

All shooting is done on a range relevant to the weapon being fired. Ranges can be indoor or outdoor and most are permanent fixtures. Distances on military ranges are either in metres (m) or yards (x). An in date WHT must be held to be able to fire any weapon on any range.

- **Air rifle (5.5 or 10 metres): Basic & one star shooting**
  These can be indoor or outdoor and can be a temporary fixture, meaning that it can be packed away and set up again as long as all rules around its use are followed.

- **CSBTR (15 - 25 yds): Basic & one star shooting**
  Shooting on the CSBTR must be on indoor or outdoor purpose built permanent range.

- **L98 A2 (25 - 300 metres): Two, three & four star shooting**
  Shooting on the L98 A2 must be done on a permanent outdoor range.

- **DCCT - Dismounted Close Combat Trainer: Two star onwards**
  This is an indoor computerised firing simulator for the L98 A2 and is extremely useful to help develop shooting skills by analysing lots of key data from the firer.

- **L81 A2 (25 metres - 1000 yds): Competition shooting**
  These are outdoor permanent ranges located at large military range complexes.

All ranges have a similar set up

- **Target area:** This is where you will place your targets and aim.
- **Firing point:** Area where you will be firing from.
- **Scoring:** An area to collect targets and return them for scoring.
- **Ammo:** A secure area to store pellets and load magazines.
- **First Aid:** First aid point in case of any incidents.
- **Waiting area:** Cadets waiting to shoot.

CHAPTER FIFTEEN: SHOOTING (SH) OVERVIEW

RANGE LAYOUT

The diagram below represents a temporary air rifle range, but the principle is the same for all ranges.

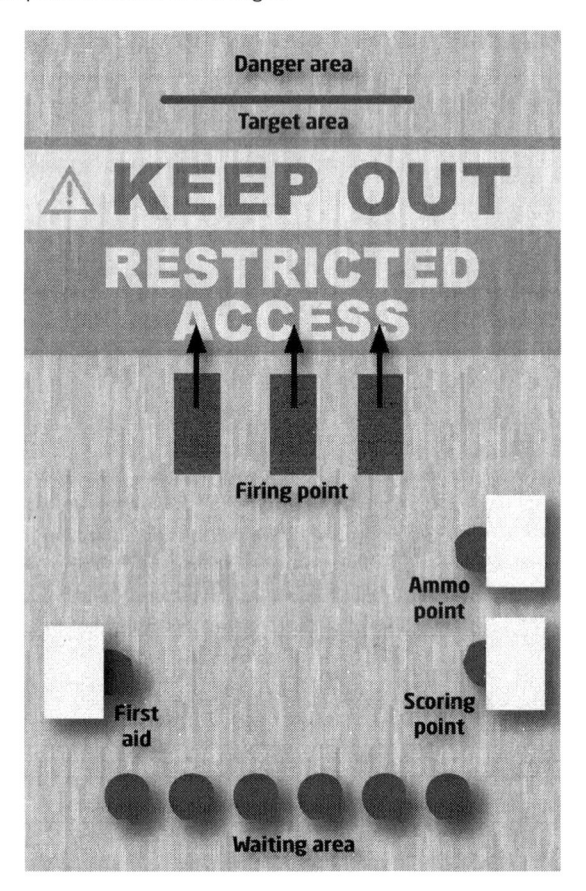

CHAPTER FIFTEEN: SHOOTING (SH) OVERVIEW

RANGE STAFF

To make your range experience safe and enjoyable, there are several key members of staff that have specific roles on every range, however large or small.

- **Range Conducting Officer (RCO):** The RCO is the person ultimately responsible for the safety and running of the range. They control all staff and cadets on the range and will be the person giving the words of command on the firing point.
- **Safety Supervisors/Coaches:** There primarily for safety and to make sure the cadets are carrying out their rifle drills correctly. They are also there to assist and advise to help everyone get the most out of their shooting experience.
- **Ammunition orderly:** Normally just one person nominated to take control of the issue of pellets/rounds. They will either load magazines or issue the correct numbers of pellets/rounds.
- **First Aider:** With the amount of training provided and the rules around how the range runs, there is very little chance of any incidents or injuries but, to be safe, there is always a qualified first aider with a full first aid kit and a stretcher.
- **Scoring:** Sometimes the safety staff will do this with you, or there may be a single person designated to score the targets and keep track of results.

CHAPTER FIFTEEN: SHOOTING (SH) OVERVIEW

RANGE PROCEDURE

There will always be variations on how a range runs depending on what the aims are and who is in charge, but this is a general idea of what to expect.

- **Arrival:** The first stage when arriving at a range is to have a safety brief and overview of the shoot. Here you will find out who the staff are, where everything is and what shoot you are doing as well as all safety details.

- **Pre-shoot:** before getting onto the range, there may be some skill at arms revision or some other 'background' activities, but when you get to the range, you will collect a target(s) and write your name and detachment on it, you will then wait in the waiting area until being called forward for your shoot.

- **Shoot:** Under the direction of the RCO, you will respond to words of command to go through the whole shooting sequence from placing targets in the target area and taking your position on the firing point and firing at your target right, through to unloading and collecting your targets back.

- **After shoot:** When the RCO dismisses you from the firing point, you will take your target to the scoring officer to see how you did and will then either return to the waiting area or return to some other form of training.

- **Departure:** Before leaving the range area, you may need to help with clearing up or tidying, but the last thing you must do is to make an 'end of shoot declaration'. The RCO will form everyone up that has been on the range and read a statement regarding the rules around ammunition/pellets being removed from the range. Everyone then takes it in turn to confirm they do not have anything by saying:

"Sir/Ma'am, I have no ammunition/pellets in my possession and will report anyone who has"

CHAPTER FIFTEEN: SHOOTING (SH) OVERVIEW

GROUPING & ZEROING

Everyone that fires a weapon will have their own way of aiming through the sights to align with a target. This means that two firers of equal skill can fire the same weapon and aim at the same point on a target but their rounds may fall in different places. This does not mean either of the firers are bad, it just means that the sights have not been adjusted specifically for them.

ZEROING THE SIGHT

Zeroing the sights to the firer, simply means adjusting them to compensate for any difference in the firers point of aim and where the rounds actually fall.

GROUPING

If after firing several rounds at a target, you see that all of your shots are really close together, but are not exactly where you aimed, this means that your shooting is good, but the rifle sights are not zeroed to you. In some firing practices, this doesn't matter as the closeness of the shots to each other is the most important factor.

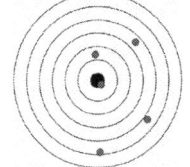

1. Poor grouping

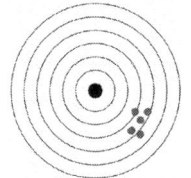

2. Good grouping Not zeroed

3. Good grouping Sights zeroed

Example 1: The firer needs more practice of the marksmanship principles.

Example 2: The firer has achieved a good group size (shots are close together), but they all fall slightly down and right of the centre of the target (the point of aim). The sights therefore need to be adjusted left and up to allow the firer to aim at the same point, yet get the rounds closer to the centre of the target.

Example 3: Shows what the same group fired from a correctly zeroed weapon with the same point of aim.

CHAPTER FIFTEEN: SHOOTING (SH) OVERVIEW

THE MARKSMANSHIP PRINCIPLES

The Marksmanship principles are covered in full during SAA lessons with the L98 A2, but it is revised again to develop good shooting.

1. **Support & position - The position and hold must be firm enough to support the weapon.**
2. **Pointing (natural alignment) - The weapon must point naturally towards the target without any undue physical effort.**
3. **Aiming (sight alignment) - Sight alignment and sight picture must be correct.**
4. **Release of shot & follow through - The shot must be released and followed through without undue disturbance to the position.**

THE PRONE UNSUPPORTED POSITION

Leg position 1.
This position ensures that the right side of the body, including the right leg is immediately behind the rifle.

Leg position 2.
This position is slightly angled to the left of the line of fire. The left leg is on the same line as the body, and the right leg is in line with the rifle.

CHAPTER FIFTEEN: SHOOTING (SH) OVERVIEW

FIRING POSITION CHECKLIST

Head low, with cheek resting on the cheek plate.

Butt of the rifle pulled firmly into the shoulder.

Left hand under the hand guard, supporting but not gripping.

Left elbow as close as possible to a central point below the rifle.

Right elbow in close to support the rifle.

Right hand is the controlling hand. Hold the pistol grip and pull into the shoulder.

+ Rife is lifted completely off of the ground
+ Firer is completely relaxed
+ Firer is breathing correctly

EYE RELIEF

To achieve the best aim, and to avoid the rear sight recoiling back into your eye when firing, the distance between the rear sight and your eye can be adjusted. This is called 'eye relief' and should be set to a minimum of 25mm.

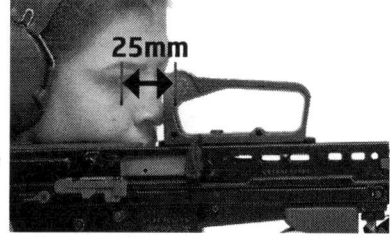

CHAPTER FIFTEEN: SHOOTING (SH) OVERVIEW

AIMING (RIGHT EYE ONLY)

E. Eye: Your right eye, looking down the sights.

A. Aperture: The centre of the rear aperture (rear sight).

S. Sights: The tip of the foresight blade.

T. Target: Your exact point of aim on the target in front of you.

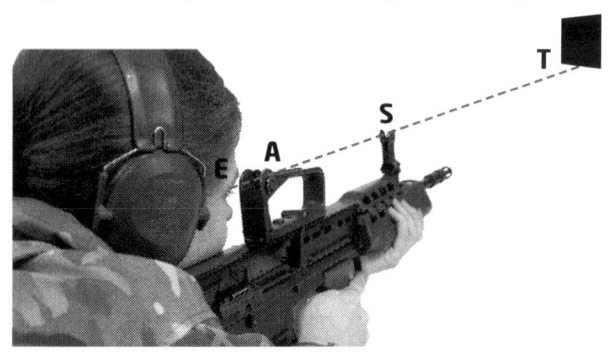

AIM PICTURE

To create the correct aim picture, ensure that the tip of the foresight blade is in the centre of the rear aperture, and at the bottom centre of the aiming patch. Switch your focus between the target and the foresight blade, but focus on the foresight more, especially as you fire.

- Aperture (Rear sight)
- Aiming patch on target
- Foresight blade
- Point of aim

CHAPTER FIFTEEN: SHOOTING (SH) OVERVIEW

BREATH CONTROL

Breathing is a natural process, so we do not want to do anything unnatural to that process which will have a negative impact on our shooting. We do however want to be aware of our breathing and control the timings of our shots around it.

- Having set up your firing position and received the words of command to start firing, set the safety catch to 'F' (Fire), and take up the first pressure on the trigger.
- Take a few slow deep breaths to increase the amount of oxygen in your blood which will help reduce strain.
- Exhale to the end of a normal breath and then slightly extend the natural pause between exhaling and inhaling.
- Do not empty your lungs completely or hold your breath for too long.
- Apply the second pressure to take the shot when the aim picture is correct but do not release the trigger straight away.
- If the aim picture is not correct soon enough, it is better to start the breathing cycle again rather than holding your breath.

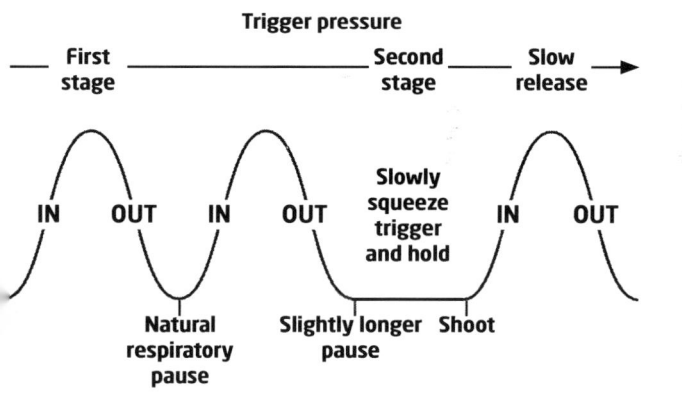

Trigger pressure

| First stage | Second stage | Slow release → |

IN — OUT — IN — OUT — *Slowly squeeze trigger and hold* — IN — OUT

Natural respiratory pause — Slightly longer pause — Shoot

CHAPTER FIFTEEN: SHOOTING (SH) OVERVIEW

BASIC SH TRAINING OVERVIEW

Basic shooting can be done on either the air rifle or the CSBTR.

01. MARKSMANSHIP PRINCIPLES *(basic training)*

The Marksmanship principles are covered in full during SAA lessons with the L98 A2, but it is revised again to develop good shooting. See pages 238 - 241 for more detail.

02. CADET LIVE FIRING PRACTICE *(basic training)*

This can be carried out on either the air rifle (AR) or CSBTR (SB). Grouping size is measured between the furthest shot holes (Extreme Spread - ES).

Option 1 - Cadet Live Firing Air Rifle 1 (CLF AR 1): Intro shoot

Firing the Air Rifle prone on a 5.5 or 10 metre range. The first practice is supported and the next is unsupported.

Option 2 - Cadet Live Firing Small Bore 1 (CLF SB 1): Intro shoot

Firing the CSBTR prone on a 15, 20 or 25 yard or 25 metre range. The first practice is supported and the next is unsupported.

BASIC TRAINING SHOOTING ASSESSMENT

To pass basic shooting on the Air Rifle or CSBTR, achieve the required grouping size while firing from the prone unsupported position. Re-tests are permitted until the required group sizes have been achieved.

The 'Trained Shot' badge can be awarded if the required group sizes are achieved based on rifle type, range distance and grouping size.

CHAPTER FIFTEEN: SHOOTING (SH) OVERVIEW

ONE STAR SH TRAINING OVERVIEW

One star shooting can be done on either the air rifle or the CSBTR.

OPTION 1 - AIR RIFLE *(one star training)*

Firing the Air Rifle from various positions on a 5.5 or 10 metre range.

CLF AR 2: Firing From Other Positions

This involves firing unsupported from the sitting, kneeling and standing positions. Before moving onto the next shoot, cadets must achieve the required grouping sizes for all positions.

CLF AR3: Zeroing (assessed to pass one star shooting)

This involves firing the air rifle in the prone unsupported position to learn about correctly zeroing the rifle and achieve a good grouping.

CLF AR 4: Establish the Point of Aim and Apply Fire (all positions)

This combines firing unsupported from various different position and zero a rifle to be able to apply fire to the centre of the target.

OPTION 2 - CSBTR *(one star training)*

Firing the CSBTR from various positions on a 15, 20 or 25 yard or 25 metre range.

CLF SB 2: Grouping & Development Grouping Prone

This involves firing unsupported from the prone position. Before moving onto the next shoot, cadets must achieve the required grouping sizes for all positions.

CLF SB3: Zeroing (assessed to pass one star shooting)

This involves firing in the prone unsupported position to learn about correctly zeroing the rifle and achieve a good grouping.

ONE STAR TRAINING SHOOTING ASSESSMENT

To pass one star shooting on the air rifle or CSBTR, achieve the required grouping size while firing from the prone unsupported position during CLF AR/SB 3. Re-tests with coaching are permitted until the required group sizes have been achieved.

The Trained Shot or Marksman badge can be awarded if the required group sizes are achieved based on rifle type, range distance and grouping size.

CHAPTER FIFTEEN: SHOOTING (SH) OVERVIEW

TWO STAR SH TRAINING OVERVIEW

Two star shooting is carried out on the L98 A2 Cadet GP rifle (GP).

01. INTRODUCTORY SHOOT *(two star training)*

There are two options for the two star introductory shoot.

Option 1 - CLF GP 1: DCCT - Grouping at 25m (prone)

This involves firing on the Dismounted Close Combat Trainer (DCCT) computerised indoor range. Shooting is done from the supported and unsupported prone position.

Option 2 - CLF GP 2: Introductory Shoot at 25m (prone)

This involves firing the L98 A2 GP rifle on a 25m range from the supported and unsupported prone position.

02. ZEROING SHOOT *(two star training)*

There are two options for the second shoot.

Option 1 - CLF GP 5: Zeroing 25m

Firing from the prone unsupported position and zeroing the rifle.

Option 2 - CLF GP 6: Zeroing 100m

This is the same as option one but on a 100m range.

TWO STAR TRAINING SHOOTING ASSESSMENT

To pass two star shooting, achieve the required grouping size while firing from the prone unsupported position during CLF GP 5 or 6. Re-tests with coaching are permitted until the required group sizes have been achieved.

The Trained Shot or Marksman badge can be awarded if the required group sizes are achieved based on rifle type, range distance and grouping size.

CHAPTER FIFTEEN: SHOOTING (SH) OVERVIEW

THREE STAR SH TRAINING OVERVIEW

Three star shooting is carried out on the L98 A2 Cadet GP rifle (GP).

01. CLF GP 3 - GROUPING OTHER POSITIONS 25M
(three star training)

This involves firing the L98 A2 Cadet GP rifle on a 25m range or a DCCT range from the sitting (unsupported) and kneeling (supported) positions.

02. CLF GP 9 - ESTABLISH THE POINT OF AIM AND APPLY FIRE AT 100M (ALL POSITIONS) *(three star training)*

Firing from 100m in the prone, sitting, kneeling (unsupported) and fire trench positions and apply fire to the centre of the target.

THREE STAR TRAINING SHOOTING ASSESSMENT

To pass three star shooting, achieve the required score while firing from all positions during CLF GP 9. Re-tests with coaching are permitted until the required scores have been achieved.

The Trained Shot or Marksman badge can be awarded if the required score is achieved for each firing position.

CHAPTER FIFTEEN: SHOOTING (SH) OVERVIEW

FOUR STAR SH TRAINING OVERVIEW (optional)

Four star shooting is optional and is carried out on the L98 A2 Cadet GP rifle (GP).

01. CLF GP 10 - ADVANCED APPLICATION OF FIRE FROM ALL POSITIONS UP TO 100M *(four star training)*

Applying different rates of fire (snap and rapid) at targets with different exposure times. Firing is done from the prone, sitting, kneeling and fire trench positions on a 100m (or 75yd) range.

02. CLF GP 12 - ESTABLISH THE POINT OF AIM AND APPLY FIRE AT 200M - 300M (ALL POSITIONS) *(four star training)*

Fire in various positions at distances of 200m - 300m and apply fire to the centre of the target.

03. CLF GP 13 - APPLICATION OF FIRE UP TO 300YDS (ALL POSITIONS) *(four star training)*

Applying different rates of fire (snap and rapid) at targets with different exposure times. Firing is done from various positions at 100m - 300m.

FOUR STAR TRAINING SHOOTING ASSESSMENT

To pass four star shooting, achieve the required scores from CLF GP 13. Re-tests with coaching are permitted until the required scores have been achieved.

The Trained Shot, Marksman or Advanced Marksman badge can be awarded if the required score is achieved for each firing position.

CHAPTER SIXTEEN
FIRST AID (FA) OVERVIEW

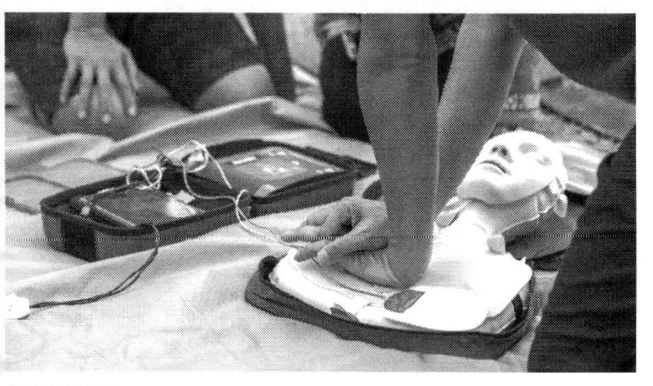

CONTENTS:
- Introduction
- Primary Survey
- Syllabus First Aid
- Basic FA Training Overview
- One Star FA Training Overview
- Two Star FA Training Overview
- Three Star FA Training Overview
- Four Star FA Training Overview

REFERENCES:
- *Army Cadet Syllabus - AC71101 (Version 1.2 - July 2022)*
- *The First Aid Manual written & authorised by the UK's leading Fist Aid providers (Latest Edition)*
- *St John Ambulance Powerpoint Presentations*
- *Army Cadet Resource Centre via Westminster*

CHAPTER SIXTEEN: FIRST AID (FA) OVERVIEW

INTRODUCTION

First Aid is one of the most important and relevant subjects you will learn in the cadets, as it is an important skill that can be used in every walk of life. Many cadets have been in situations where their actions have saved lives.

- **Badges available:** St John Ambulance red Young First Aider badge is available on successful completion of 2 star training.
- **Specialist qualifications required to teach:** Instructors must hold a minimum of an in date First Aid At Work (FAAW) qualification and be familiar with the St John Youth First Aid pack.
- **Further progression beyond the syllabus:** Cadets continuing with First Aid at three and four star level will gain qualifications with certificates and the achievement of four star allows them to teach other cadets.

PRIMARY SURVEY

The aims of First Aid can be remembered as the 3 Ps:

- **Preserve life**
- **Prevent the casualty's condition from worsening**
- **Promote recovery**

The primary survey is the first assessment of a casualty to find out their condition and work out what to do next.

DANGER

- On approaching a casualty, check for any danger that might affect you, the casualty or any bystanders.

RESPONSE

Check for a response from the casualty.

- Tap the casualty's shoulders and ask **"Are you all right?"**

CHAPTER SIXTEEN: FIRST AID (FA) OVERVIEW

Outcome A: The casualty responds:

If the casualty responds by answering or moving, check their condition and call for help and/or 999/112 if required.

- Leave casualty in the position found unless they are in further danger.
- After calling 999/112 stay with the casualty and continue to monitor their condition.

Outcome B: The casualty does not respond:

If the casualty does not respond, their condition may be more serious so there is more we can do.

- Shout for help if no-one is around.
- If you can get help, ask them to wait until you check to see if the casualty is breathing. (They can then call the emergency services on 999/112 and advise them if the casualty is breathing or not).

AIRWAY

A casualty's airway may be blocked by their tongue which can stop them from being able to breath. We therefore need to open the casualty's airway.

- If safe to do so, turn the casualty onto their back.
- Gently tilt the head back using the tip of the first two fingers under the top of the chin and a hand on the forehead. This will lift the tongue away from the back of the throat.

BREATHING

Check if the casualty is breathing normally.

- Keeping the airway open look, listen and feel for signs of normal breathing for no more than ten seconds. Feel for air on the side of your cheek, listen for breath and look down the casualty's chest to see signs of breathing.
- If you observe infrequent, noisy gasps this is not 'normal breathing' and the casualty has gone into cardiac arrest. (This is known as Agonal breathing).
- If you are not sure if the casualty is breathing normally or not, assume they are not.

CHAPTER SIXTEEN: FIRST AID (FA) OVERVIEW

CASUALTY IS BREATHING NORMALLY - RECOVERY POSITION

If the casualty is breathing normally but remains unresponsive, stay with them, leave them on their back, monitor them and await the emergency services. If they need to be left unattended for any reason, or if their airway becomes blocked either by their tongue or by vomit etc. you will need to put them into the recovery position.

- Kneel beside the casualty (injured side). Remove bulky objects from pockets, and glasses or large rings.
- Place their nearest arm straight out or bent at a right angle with their palm facing up.
- Make sure both legs are straight.
- Bring their furthest arm across their chest by holding the back of their hand against their cheek on your side. Keep hold of their hand.
- With your other hand, grasp their far leg just above the knee and pull it up, keeping their foot flat on the ground.
- Keeping their hand under their cheek, pull on their leg and roll the casualty towards you onto their side.
- Adjust their upper leg so their hip and knee is at a right angle.
- Tilt their head and chin back to open their airway.
- Monitor the casualty's breathing until the ambulance arrives.

CHAPTER SIXTEEN: FIRST AID (FA) OVERVIEW

CASUALTY IS NOT BREATHING - CPR

CPR (Cardiopulmonary Resuscitation) is used when a casualty has stopped breathing or has irregular (agonal) breathing. It pushes blood through the body and can help keep someone alive until the emergency services arrive.

After carrying out the Primary Survey, get someone to call for the emergency services and let them know there is a casualty that is not breathing.

Note: If you are alone and need to call the emergency services yourself, put your phone onto speaker so you can talk and start CPR.

- Put casualty on their back.
- Place the heel of one hand in the centre of the casualty's chest. Place the heel of the opposite hand on top and interlock your fingers.
- Keeping your arms straight repeatedly push down onto the chest quite fast 30 times. Speed should be around 100-120 bpm so 30 compressions takes approx. 15-18 seconds.

Depth of compressions should be around 5 - 6cm

After 30 compressions, give two rescue breaths:

- Tilt head back using two fingers under the chin on one hand with the other hand on the forehead. Pinch nose and blow into mouth, watch to see chest fall. Do no more than two attempts.
- Continue the cycle of 30:2 until either, professionals arrive and take over, the casualty starts breathing or you are too exhausted to continue.

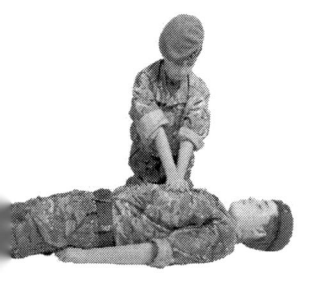

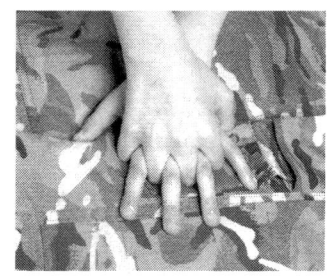

CHAPTER SIXTEEN: FIRST AID (FA) OVERVIEW

Hands-only CPR
If you are unable or unwilling to give rescue breaths, then give chest compressions only, it is certainly better than doing nothing.

Regurgitation During CPR
The casualty's stomach contents may get regurgitated during CPR, if this happens, turn the casualty away from yourself onto their side to allow fluid to drain away, once done, commence CPR again asap.

SUMMONING ASSISTANCE
You can call the emergency services free on 999 or 112 from any phone. You will need to know the following:

- The number you are calling from.
- The Emergency service you need (once you are through, you will be asked some questions, but it will not effect the response time).

Emergency SMS
If you cannot make voice calls, you can contact 999 emergency services by SMS text from your mobile phone. To register text 'register' to 999 and then follow the instructions.

Citizen Aid Application
This is an app that is available to download for free. it has lots of easy to follow guides on a whole host of emergency scenarios.

What 3 Words Application
This is another free to download app that can help pinpoint your location to the nearest metre. It is used widely now by the emergency services and can be helpful in all kinds of emergency and non-emergency situations.

/// what3words

CHAPTER SIXTEEN: FIRST AID (FA) OVERVIEW

INTRODUCTION TO AEDs

An AED (Automated External defibrillator) is a small lightweight 'shock box' that can restart the heart by giving an electric shock when a casualty is in cardiac arrest (heart has stopped pumping properly).

It analyses the casualty's heart rhythm and determines whether a shock is needed to restore the normal rhythm and pumping action of the heart to get the blood circulating again to get oxygen to the body's vital organs.

As part of 'The Chain of Survival' early de-fibrillation is vital.

Using AEDs

AEDs are user-friendly devices that untrained bystanders can use. They can be found in many public places i.e. shopping centres, airports, schools.

Turn on power button and follow the instructions and voice prompts.

- **Switch on AED.**
- **Remove or cut through clothing on chest.**
- **Take pads out, remove backing paper and attach to chest in positions indicated.**
- **The AED will start analysing the heart rhythm.**
- **Ensure no-one is touching the casualty**
- **Follow the voice &/or visual prompts given by the machine.**

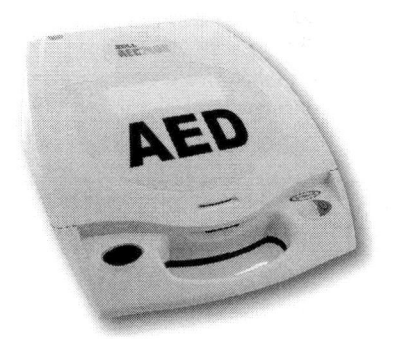

CHAPTER SIXTEEN: FIRST AID (FA) OVERVIEW

SYLLABUS FIRST AID

Army Cadet Syllabus First Aid is taught using the St John Ambulance lesson plans and presentations and must be taught by an instructor with a minimum of an in date First Aid At Work (FAAW) qualification. Because of this, lessons for each star level are simply listed.

First Aid Manual

This First Aid Manual is considered the definitive first aid reference in the UK and is written and endorsed by St John Ambulance, the British Red Cross and St Andrew's First Aid.

The First Aid syllabus is based on this manual (latest edition) along with the online lesson plans and presentations.

It is available to buy from various websites and from most major book retailers.

The Chain of Survival

This represents the sequence of actions that need to occur as quickly as possible in a life-threatening emergency.

Most First Aid situations start with the primary survey as this allows us to make a judgement call on what to do next without putting ourselves or others in danger. This along with the ability to contact the emergency services, put someone in the recovery position, administer CPR and use a defibrillator can make us effective in an emergency situation and possibly save someone's life.

You should not expect to see casualty recover spontaneously; the important thing is to buy time until professional help arrives.

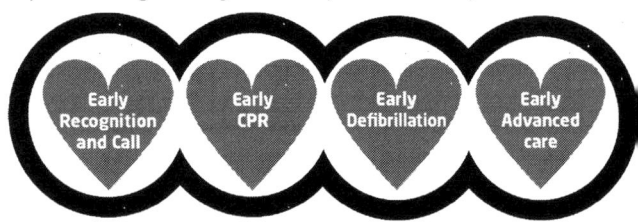

- Early Recognition and Call
- Early CPR
- Early Defibrillation
- Early Advanced care

CHAPTER SIXTEEN: FIRST AID (FA) OVERVIEW

BASIC FA TRAINING OVERVIEW

First Aid at a Basic level is designed to introduce cadets to first aid and how to deal with a life-threatening emergency.

01. PRIMARY SURVEY *(basic training)*

This is the starting point of all first aid situations. See pages 248 - 253 for more details on this along with how to put someone in the recovery position and contact the emergency services.

02. CARDIOPULMONARY RESUSCITATION (CPR) *(basic training)*

CPR (Cardiopulmonary Resuscitation) is used when a casualty has stopped breathing or has irregular (agonal) breathing. It pushes blood through the body and can help keep someone alive until the emergency services arrive. More info is on pages 251 - 253.

03. HEART ATTACK, BLEEDING AND CHOKING *(basic training)*

This lesson looks at three time sensitive injuries to allow cadets to administer more emergency care and buy the casualty more time while waiting for the emergency services to arrive.

BASIC TRAINING FIRST AID ASSESSMENT

Instructors must hold a minimum of an in date First Aid At Work (FAAW) qualification and be familiar with the St John Youth First Aid pack to assess basic first aid.

There is no formal assessment of first aid skills covered during basic training but instructors must ensure cadets can effectively demonstrate what they have learnt during lessons before moving on.

To finish basic training, cadets must take part in a role play where they make a phone call to the emergency services to summon help for a scenario set to them by an instructor.

Cadets will pass if the instructor believes the phone call would have been effective in getting assistance to the scene.

If a cadet fails (is referred), they may be assessed again immediately. If they do not pass after a second attempt, re-training is required before further assessment.

CHAPTER SIXTEEN: FIRST AID (FA) OVERVIEW

ONE STAR FA TRAINING OVERVIEW

LESSONS MUST BE DELIVERED USING THE ST JOHN AMBULANCE LESSON PLANS

One star first aid training looks at identifying and treating several other common injuries. When both basic and one star first aid have been completed they match the requirements for Bronze level DofE first aid so, if registered, this can be signed off.

01. BONES, MUSCLES & JOINTS *(one star training)*

This looks at dislocations, fractures, strains and sprains.

- **Fracture** - a crack or break in the bone.
- **Dislocation** - a bone in a joint that has moved out of place.
- **Sprains & strains** - damage to soft tissues.

02. HYPOTHERMIA *(one star training)*

Hypothermia occurs when the body's core temperature falls too low (below 35 degrees) for normal bodily functions and can be fatal. It is important to be able to recognise its early stages and take action to reverse it. This topic is particularly important in cadets when training and/or staying out overnight in cold temperatures.

03. HEAT EXHAUSTION *(one star training)*

Heat exhaustion is caused by a loss of salt and water from your body through excessive sweating. Be sure to look out for the signs and symptoms below as this can affect many cadets whilst out training. Make sure you drink plenty of water and wear layered clothing. If your body temperature gets above 40 degrees you may well develop heat stroke, which, if ignored can become fatal.

04. BITES, STINGS & MINOR INJURIES *(one star training)*

Insect bites and stings are very common, so it is important you know how to deal with them correctly. Ticks are small arachnids commonly found in grassy and wooded areas in southern England and the Scottish highlands. It is important to remove ticks safely using a tick removal tool. An early symptom of lyme disease caused by ticks is a circular rash. Ideally use a tick removal tool and not tweezers to remove.

Other minor injuries covered are minor bleeding and nose bleeds.

CHAPTER SIXTEEN: FIRST AID (FA) OVERVIEW

ONE STAR TRAINING FIRST AID ASSESSMENT

The one star first aid assessment is made up of three practical assessments carried out in the form of role play scenarios.

- Deal with a casualty who is not breathing (CPR).
- Deal with a casualty who is breathing but unconscious.
- Deal with a conscious casualty with a bleeding wound.

Full details are in the syllabus guide and on the resource centre.

If a cadet fails (is referred), they may be assessed again immediately. If they do not pass after a second attempt, re-training is required before further assessment.

TWO STAR FA TRAINING OVERVIEW

LESSONS MUST BE DELIVERED USING THE ST JOHN AMBULANCE LESSON PLANS

Two star first aid revises lessons learnt at basic and one star level and continues to look at identifying and treating other common injuries.

01. DEALING WITH AN EMERGENCY *(two star training)*

This lesson helps cadets prepare for dealing with a real life emergency should they encounter one. It looks at other factors such as communicating with casualties and bystanders, taking control of a situation and dealing with the emergency services.

02. REVISION - PRIMARY SURVEY & RECOVERY POSITION
(two star training)

Revision of lessons covered during basic training (also covered on pages 248 - 250 in this chapter).

03. REVISION - CARDIOPULMONARY RESUSCITATION (CPR) *(two star training)*

Revision of lessons covered during basic training (also covered on pages 251 - 253 in this chapter).

04. REVISION - MINOR BLEEDING, BLEEDING AND SHOCK
(two star training)

Revision of lessons covered during basic and one star training.

CHAPTER SIXTEEN: FIRST AID (FA) OVERVIEW

05. CHOKING (REVISION) & FAINTING *(two star training)*
Choking was covered during basic training so revision of this is covered. Fainting is also covered.

06. ELECTRIC SHOCK *(two star training)*
Dealing with someone who has received an electric shock and dealing with extra hazards that may be encountered.

07. BURNS & SCALDS *(two star training)*
Burns are created from dry heat such as a naked flame, whereas a scald is from a liquid heat such as boiling water or steam. This looks at safe and effective treatment of both.

08. ASTHMA *(two star training)*
Lots of people in the UK suffer from asthma so it is important to be able to identify someone having an asthma attack and be able to assist them. Different types of asthma medication is also looked at.

09. CHEST PAINS *(two star training)*
Dealing with someone who is having chest pains and identifying possible causes. Early treatment and emergency aid is often crucial.

10. FOREIGN OBJECTS *(two star training)*
How to deal with someone who has a foreign object stuck in their ear, eye and nose.

11. HEAD INJURIES *(two star training)*
How to deal with someone who has had a head injury and looking at seeking medical advice or emergency aid after an incident in case of future complications.

12. LOW BLOOD SUGAR *(two star training)*
Lots of people in the UK have some form of diabetes and are on medication or need certain food types at set times to maintain their blood sugar levels. If this is not done it can have serious effects so knowing what can be done in this situation is important.

CHAPTER SIXTEEN: FIRST AID (FA) OVERVIEW

13. POISONS *(two star training)*

Looking at what a poison is and where it may be found. Also looks at identifying different labels and taking appropriate action for anyone that has ingested any type of poison.

14. SEVERE ALLERGIC REACTION *(two star training)*

Lots of people in the UK have severe allergies to items such as nuts, bee stings etc. and can go into anaphylactic shock if exposed. If not identified and dealt with quickly, results can be deadly. People who know about their allergies may carry medication with them in the form of Epi pens so being able to assist people using them is useful.

15. SEIZURES *(two star training)*

Seizures are fairly common and are quite often not dangerous. This lesson looks at being able to assist someone having a seizure and knowing when extra emergency aid is required.

16. SPINAL INJURIES *(two star training)*

Anyone who has sustained a spinal injury is at serious risk of permanent damage which could lead to paralysis or worse. Knowing how to safely deal with someone with a suspected spinal injury is therefore essential.

TWO STAR TRAINING FIRST AID ASSESSMENT

The two star first aid assessment is made up of three practical assessments carried out in the form of role play scenarios.

- Deal with a casualty who is not breathing (CPR).
- Deal with a casualty who is breathing but unconscious.
- Deal with a conscious casualty with a bleeding wound.

Full details are in the syllabus guide and on the resource centre.

When basic, one star and two star first aid have been completed successfully, cadets will have gained the St John Ambulance Youth First Aid qualification and receive the associated badge and certificate.

If a cadet fails (is referred), they may be assessed again immediately. If they do not pass after a second attempt, re-training is required before further assessment.

CHAPTER SIXTEEN: FIRST AID (FA) OVERVIEW

THREE STAR FA TRAINING OVERVIEW (optional)

Three star first aid is optional and is done in the form of an adult Emergency First Aid At Work (EFAAW) course which must be delivered by a qualified Army Cadet First Aid Trainer/Assessor.

EMERGENCY FIRST AID AT WORK QUALIFICATION
(three star training)

The course covers the following:

- Role and responsibilities of first aider.
- Incident and casualty assessment.
- Unconscious casualty breathing normally.
- Unresponsive casualty not breathing properly.
- Choking casualty.
- Shock and bleeding.
- Minor injuries.

THREE STAR TRAINING FIRST AID ASSESSMENT

The assessment for the EFAAW qualification is continuous throughout training. There is a theory exam and practical observations. Full details are within the assessment guide.

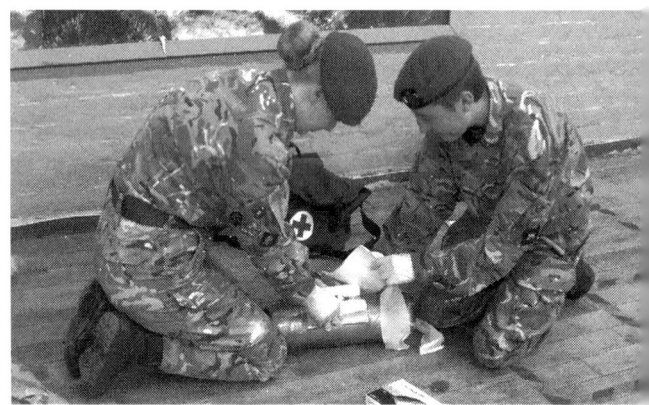

CHAPTER SIXTEEN: FIRST AID (FA) OVERVIEW

FOUR STAR FA TRAINING OVERVIEW (optional)

Four star first aid is optional and is done in the form of an adult First Aid At Work (FAAW) course which must be delivered by a qualified Army cadet first aid trainer/assessor. Cadets also need to complete an additional first aid instructors course to pass.

Cadets do not need to complete three star first aid in order to move onto four star training and on completion cadets are also permitted to teach junior cadets all first aid up to and including two star.

FIRST AID AT WORK QUALIFICATION *(four star training)*
See over the page for a list of lessons covered.

FOUR STAR TRAINING FIRST AID ASSESSMENT
The assessment for the FAAW qualification is continuous throughout training. There is a theory exam and practical observations. Full details are within the assessment guide.

CHAPTER SIXTEEN: FIRST AID (FA) OVERVIEW

FIRST AID AT WORK QUALIFICATION *(four star training)*

The following lessons are covered during the FAAW qualification:

- Role & responsibilities of first aider
- Incident & casualty assessment
- Unconscious casualty breathing normally
- Unresponsive casualty not breathing normally
- Choking casualty
- Shock & Bleeding
- Minor injuries
- Catastrophic Bleeding
- Secondary Survey
- Bone Muscle & Joint Injuries
- Head Injuries
- Spinal Injuries
- Chest Injuries
- Burns & Scalds
- Eye Injuries
- Poisons
- Anaphylaxis
- Heat & Cold Injuries
- Asthma
- Stroke
- Heart Attack & Angina
- Epilepsy
- Diabetes
- Scenario skills stations

Cadets also need to complete a two hour Cadet First Aid instructor course and then be observed for 30 minutes delivering a basic, one star or two star First Aid lesson. A reflective statement from the cadet is also required.

CHAPTER SEVENTEEN
COMMUNITY ENGAGEMENT (CE) OVERVIEW

CONTENTS:
- Introduction
- Basic CE Training Overview
- One Star CE Training Overview
- Two Star CE Training Overview
- Three Star CE Training Overview
- Four Star CE Training Overview

REFERENCES:
- *Army Cadet Syllabus - AC71101*
  (Version 1.2 - July 2022)
- *Army Cadets Community Engagement Training Manual - AC72145*
  (Version 1 - 2021)
- *Army Cadet Resource Centre via Westminster*

CHAPTER SEVENTEEN: CTY ENGAGEMENT (CE) OVERVIEW

INTRODUCTION

Community Engagement (CE) does not have many lessons but instead encourages cadets to get involved in their community.

"Its aim is to inspire young people to achieve success in life with a spirit of service to the King, their Country and their local community, and to develop in them the qualities of a good citizen".

- **Badges available:** None.
- **Specialist qualifications required to teach:** None.
- **Further progression beyond the syllabus:** Involvement in local, regional or national events such as parades and fund raising.

BASIC CE TRAINING OVERVIEW

Basic CE provides an introduction to the subject and looks at how local Emergency Services work together.

01. INTRODUCTION *(basic training)*

Members of the Armed Forces have very varied roles. Servicemen and women can often be seen in the local community taking part in a whole array of different tasks, from attending parades and memorials to helping with major disasters and national events.

This approach extends out to the Army Cadet Force, and you will often see cadets helping in the local community by attending remembrance and Armed Forces day parades, selling poppies, helping maintain public monuments and attending fêtes etc. It is a great way to help build a strong sense of belonging.

It is important that when cadets are seen in public, they display extremely high standards of personal appearance and conduct. In some instances, cadets may be the only military representation at an event and should take extreme pride in wearing the uniform issued to them and show the utmost respect to the men and women that currently serve, have served or lost their lives in the Armed Forces.

02. EMERGENCY SERVICES *(basic training)*

To contact any of the Emergency Services, call 999 or 112 from any phone. You can also set up the ability to contact them via SMS text message by texting 'REGISTER' to 999.

CHAPTER SEVENTEEN: CTY ENGAGEMENT (CE) OVERVIEW

There are 4 main Emergency Services in the UK that all have full time control centres. These services also work with local councils and regularly train together.

- **Police**
- **Fire & Rescue**
- **Ambulance**
- **His Majesty's Coastguard**

As well as the 4 main services, there are others that do not maintain full time control centres, but are called on when needed:

- **Voluntary Lifeboats**
- **Voluntary Search and Rescue Associations (SAR)**
- **Bomb Disposal**

All of the Emergency Services prime aim is to save lives, protect the public and prevent incidents from happening where possible. Each service has it's own specific role to play though.

Joint Emergency Services Interoperability Programme (JESIP)

Projects such as JESIP have been established to ensure the Emergency Services work well together during major incidents and each know their own roles and responsibilities to avoid confusion or misunderstanding. It also allows for information and expertise sharing and can save valuable time when dealing with a major incident.

BASIC TRAINING COMMUNITY ENGAGEMENT ASSESSMENT

The Community Engagement assessment at basic level is a simple written or verbal test with five questions on topics covered.

CHAPTER SEVENTEEN: CTY ENGAGEMENT (CE) OVERVIEW

ONE STAR CE TRAINING OVERVIEW

One star Community Engagement continues to look at how local communities work and also introduces the cadets to carrying out voluntary work and assisting with domestic tasks at their detachments.

01. COMMUNITY DIVERSITY *(one star training)*

A community is a group of people that have something in common such as an interest, their background or where they live and most people are part of more than one community. Here are some examples:

- **Local community** - People that live in the same area.
- **Religious community** - People that share the same religious beliefs.
- **Cultural community** - People that share the same background.
- **School community** - People that go to or work at the same school.
- **Social community** - A group of friends or members of a club.
- **Online community** - A global community that exists online.

Discrimination

Being part of a community gives people a sense of identity and belonging, but it is important to understand and accept others to be able to get along. Some people do not allow this to happen and, through a lack of understanding, are prejudiced against those that are not the same as themselves. Judging people based on their skin colour, nationality, background, religion, weight, age etc. and treating them differently or unfairly is called discrimination and is unacceptable.

02. DOMESTIC TASKS *(one star training)*

As you progress as a cadet you will be given more responsibility at your detachment to look after junior cadets and to show leadership. A good way to develop this is to take ownership of some of the domestic tasks required to keep your detachment looking good and be proud of where you parade.

Tasks can include sweeping the drill hall and other areas, emptying rubbish bins, organising notice boards, wiping down tables, washing up cups, mopping floors, litter picking, cleaning wipe boards, hoovering, dusting classrooms, tidying and organising the stores etc.

CHAPTER SEVENTEEN: CTY ENGAGEMENT (CE) OVERVIEW

03. INTRODUCTION TO VOLUNTEERING *(one star training)*

There are lots of opportunities for volunteering so it is quite easy to find something that interests you and can commit to with the free time you have available. From working in a big group on a large one off community project such as renovating a local play area right through to regular visits to a care home to talk to residents, there is something to suit everyone.

Here are some types of volunteering:

- **Caring** - Helping out in the health and social sector with elderly or disabled people.
- **Environment** - Helping to look after the environment either at a local, national or global level.
- **Food banks** - Helping those in need get free food and supplies by collecting, packing and delivering donations.
- **Fundraising** - Helping to raise money through collections or other admin tasks.
- **Working with animals** - From assisting at local animal shelters or sanctuaries through to assisting large charities.
- **Children or youth organisations** - Helping with young children or volunteering for organisations like the cubs, scouts or ACF.

Benefits to the Volunteer

Volunteering is a way to help others and give something back but there are lots of benefits to the volunteer such as career development, health and fitness, learning new life skills and making new friends.

ONE STAR TRAINING CE ASSESSMENT

The one star CE assessment is in three parts.

1. **Community diversity quiz** - Ten questions.
2. **Domestic tasks** - Complete three domestic tasks around detachment or on a cadet overnight activity.
3. **Introduction to volunteering** - Participate in a community-based activity and then discuss it back at detachment with an instructor or in a group.

CHAPTER SEVENTEEN: CTY ENGAGEMENT (CE) OVERVIEW

TWO STAR CE TRAINING OVERVIEW

Two star CE looks at different types of emergencies, who can help and who is likely to be most vulnerable. It also encourages cadets to get involved in practical community activities.

01. PRACTICAL ACTIVITY *(two star training)*

Cadets need to take part in two local community activities or functions as part of a group. The background and relevance needs to be briefed to the cadets before attending.

02. UNDERSTANDING EMERGENCIES *(two star training)*

An emergency is a serious incident that may put peoples lives, property or wildlife at risk that requires immediate action.

Examples of emergencies:

- **Natural hazards** - Floods, high winds, earthquakes etc.
- **Diseases** - Human diseases and pandemics or animal based.
- **Major accidents** - Traffic collisions, fires, system failures.
- **Societal risks** - Public disorder, riots, industrial action etc.
- **Malicious attacks** - Criminal, terrorist or cyber attacks.

Who Can Help?

Most emergencies are dealt with by local Emergency Services and other local authorities such as the NHS and Environment Agency.

These multi-agency groups are known as Local Resilience Forums (LRFs) and they not only work together to deal with emergencies, they also plan in advance for potential incidents.

Vulnerable Persons

In most emergencies there are certain people such as the elderly, disabled, pregnant women, single parents, families with very young children etc. that may require extra assistance or help. Being aware of who these people are in your community can help identify who to check on and look out for.

CHAPTER SEVENTEEN: CTY ENGAGEMENT (CE) OVERVIEW

Word cloud around "Emergency": incident, threat, life, risk, protection, disease, danger, health, disaster, loss, damage, plan, critical, property

03. PREPARE A STREET PLAN *(two star training)*

Just as local authorities and governments make plans in case of emergencies, it is useful for individuals to do a similar thing. Being aware of where Emergency Services, hospitals, doctors, defibrillators are located in your local area can be life saving. Knowing where the vulnerable people are in your local community too can also help if dealing with a major emergency.

TWO STAR TRAINING CE ASSESSMENT

The two star CE assessment is in three parts.

1. **Practical activity -** Take part in two local community events.
2. **Understanding emergencies quiz -** Written test.
3. **Prepare a street plan -** Create a plan of your local area that includes locations of all things you might find important in an emergency such as the Emergency Services, hospitals, doctors, defibrillators and anything else you feel would be relevant.

CHAPTER SEVENTEEN: CTY ENGAGEMENT (CE) OVERVIEW

THREE STAR CE TRAINING OVERVIEW (optional)

Three star Community Engagement is optional and is all about getting cadets to plan and execute their own volunteering activity.

01. PLANNING VOLUNTEERING *(three star training)*

Planning for a volunteering activity is in four stages:

1. **Identify need** - Find out where a volunteering activity is required.
2. **Plan action** - Decide on what can be done to make a difference.
3. **Act** - Carry out the volunteering individually or as part of a group.
4. **Reflect** - Looking back after the event to see what differences have been made for the cause and to the individual.

02. RISKS OF VOLUNTEERING *(three star training)*

Volunteering can be extremely rewarding, but there are some factors to consider when participating.

Responsibilities

Although volunteering is normally done for free, volunteers have certain responsibilities that are just the same as if being paid. This means that certain standards of dress, etiquette and behaviour need to be met and people need to be kept safe and be treated with respect. Not being paid is not an excuse to not follow the rules.

As a volunteer you also have certain rights and, if working for an organisation, you should expect to have the relevant training and assistance to be able to fulfil your duties safely and effectively.

Risks

Volunteering is generally done with great intentions and everyone involved tends to be very positive, but there are certain risks present.

- **Physical** - Working in a dangerous environment, without the correct clothing or PPE or not following health & safety rules.
- **Emotional** - Receiving verbal abuse, criticism or getting emotionally involved in an upsetting or disturbing environment.
- **Morale** - Not understanding your role fully or not feeling that your time is being used wisely or working too long without breaks.
- **Reputation** - Poor conduct that impacts personal or ACF reputation.

CHAPTER SEVENTEEN: CTY ENGAGEMENT (CE) OVERVIEW

Control Measures

To minimise the occurrence of these risks it is important to take steps to receive the correct training and follow all rules and guidelines laid out. Volunteering within the ACF should be carried out with direct CFAV supervision and assistance must be provided in the planning and execution of any activities.

It is important to have good communication with all people involved, always speak up if you are unsure about something or if you have questions. Let people know where you are going to be and what your timetable is and let people know if you have any issues or are not comfortable with anything asked of you. Also remember to wear the appropriate clothing, avoid working alone and take regular breaks.

Support

There are various organisations that support volunteers across the UK such as Volunteering England/Scotland/Wales, Volunteer now NI, Jersey/Guernsey charities and Volunteering matters. ACF/CCF support is available through the Army Cadet Force Association (ACFA) or the Combine Cadet Force Association (CCFA).

In addition, there are many local volunteer centres which can be found through the NCVO (England), Volunteer Scotland local support, Third Sector Support Wales and NI Direct Government Services websites.

The following can help young people or those working with them:

NSPCC - 0808 800 5000

Childline - 0800 1111

03. PRACTICAL ACTIVITY *(three star training)*

Having looked at the planning of a volunteering activity and thought about the responsibilities and risks involved, cadets should then take part in a practical activity.

THREE STAR TRAINING CE ASSESSMENT

The three star CE assessment is in three parts.

1. **Risks of volunteering quiz** - Written or verbal test.
2. **Planning volunteering** - Plan a volunteering activity.
3. **Practical activity** - Organise and take part in 15 hours of volunteering over a six month period.

CHAPTER SEVENTEEN: CTY ENGAGEMENT (CE) OVERVIEW

FOUR STAR CE TRAINING OVERVIEW (optional)

Four star Community Engagement is optional and is all about cadets planning, organising and leading a community-based engagement project. There are no extra lessons, however revision of previous lessons should be covered.

PREPARATION FOR PRACTICAL ACTIVITY *(four star training)*

This should include revision of previous CE lessons followed by putting a plan together for their project.

FOUR STAR TRAINING CE ASSESSMENT

Cadets are to plan, organise and conduct a community-based project over a six month period. Instructors are to assist with elements of paperwork or admin such as Cadet Action safety Plans (CASPs) etc. and are to ensure the activity follows the Safe System of Training (SST) before allowing it to proceed.

Assessment is ongoing throughout all stages and should include planning, conduct, communication and after activity procedures.

CHAPTER EIGHTEEN
KEEPING ACTIVE (KA) OVERVIEW

CONTENTS:
- Introduction
- Basic KA Training Overview
- One Star KA Training Overview
- Two Star KA Training Overview
- Three Star KA Training Overview
- Four Star KA Training Overview

REFERENCES:
- *Army Cadet Syllabus - AC71101*
  (Version 1.2 - July 2022)
- *Army Cadets Keeping Active Training Manual - AC72154*
  (Version 1 - 2021)
- *Army Cadet Resource Centre via Westminster*

CHAPTER EIGHTEEN: KEEPING ACTIVE (KA) OVERVIEW

INTRODUCTION

Fitness is an important part of army cadet training and helps prepare cadets for some of the strenuous activities they take part in.

- **Badges available:** None.
- **Specialist qualifications required to teach:** None.
- **Further progression beyond the syllabus:** Area, regional or national sporting events.

BASIC KA TRAINING OVERVIEW

Basic Keeping Active (KA) provides an introduction to the subject and highlights the importance of regular exercise and a healthy diet.

01. INTRODUCTION TO KEEPING ACTIVE AND THE IMPORTANCE OF HYDRATION *(basic training)*

Fitness is the ability to take part in strenuous activities and recover in a reasonable time. Being healthy means not having injuries or illness. Both work together and compliment each other.

Cadets need to focus on keeping active by taking part in cadet physical training as well as their own activities away from cadets. Cadets should be doing at least 60 minutes per day of physical activity and should avoid prolonged periods of being sedentary (sitting).

To have a good overall fitness level, there are four main areas:

1. **Stamina:** This is the ability to sustain prolonged physical effort. This is the kind of exercise that can get you out of breath quickly as your heart and lungs do their best to move oxygen around the body. This is known as 'aerobic' exercise and includes activities such as running, cycling, walking and swimming.

2. **Strength:** This requires building muscles to be able to exert large amounts of force. Building muscular strength can allow you to lift more weight whereas developing explosive strength can help with movement and other activities. Building strength can be achieved by completing compound exercises such as squats and press ups that use more than one muscle group.

CHAPTER EIGHTEEN: KEEPING ACTIVE (KA) OVERVIEW

3. **Speed:** This is how fast your muscles can exert force which is normally used over shorter periods of time. Sprinting or doing shuttle runs allow you to move at maximum speed but requires less oxygen than when taking part in longer activities so is 'anaerobic'.
4. **Flexibility:** Developed by regular stretching, this increases the range of movements at your joints and is important for almost all sports and activities.

Hydration

Around 60% of the human body is made of water and water is required for all bodily functions so it is really important to keep ourselves hydrated. Water is present in some foods, but we should still drink two litres (eight glasses) of water every day under normal circumstances. If we are exercising or getting very hot, we need to drink even more than that though.

Diet

In just the same way that an engine needs fuel to work, our bodies need fuel to be able to function properly. Fuel produces energy and we require energy to do everything from making our internal organs such as heart and lungs work, right through to fighting off illness.

Calories

Fuel in food is measured in calories and the amount of calories in most packet foods is shown on the label somewhere. It's important to be aware of this as some foods have lots of calories, whereas others don't have many at all.

Nutrients

Calories are actually made up of many different 'nutrients' which the body needs in different quantities. Unfortunately, a lot of the foods we love such as crisps, sweets, fizzy drinks and chocolate contain huge amounts of the things we need the least of, so getting our calories just from those types of food is not good.

The main nutrients in food are carbohydrates, proteins, fats, vitamins, minerals, fibre and water. On most packet foods in the UK there is a traffic light code to help you understand what foods you should be eating more of and what to avoid.

CHAPTER EIGHTEEN: KEEPING ACTIVE (KA) OVERVIEW

02. HOW TO WARM UP AND COOL DOWN *(basic training)*

Warm up before exercise

Before any physical training or exercise it is important to prepare your heart, lungs and muscles by warming up. This helps avoid injury, improves performance and can prepare you mentally for whatever activity you are doing.

RAMP

A good way to structure your warm up is to use RAMP.

R: Raise: Raise your heart rate through movement such as walking, jogging. Lift your knees, flick your heels out and side step to warm up and stretch more muscles.

A & M: Activate and Mobilise: Activate and mobilise joints and muscles by making big circles with your arms, bending to the side and front and doing squats and lunges etc.

P: Potentiate: Use movements relevant to the activity you are about to take part in to increase the effect of key muscle groups.

Cool Down After Exercise

After any period of exercise or strenuous activity, it is important to cool down to gradually return your body to how it was before you started. Stopping exercise completely without a cool down period can lead to dizziness and possibly fainting as your blood pressure drops.

To cool down effectively only takes around 8 to 10 minutes and should include some pulse rate reduction by gentle walking while breathing deeply, some joint mobility such as making big circles with your arms, bending to the side and front and doing squats and lunges etc.

Holding some stretches for 30 seconds each are also required to avoid muscles tightening and causing discomfort. Stretches can include standing hamstring and quadricep stretches, gluteal stretches and abdominal stretches.

BASIC TRAINING KA ASSESSMENT

There is no formal assessment for basic KA, although both lessons need to be delivered properly to ensure cadets understand the importance of regular exercise, hydration and diet.

CHAPTER EIGHTEEN: KEEPING ACTIVE (KA) OVERVIEW

ONE, TWO & THREE STAR KA TRAINING OVERVIEW (optional at three star) (no four star KA)

Keeping Active is the same at one, two and three star levels and is all about encouraging cadets to be more active in general and not about getting great scores at individual activities. For this reason, cadets get points for taking part in activities at detachment and at home which all count towards passing their star level.

There is no KA at four star level.

DETACHMENT KEEPING ACTIVE NIGHTS

Detachment Keeping Active nights are made up of exercises designed to help develop fitness and strength to allow cadets to take part in the demanding activities covered at each star level.

Scoring: These exercises can be scored to gauge cadet's progress. Keep a record of each cadet's individual scores each night to be able to compare results and monitor progress. Points do not count towards passing star levels. (See page 279 for how to pass star levels).

Broad jump: This is a long jump from a standing position that tests lower body, explosive strength. Cadets bend their arms, hips and knees and then propel themselves as far forward as possible while remaining upright. Cadets have three attempts and the distance is measured from the start line to the heel after landing.

DISTANCE (cm)	100	130	150	170	200
POINTS	1	2	3	4	5

Squat test: These test lower body strength by seeing how many squats can be done in one minute. Cadets start with their legs straight and arms out to the front. To perform a squat, bend your knees and go into a position as if sitting on a chair with thighs and hips parallel to the floor and then return to the start position.

NUMBER	5	10	15	21	28
POINTS	1	2	3	4	5

CHAPTER EIGHTEEN: KEEPING ACTIVE (KA) OVERVIEW

Press ups: Tests upper body strength by seeing how many press ups can be done in one minute. Starting with your stomach flat on the floor, legs straight behind you and palms of your hands flat on the floor under your shoulders, push your body up until your arms are straight. Keeping your back straight, lower your body until your upper arms are parallel to the floor and then push back up.

NUMBER	5	11	17	20	28
POINTS	1	2	3	4	5

100m shuttle sprint: Tests anaerobic capacity by seeing how quickly you can run 5 x 20 metre shuttle runs. Start by laying down in the prone position, on the command 'Go', stand up and sprint to the end of a 20 metre lane. Making sure your foot touches the line, turn 180 degrees and sprint back. Repeat until you have run five lengths.

TIME (sec's)	45	35	29	25	23
POINTS	1	2	3	4	5

Multi-Stage fitness test (MSFT): Tests aerobic capacity by running at increasing speeds until you cannot continue. Run 20 metre lengths in time with recorded beeps that start very slow and increase speed every level. Cadets are given up to two warnings if they are not in time with the beep and on the third warning cadets must stop and their last level is recorded.

LEVEL	5	7	8.1	9	10.2
POINTS	1	2	3	4	5

CHAPTER EIGHTEEN: KEEPING ACTIVE (KA) OVERVIEW

ONE, TWO & THREE STAR TRAINING KA ASSESSMENT

Taking part in detachment Keeping Active nights, ACF sports events and other fitness activities away from cadets earns points that are added together. Each star level requires a different amount of points to pass and progress to the next star level.

Points can be obtained in two ways:

1. Participation Points

Cadets get 2 points for every 30 minutes of physical activity they carry out in the following situations:

- Organised training activity as part of the ACF in line with the Keeping Active manual.
- Organised sports events with the ACF in line with the sports manual.
- Physical activity conducted in their own time with a parent/guardian/coach supervising.

2. Bonus Points

If taking part in ACF activities, a bonus point can be issued in the following ways:

- Improving on previous score, times etc. from Keeping Active sessions.
- Getting the highest score/best performance within a group of cadets during a keeping Active session.

All activities need to be completed under supervision from an instructor (or family member/sports coach etc. if away from the ACF) and be done in full sports kit with trainers instead of boots.

Score requirements by star level (no four star option):

STAR LEVEL	ONE STAR	TWO STAR	THREE STAR	FOUR STAR
POINTS REQUIRED	22	27	32	N/A

2 points for every 30 minutes of physical activity

Use the diary on the next page to record activities

CHAPTER EIGHTEEN: KEEPING ACTIVE (KA) OVERVIEW

Date	Activity	Witness	Duration (mins)	Score	Running total

CHAPTER NINETEEN
ADVENTUROUS TRAINING (AT) OVERVIEW

CONTENTS:
- Introduction
- Basic AT Training Overview
- One Star AT Training Overview
- Two Star AT Training Overview
- Three Star AT Training Overview
- Four Star AT Training Overview

REFERENCES:
- *Army Cadet Syllabus - AC71101 (Version 1.2 - July 2022)*
- *Army Cadets Expeditions (ACS 21 & DofE) and Adventurous Training Manual - AC71849 (Version 2 - 2022)*
- *Army Cadet Resource Centre via Westminster*

CHAPTER NINETEEN: ADV. TRAINING (AT) OVERVIEW

INTRODUCTION

Adventurous Training (AT) is a non-military subject in the Army Cadet Syllabus that, apart from being great fun, develops lots of personal skills that can transfer into everyday life.

The activities that are available may at first seem to be dangerous or extreme, but they are completely safe when the correct training is given and adequate Personal Protective Equipment (PPE) is used. This is what can make taking part so exciting though and the reason it is so beneficial to personal development.

- **Badges available:** None.
- **Specialist qualifications required to teach:** Relevant AT qualifications required from National Governing Body (NGB).
- **Further progression beyond the syllabus:** Area, regional, national or international trips and activities.

BASIC AT TRAINING OVERVIEW

Basic AT is theory based only and provides an introduction to AT along with a look at the key aims, opportunities and benefits.

01. AIMS & BENEFITS OF ADVENTUROUS TRAINING
(basic training)

AT activities are broken down into three main categories:

- **Land Activities:** Mountain biking, climbing, mountaineering, hill walking, abseiling, gorge walking, skiing and snow boarding etc.
- **Water Activities:** Kayaking, canoeing, sailing, sub-aqua and coasteering etc.
- **Air Activities:** Parachuting, gliding and paragliding etc.

In the ACF all of these activities are available either at local, regional or national level. Some are delivered as part of the syllabus and others are not.

CHAPTER NINETEEN: ADV. TRAINING (AT) OVERVIEW

Aims of AT

The importance of AT goes beyond having fun and doing some great activities as it develops lots of transferable skills that might not be obvious straight away.

The aims of AT in the Army Cadet Force are as follows:

- Influence the cadet's personal development.
- Inspire cadets to achieve their full potential.
- Provide opportunities to engage in progressive, arduous and challenging activities.
- Develop teamwork and leadership.
- Enable values and standards.
- Provide an alternative learning environment.

Benefits of AT

There are many benefits to participating in AT:

- **Physical benefits:** Improve fitness and health and develop stamina, endurance, strength and flexibility.
- **Mental benefits:** Build confidence and mental robustness. In addition, it helps develop moral courage and discipline and encourages problem solving and risk awareness.
- **Develops teamwork:** Some aspects of AT can initially be quite daunting but working in a team makes everything achievable. From checking each others kit and discussing how to tackle a tricky situation right through to offering encouragement and support.
- **Develops leadership:** Teams need leadership and as cadets develop through various activities, this comes from them.
- **Transferable skills:** All of the aspects above transfer into our daily lives and can help with future employment of any kind. Key transferable skills include communication, leadership, motivation, organisation/admin, decision making and people skills.
- **Travel:** Quite often you will need to travel to get to a suitable AT location. Sometimes this means visiting different areas of the UK, but on occasions, you may need to go even further and visit a different country where you also get to learn about new cultures.

CHAPTER NINETEEN: ADV. TRAINING (AT) OVERVIEW

AT Opportunities

There are lots of ways to get involved in Adventurous Training and through the Army Cadet Syllabus, you will get to sample at least a few different activities. If you want to do more thought, there are lots of opportunities available locally or at regional or national level.

Cadet Centre for Adventurous Training (CCAT)

This is the ACF & CCF Centre of Excellence for all AT training and offers beginner and intermediate courses as well as full qualification courses. There is a list of activities available, a diary of events and course application forms.

Check out the website to find out more:
www.armycadetadventure.co.uk

Royal Canadian Army Cadets (RCAC) Exchange

This is an annual six week leadership and challenge course held in the Rocky Mountains of Canada and is open to four star passed cadets that are aged 15 or over. It comprises of six training cycles including mountaineering expeditions, glacier travel, canoeing/kayaking, horse riding, climbing and mountain biking.

National Army Cadet Expedition

An annual event that takes place in a different country each year.

BASIC ADVENTUROUS TRAINING ASSESSMENT

This is a written or verbal assessment based on information covered during the AT theory lessons.

If a cadet fails they can take the test again but, if they fail after a second attempt, re-training is required before attempting again.

CHAPTER NINETEEN: ADV. TRAINING (AT) OVERVIEW

ONE STAR AT TRAINING OVERVIEW

At one star level, you will get to take part in a low level AT taster session. This will be a minimum of two hours and will introduce the basics of a specific activity.

Training

The activity you will get to take part in will vary depending on where you are and what is available but will be something along the lines of kayaking, trail walking or using a climbing wall etc. Whichever it is, you will need to learn what is involved and how to take part safely before getting fully involved.

- **Location:** The location of your activity will create several factors that need to be considered such as the weather, other users, layout and facilities, environmental risks such as lakes, cliffs, roads etc. and access/exits.
- **Equipment:** Every AT activity will have some sort of equipment required from essential hardware such as kayaks or mountain bikes through to Personal Protective Equipment (PPE) such as helmets, life jackets and climbing harnesses.
- **Participation**: Full training will be given to allow you to safely take part in a supervised activity. You will have time to practice and ideally interact with others to encourage teamwork and communication skills.
- **Finish up** At the end of your session you will be required to clean, check, return and help store any equipment used and will have time to discuss the event with staff and other cadets.

ONE STAR ADVENTUROUS TRAINING ASSESSMENT

The one star AT assessment is in two parts:

1. Ongoing assessment during the practical AT activity to check the cadet has participated fully and safely and used the relevant PPE.
2. Written, verbal or group discussion to check understanding of skills used during activity and the importance of team work.

If a cadet fails they can take the test again but, if they fail after a second attempt, re-training is required before attempting again.

CHAPTER NINETEEN: ADV. TRAINING (AT) OVERVIEW

TWO STAR AT TRAINING OVERVIEW (optional)

Two star AT is optional and involves taking part in a two day multi activity AT package which should ideally be residential.

When taking part in AT there are other things to consider such as the environment and access issues, so these are also looked at.

01. BACKGROUND OF ACTIVITIES *(two star training)*

Over a two day period, cadets find out more and take part in at least two different activities. This exposes them to different types of AT and can help with choosing an activity to focus on during three star training if they wish to continue.

Cadets learn about the background, disciplines and grading schemes of each along with which National Governing Bodies (NGB) covers them and what qualifications can be gained by participating or are required to teach.

02. EQUIPMENT *(two star training)*

For each activity there will be specific equipment required so cadets need to know how to check that everything is in good working order, fits correctly and is suitable for use. Maintenance, handling and storage is also covered.

03. PARTICIPATION *(two star training)*

Learning the basic skills to participate is obviously a massive part of training but warming up, communication, safety, teamwork the effects of weather and cooling down are also elements that are covered.
It is also expected that the Army Cadet Values and Standards are developed and demonstrated through AT.

04. ENVIRONMENT *(two star training)*

Understanding the impact each activity has on the environment is also important as it allows us to minimise its effect. Issues can include erosion, pollution, disturbance, tourism, fire and infection.

05. ACCESS *(two star training)*

Access issues and guidelines were looked at during Expedition and Navigation training and the same applies to carrying out AT. (Refer back to pages 190, 191, 205, 209 & 210 for a reminder).

CHAPTER NINETEEN: ADV. TRAINING (AT) OVERVIEW

06. LOGBOOK *(two star training)*

Keeping a logbook of AT activities is important and these can be kept as paper, electronic copies or online. Information about each activity along with dates, progress, awards etc. can then be documented.

TWO STAR TRAINING AT ASSESSMENT

The two star AT assessment is in two parts.

1. Ongoing practical assessment throughout all activities.
   - Correct use of equipment, clothing and PPE.
   - Understanding of risk and safety procedures.
   - Basic skills to participate in activities under supervision.
   - Environmental awareness.
2. Verbal, written, individual or team assessment to check understanding of access, log books, transferable skills and application of values and standards during participation.

CHAPTER NINETEEN: ADV. TRAINING (AT) OVERVIEW

THREE STAR AT TRAINING OVERVIEW (optional)

Three star AT is optional and involves taking part in a two day single activity progressive AT package of the cadet's choice which should ideally be part of a journey and residential.

Cadets must have completed basic and one star AT but they do not have to have done two star AT to take part. Full revision must be done to ensure cadets have the relevant knowledge though.

01. BACKGROUND OF ACTIVITY *(three star training)*

AT at this level is more advanced and focusses on just one activity. Cadets are allowed to choose what activity they take part in based on options within the CCAT (Cadet Centre for Adventurous Training - see page 284) and the NGBs (National Governing Bodies).

Cadets get to look more in depth at the origins of their chosen activity and can gain an intermediate level qualification whilst also learning about further options and instructor qualifications.

02. ENVIRONMENT *(three star training)*

This looks at weather and how this can drastically effect the safety and enjoyment of certain activities. It also looks at different types of forecasts and where to find them (see page 210 - 211).

03. RISKS *(three star training)*

It is always important to be able to identify risks as early as possible and make plans to avoid or reduce their impact. This is covered in part during Expedition training (see page 194 & 205).

When assessing risk, you need to look at the likelihood of something happening and what the impact that would have. This forms the basis of a standard written risk assessment which encourages the use of control measures to reduce the likelihood and/or severity of the impact to make an activity safe.

Despite standard practices and other control measures being in place, there may still be some residual risk. If this is still too high then an activity cannot take place.

CHAPTER NINETEEN: ADV. TRAINING (AT) OVERVIEW

04. LEADERSHIP CODE *(three star training)*

The leadership code was looked at on page 214 as part of Expedition training. AT also helps develop great leadership and can be essential to help motivate a team and achieve goals.

05. EQUIPMENT *(three star training)*

During the chosen activity there will be specific equipment required so cadets need to know how to check that everything is in good working order, fits correctly and is suitable for use. Correct maintenance, handling and storage is also important.

06. PARTICIPATION *(three star training)*

Learning the basic skills of a chosen activity along with the boundaries and emergency procedures is obviously a massive part of training but warming up, communication, safety, teamwork and cooling down are also element that are covered. It is also expected that the Army Cadet Values and Standards are developed and demonstrated through AT.

THREE STAR TRAINING AT ASSESSMENT

The three star AT assessment is in two parts.

1. Ongoing practical assessment throughout all activities
   - Correct use of equipment, clothing and PPE.
   - Understanding of risk and safety procedures.
   - Intermediate skills to participate under supervision.
   - Awareness and use of leadership code.
2. Verbal, written, individual or team assessment to check understanding of access issues and support and application of leadership code and values and standards during participation.

CHAPTER NINETEEN: ADV. TRAINING (AT) OVERVIEW

FOUR STAR AT TRAINING OVERVIEW (optional)

Four star AT is optional and involves taking part in a five day single activity progressive AT package which is residential and contains elements of journeying.

Cadets can choose from the following:

- **A relevant activity from the CCAT website (see page 284)**
- **Take part in an area led five day expedition**
- **Rocky Mountain exchange**
- **National Cadets AT expedition**

Cadets must have completed basic and one star AT but they do not have to have done two or three star AT to take part. Full revision must be done to ensure cadets have the relevant knowledge.

01. ENVIRONMENT *(four star training)*

This consolidates previous learning by looking at all environmental issues from AT activities impact on the local environment through to looking at weather conditions and advanced forecasting resources.

02. EQUIPMENT *(four star training)*

During the chosen activity there will be specific equipment required so cadets need to know how to check that everything is in good working order, fits correctly and is suitable for use. Correct maintenance, handling and storage is also important.

03. PARTICIPATION *(four star training)*

Learning more skills of a chosen activity to allow cadets to participate in mentored groups away from cadets. Warming up, communication, safety, teamwork and cooling down are also elements that are covered as well as the Army Cadet Values and Standards and leadership code.

FOUR STAR TRAINING AT ASSESSMENT

This is an ongoing practical assessment throughout the activity done through observation and use of the log book.

CHAPTER TWENTY
COMMUNICATIONS (CIS) OVERVIEW

CONTENTS:
- Introduction
- Basic CIS Training Overview
- One Star CIS Training Overview
- Two Star CIS Training Overview
- Three Star CIS Training Overview
- Four Star CIS Training Overview

REFERENCES:
- *Army Cadet Syllabus - AC71101* (Version 1.2 - July 2022)
- *Army Cadets CIS Training Manual - AC72143* (Version 1.0 - September 2021)
- *Voice Procedure Manual - AC70816(C)* (Version 1.0 - September 2021)
- *Army Cadet Resource Centre via Westminster*

CHAPTER TWENTY: COMMS TRAINING (CIS) OVERVIEW

INTRODUCTION

Communication & Information Systems (CIS) teaches cadets about forms of military communication and cyber security. Working through the Army Cadet Syllabus, training starts with some very simple concepts, but as cadets progress, there are lots of opportunities to use communication equipment and, at the highest level, cadets can achieve qualifications that are useful if looking to move into a career in communications or cyber.

- **Badges available:** Badges available at two, three and four star.

Radio
Achievable at two star level

NEW BADGE AVAILABLE SOON

Line
Achievable at three star level

Crossed flags
Achievable at four star level

- **Specialist qualifications required to teach:** No specialist qualifications are required to teach basic and one star CIS with the exception of the PRR (Personal Role Radio). To teach the PRR and two star CIS, instructors need to hold the basic CIS instructor qualification. To teach three and four star CIS, instructors need to hold the intermediate CIS instructor qualification. To assess four star CIS, instructors need to hold the advanced CIS instructor qualification.

- **Further progression beyond the syllabus:** In addition to the training available through the Army Cadet Syllabus, there are other courses available either locally or at CIS HQ, Blandford.
  - **Cadet Advanced Radio:** Cadets must be 4 star passed to attend.
  - **Cyberfirst Adventurers:** One day introduction to cyber.
  - **Cyberfirst Defenders:** Five day course that looks at building small networks, ethical hacking, password cracking and cryptography.
  - **Cyberfirst Advanced:** Five day course that allows cadets to hone their skills and behaviours needed to enter the cyber security or computing workplace for real.

CHAPTER TWENTY: COMMS TRAINING (CIS) OVERVIEW

BASIC CIS TRAINING OVERVIEW

Basic CIS is made up of three lessons that introduces cadets to military communications and its early history. Assessment is both practical and theory based.

01. PHONETIC ALPHABET *(basic training)*

When talking over a phone or radio or when in a loud environment, sometimes it is difficult to hear a word or letter accurately. For these occasions, we use the NATO Phonetic Alphabet. Every letter has a word associated with it that starts with that corresponding letter which can then be used to spell out words or give call signs, passwords etc. There is also a correct way to pronounce each word.

Letter	Phonetic	Pronounced	Letter	Phonetic	Pronounced
A	ALPHA	AL-FAH	N	NOVEMBER	NO-VEM-BER
B	BRAVO	BRAH-VO	O	OSCAR	OSS-CAH
C	CHARLIE	CHAR-LIE	P	PAPA	PAH-PAH
D	DELTA	DELL-TAH	Q	QUEBEC	KEH-BECK
E	ECHO	ECK-OH	R	ROMEO	ROW-ME-OH
F	FOXTROT	FOKS-TROT	S	SIERRA	SEE-AIR-RAH
G	GOLF	GOLF	T	TANGO	TANG-GO
H	HOTEL	HOH-TELL	U	UNIFORM	YOU-NEE-FORM
I	INDIA	IN-DEE-AH	V	VICTOR	VIK-TAH
J	JULIET	JEW-LEE-ET	W	WHISKEY	WISS-KEY
K	KILO	KEY-LOH	X	X-RAY	ECKS-RAY
L	LIMA	LEE-MAH	Y	YANKEE	YANG-KEY
M	MIKE	MIKE	Z	ZULU	ZOO-LOO

CHAPTER TWENTY: COMMS TRAINING (CIS) OVERVIEW

02. 24 HOUR CLOCK & DATE, TIME GROUPS (DTG) *(basic training)*

There are 24 hours in a day which is generally broken down into 12 hours before midday (AM) and 12 hours after midday (PM).

To avoid confusion, the military use a 24 hour clock.

BEFORE MIDDAY

12hr CLOCK	24HR CLOCK
12AM	0000
1AM	0100
2AM	0200
3AM	0300
4AM	0400
5AM	0500
6AM	0600
7AM	0700
8AM	0800
9AM	0900
10AM	1000
11AM	1100

AFTER MIDDAY

12hr CLOCK	24HR CLOCK
12PM	1200
1PM	1300
2PM	1400
3PM	1500
4PM	1600
5PM	1700
6PM	1800
7PM	1900
8PM	2000
9PM	2100
10PM	2200
11PM	2300

Examples:

12 hour clock	24 hour clock	Pronounced
6.30am	0630hrs	Zero Six Thirty Hours
10.25am	1025hrs	Ten Twenty Five Hours
5.15pm	1715hrs	Seventeen Fifteen Hours
10.08pm	2208hrs	Twenty Two Zero Eight Hours
2am	0200hrs	Zero Two Hundred Hours
2pm	1400hrs	Fourteen Hundred Hours

CHAPTER TWENTY: COMMS TRAINING (CIS) OVERVIEW

Writing Letters and Numbers

When writing letters and numbers down, it is quite easy to confuse some of them, so there are specific ways to write them.

Number zero written as Ø **Number seven written as 7̶**

Number one written as 1 **Letter Z written as Z̵**

How to Pronounce Numbers Correctly

Number	Pronounced
1	WUN
2	TOO
3	TH-REE
4	FOE-ER
5	FIE-YIV

Number	Pronounced
6	SIX
7	SEV-EN
8	ATE
9	NINE-ER
Ø	ZE-RO

Time Zones

Around the world time is based on Coordinated Universal Time (UTC) or Greenwich Mean Time (GMT). The UK time is in-line with UTC and is known as ZULU (Z) whereas other countries will be ahead or behind this time. Each time zone around the world is allocated a letter A - Z.

Date Time Groups (DTG)

When writing down a date and a time, the military use a specific format that can be broken down into 5 parts and looks like this:

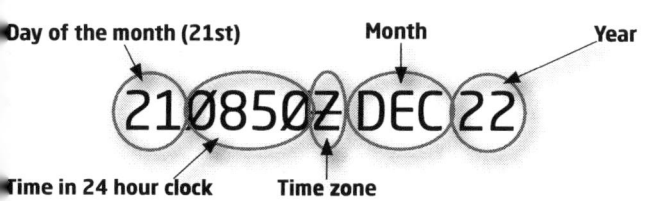

Day of the month (21st) **Month** **Year**

21Ø85ØZ DEC 22

Time in 24 hour clock **Time zone**

CHAPTER TWENTY: COMMS TRAINING (CIS) OVERVIEW

03. HISTORY OF EARLY MILITARY COMMS *(basic training)*

Communication for the military has always been essential and although early forms were very simple, a lot of them are still used today. Here are some examples that were used up until World War Two.

- **Vocal Communication:** Vocal commands on the battlefield.
- **Runners:** Taking written messages or verbal orders.
- **Sun reflections:** Using mirrors or shiny metal to reflect the sun.
- **Fire:** Lighting beacons or using smoke from fires.
- **Horn, Trumpet & Bugle:** Melodies have different meanings.
- **Drums:** Indicate times of the day and give orders on a battlefield.
- **Flags:** Identify individual units or send messages.
- **Telegraphy:** A way to send messages over longer distances.
- **Animals:** Horses, carrier pigeons and dogs used to take messages.

Codes & Ciphers

Codes and ciphers are used to send messages that can only be understood by the people they are intended for. They use letters, numbers, words, symbols or gestures and anyone using the code needs to understand how it works. The British Army use a system called BATCO (Battle Code) to send low level encrypted messages.

BASIC TRAINING CIS ASSESSMENT

This is made up of a mixture of practical assessment and written/verbal questioning to check understanding. If a cadet fails any section they can retake straight away. If a cadet fails after a second attempt, re-training is required before attempting again.

CHAPTER TWENTY: COMMS TRAINING (CIS) OVERVIEW

ONE STAR CIS TRAINING OVERVIEW

One star CIS is made up of six lessons and both practical and theory assessments. Lessons continue to look at the history of military communications as well as introducing elements of communication security and cyber warfare. The PRR radio system is also introduced.

01. SECURITY - COIL *(one star training)*

When using radios we need to always assume that someone is listening in and make sure to protect all sensitive information. To remember what information is considered sensitive and needs protecting, we use the mnemonic 'COIL'.

C - COMBAT EFFECTIVENESS (how effective we are).
   Number and type of any casualties, condition and availability of equipment and ration and ammunition levels.

O - ORDER OF BATTLE (what units we have).
   Identities of senior officers, unit identities and command structure.

I - INTENTIONS (what we are planning).
   Attacks or withdrawals, timings of movements and activities.

L - LOCATIONS (where we are).
   Unit and HQ locations, formation and unit boundaries. Areas of operations and movement routes.

02. SECURITY CLASSIFICATION *(one star training)*

Messages, files and written communications are given a security classification based on how sensitive the information is within them.

Highly sensitive

TOP SECRET

SECRET

OFFICIAL - SENSITIVE

OFFICIAL

UNCLASSIFIED

Not sensitive

CHAPTER TWENTY: COMMS TRAINING (CIS) OVERVIEW

03. HISTORY OF EARLY MILITARY COMMS PT2 *(one star training)*

During basic training, you looked at the early history of military comms, this is a look at more recent developments.

- **Telephony:** Using cables to carry real time voice communications.
- **Telex:** Messages typed on a typewriter could be sent as telephone signals and be printed at a different location.
- **Fax:** Short for facsimile (copy). Allowed documents to be scanned in one place and sent to the other to be printed.
- **Modems/Routers:** These use phone lines to allow computers to communicate.
- **Radio:** Wireless short to mid range communications.
  The British Army have used the following radio systems:

  Larkspur - 1962 (approx)
  Clansman - 1976 (approx)
  Bowman - 2004 (approx)

  Army Cadets get to use the following during CIS training:

  Personal Role Radio (PRR) - UK PRC 343
  Mercury radio system - UK PRC 710, 715 & 720

- **Satellites:** Signals are sent to satellites orbiting the earth that then send the signal back down to ground stations.
- **Fibre Optics:** Cables made from thin glass wrapped in plastic with laser light passing through them.

Analogue and Digital

Modern forms of transmission that work slightly differently.

- **Analogue:** A continuous electrical signal in its natural form.
- **Digital:** A non-continuous electrical signal that is converted into binary numbers.

The digital signal allows for far more information to be sent which is why digital TV and radio has far more channels than analogue.

Cyber

This is a word used to describe anything in the computer and digital age. It is now more relevant than ever and specialist cyber units are now part of the Army.

CHAPTER TWENTY: COMMS TRAINING (CIS) OVERVIEW

04. MORSE CODE & SEMAPHORE *(one star training)*

Invented in 1837, Morse Code is considered to be the first form of digital communication. Messages are sent by turning a signal on and off and can be sent in audio or visual form using radios, buzzers, lamps, torches etc. Switching on and off creates long and short signals that represent letters of the alphabet and numbers. Speed in Morse is measured in Words Per Minute (WPM).

- **Short signal** - referred to as a 'Dit' (shown as a dot •).
- **Long signal** - referred to as a 'Dah' (shown as a dash –) and lasts the same time as three Dits.

Always leave an adequate pause between letters and between words.

A • –	N – •	1 • – – – –
B – • • •	O – – –	2 • • – – –
C – • – •	P • – – •	3 • • • – –
D – • •	Q – – • –	4 • • • • –
E •	R • – •	5 • • • • •
F • • – •	S • • •	6 – • • • •
G – – •	T –	7 – – • • •
H • • • •	U • • –	8 – – – • •
I • •	V • • • –	9 – – – – •
J • – – –	W • – –	0 – – – – –
K – • –	X – • • –	
L • – • •	Y – • – –	
M – –	Z – – • •	

CHAPTER TWENTY: COMMS TRAINING (CIS) OVERVIEW

Semaphore: A visual communication system that evolved from the French Revolution in 1792. Two flags are held in specific positions to represent letters of the alphabet and numbers. Letters and numbers use the same positions so you need to specify which you are sending.

To get signals across correctly, keep arms straight, hold flags at correct angles and return them to the front after each letter or number.

A (1) B (2) C (3) D (4) E (5)

F (6) G (7) H (8) I (9) J (0)

K L M N O

P Q R S T

U V W X Y

Z NUMERICAL ALPHA ACKNOWLEDGE REST

CHAPTER TWENTY: COMMS TRAINING (CIS) OVERVIEW

04. PERSONAL ROLE RADIO (PRR) *(one star training)*

Must be taught by an instructor that has the minimum of a basic CIS instructor qualification.

The Personal Role Radio (PRR) is a small, Ultra High Frequency (UHF) transmitter and receiver that is designed to allow infantry soldiers within an eight person section to communicate over short distances.

It allows them to talk to each other when patrolling and moving through different terrain or when in contact with an enemy. The range is not vast and is not effective at distances over 500 metres, but signal will still pass through cover and walls etc. when close enough.

Specifications

- Size (approx): 14 x 85 x 2.5 cm
- Weight: 1.5kg
- Range: 500 metres (or three floors of a building)
- Channels: 256 (16 directly available to user)
- Power: 2 x AA batteries
- Battery life: 20 - 24 hours

A picture with parts labelled is on the next page.

05. BASIC MESSAGES & SIMPLE NET *(one star training)*

Must be taught by an instructor that has the minimum of a basic CIS instructor qualification.

Talking over a radio is similar to using a phone but with a bit more structure and security.

Callsigns

To protect elements of COIL, when talking over a radio, callsigns are used instead of names, communication centres, organisations etc. These are a series of letters and numbers and will be allocated to cadets by staff whenever using radios.

Letters need to be pronounced phonetically and numbers said individually. For example 'A13D' (Alpha One Three Delta) or 'E30' (Echo Three Zero).

CHAPTER TWENTY: COMMS TRAINING (CIS) OVERVIEW

Prowords & Endings

Start a new radio conversation by saying 'hello' followed by the callsign of the person you want to speak to. All transmissions after that should start with the callsign of the person talking. Here are other words used in conversation.

- **Hello:** Alerts the net that you are transmitting.
- **Roger:** Last message received and understood.
- **Over:** End of transmission but a reply is needed.
- **Out:** End of transmission and no reply is needed.
- **Out to you:** End of transmission to an individual but not everyone.
- **Wait out:** Time needed to get an answer or accurate reply.

Example conversation	
A13C (person 1)	Hello Echo Two Zero, this is Alpha One Three Charlie, what is your location, over
E2Ø (person 2)	Echo Two Zero, We are currently at checkpoint three, Over
A13C (person 1)	Alpha One Three Charlie, Roger, Out

Establishing comms

Before using a communication network, it needs to be tested to make sure it is effective and reliable, this is a 'radio check'. One of three responses can be given.

- **OK:** Transmission is satisfactory.
- **Difficult:** Workable but difficult so extra care is required.
- **Unworkable:** Unable to use until comms have been improved.

Example conversation	
W4ØT (person 1)	Hello Foxtrot Three Nine Yankee, this is Whiskey Four Zero Tango, Radio check, Over.
F39Y (person 2)	Foxtrot Three Nine Yankee, OK, Over
W4ØT (person 1)	Whiskey Four Zero Tango, Roger, Out

CHAPTER TWENTY: COMMS TRAINING (CIS) OVERVIEW

Personal Role Radio (PRR) Parts

Antenna — Keep a min of 4cm from face

Channel 1 - 16

Volume (on/off)

Headset socket

Switch — Various versions

Transceiver — Various manufacturers

Microphone

Battery compartment

Headset — Adjustable

Carrying pouch — Fitted onto webbing

Other items include:

- **Wireless Push To Talk (PTT) switch** - Attached to a rifle, this allows the user to communicate without taking their hands away.
- **Windshield adapter** - Attached to the microphone, it is only effective in high wind.

CHAPTER TWENTY: COMMS TRAINING (CIS) OVERVIEW

06. INTRODUCTION TO CYBER *(one star training)*

Cyberspace is an imaginary place without a physical location where digital information and communication exists. It is created through interconnecting technologies and is made up of three aspects.

- **Physical:** The physical parts that allow cyberspace to exist such as computers, phones, cables, switches, routers and servers etc.
- **Virtual:** What is created using the physical aspects such as networks, apps, content providers, online services and security etc.
- **Social:** This is how people interact in cyberspace acting as real people, personas, avatars, characters, artificial intelligence or bots.

Cyberspace is everywhere and effects our personal day to day lives as well as all major infrastructure such as hospitals, energy suppliers, air traffic and more. Because of this it is a vulnerable area, subject to interference and attack, and is now considered another aspect of warfare alongside air, sea, land and space. Influencing people's thoughts, opinions and actions is also easily done in cyberspace and the use of 'fake news' is now extremely common.

Cyber and the Military

This is broken down into three main elements:

1. **Cyber security:** Protect and look after infrastructure, systems and data. Prevent attacks and withstand and recover from attacks. Discover and respond to potential attacks early.

The military unit tasked with this is the 13th Signal Regiment which is home to the Army Cyber Information Security Operations Centre (SOC).

2. **Offensive cyber:** Using cyber against potential enemies or threats to attack and interfere with enemy infrastructure, systems and data to deceive, degrade, deny, disrupt and destroy.

The unit tasked with this is the national cyber force tri-service MOD partnership with GCHQ (Government Communications Headquarters) and DSTL (Defence Science and Technology Laboratory).

3. **Intelligence, Surveillance and Reconnaissance (ISR):** Collects, processes and distributes info to help with cyber operations.

The unit tasked with this is the Special Reconnaissance Regiment which is part of the UK Special Forces.

CHAPTER TWENTY: COMMS TRAINING (CIS) OVERVIEW

ONE STAR TRAINING CIS ASSESSMENT

This is made up of a practical assessment and a written assessment. If a cadet fails any section they can retake straight away. If a cadet fails after a second attempt, they will fail the course and re-training is required before attempting again.

TWO STAR CIS TRAINING OVERVIEW (optional)

Two star CIS is optional but cadets that want to complete it must have completed basic and one star CIS along with the PRR training.

At two star level, cadets get to use the PRC 710 radio and further their knowledge of military voice procedure.

Two star CIS must be taught and assessed by an instructor that holds the basic CIS Instructor qualification and is often carried out during a full training day/weekend.

Lessons covered are as follows:
- **Security & callsigns**
- **Accuracy, aids to accuracy**
- **Discipline**
- **Basic radio net & establishing comms**
- **PRC 710 VHF section**
- **PRC 710 VHF section practical**
- **No play**
- **VP exercise (practical)**
- **Calling & answering**
- **Corrections & repetitions**

TWO STAR TRAINING CIS ASSESSMENT

This is made up of a practical assessment and a written assessment. If a cadet fails any section they can retake straight away. If a cadet fails after a second attempt, they will fail the course and re-training is required before attempting again.

CHAPTER TWENTY: COMMS TRAINING (CIS) OVERVIEW

PRC 710 *(two star training)*

Below is an image of the PRC 710 with major components listed.

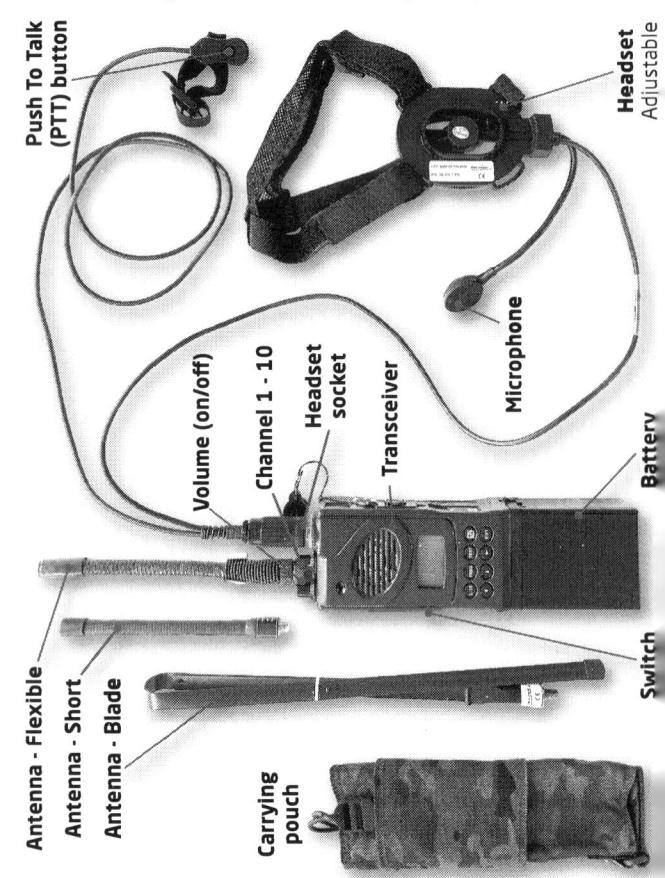

Push To Talk (PTT) button
Headset - Adjustable
Microphone
Volume (on/off)
Channel 1 - 10
Headset socket
Transceiver
Battery
Antenna - Flexible
Antenna - Short
Antenna - Blade
Switch
Carrying pouch

CHAPTER TWENTY: COMMS TRAINING (CIS) OVERVIEW

THREE STAR CIS TRAINING OVERVIEW (optional)

Three star CIS is optional but cadets that want to complete it must have completed basic, one and two star CIS.

At three star level, cadets get to use the PRC 715 radio set up (PRC 710 + amplifier for further distance comms), carry out basic field cable laying and gain knowledge of VHF antennas and propagation.

Three star CIS must be taught and assessed by an instructor that holds the intermediate CIS Instructor qualification and is often carried out over a full training weekend.

Lessons covered are as follows:

- **Introduction to line (advantages/disadvantages) & field cables**
- **PTC 414 & phone circuit**
- **Field cables & jointing & repacking**
- **Construction of the line including knots**
- **Tasks of a line party**
- **Practical line exercise**
- **Aids to security**
- **BATCO (grid ref only)**
- **BATCO (practical)**
- **Relays & time**
- **PRC 715, description**
- **PRC 715, operation**
- **Basic A&P (surface & space)**
- **5.4m mast & GSA, description**
- **5.4m mast & GSA, practical**
- **Cancellations & verifications**

THREE STAR TRAINING CIS ASSESSMENT

This is made up of a practical assessment and a written assessment. If a cadet fails any section they can retake straight away. If a cadet fails after a second attempt, they will fail the course and re-training is required before attempting again.

CHAPTER TWENTY: COMMS TRAINING (CIS) OVERVIEW

FOUR STAR CIS TRAINING OVERVIEW (optional)

Four star CIS is optional but cadets that want to complete it must have completed three star CIS. Cadets will be expected to use a variety of radio systems including the PRC 720 (Company/Battalion level comms) and be able to communicate accurately and securely.

Four star CIS must be taught by an instructor that holds the intermediate CIS Instructor qualification over two to three days.

Lessons covered are as follows:
- **Advanced VP**
- **Cable laying, line orders, routing**
- **Calls to specified person, long message**
- **Crossings**
- **Teeing in, testing, fault location**
- **Practical line exercise**
- **BATCO spelling, authentication**
- **BATCO vocab cards**
- **Directed nets**
- **Delegating & assuming control**
- **VP/BATCO exercise**
- **A&P fundamentals (freq, wavelength)**
- **A&P**
- **Comms plan, day sheet**
- **Pathfinder HF, description**
- **Pathfinder HF, operation**
- **Clark PU 12, description**
- **Clark PU 12, practical**
- **Practical HF & A&P exercise**

FOUR STAR TRAINING CIS ASSESSMENT

This is made up of a practical assessment and a written assessment and must be assessed by an instructor that holds the advanced CIS instructor qualification or CCISTT (Cadet Communication Information Systems Training Team) instructors. If a cadet fails any section they can retake straight away. If a cadet fails after a second attempt, they will fail the course and re-training is required before attempting again.

CHAPTER TWENTY ONE
MUSIC OVERVIEW

CONTENTS:
- Introduction
- Music detachments

REFERENCES:
- *Army Cadet Syllabus - AC71101 (Version 1.2 - July 2022)*
- *Army Cadet Resource Centre via Westminster*

CHAPTER TWENTY ONE: MUSIC OVERVIEW

INTRODUCTION

Music is not a requirement of the standard Army Cadet Syllabus and is only covered in specific music detachments in place of all other ACS subjects. Cadets need to pass basic ACS training the same as all other cadets but then focus entirely on music training instead of any other military training. Opportunity to take part in DofE, BTEC etc. is still there but cadets also get to gain official music qualifications.

- **Badges available:** Star level badges have an 'M' before the number to indicate the cadet is a musician. There is also a Cadet Drum Major rank available which is unique to cadet musicians.
- **Specialist qualifications required to teach:** Qualifications relevant to the type of music being taught is required at all levels. Assessments are carried out locally or at a higher level depending on type of music and star level.
- **Further progression beyond the syllabus:** Participation in official local, regional and National parades, displays and concerts.

MUSIC DETACHMENTS

The three types of music detachments are as follows:

MUSIC: PIPING AND DRUMMING

This covers the side (snare) drum and bagpipes only. The syllabus and instructor qualifications are from the Scottish Qualifications Authority (SQA), the Royal Scottish Pipe Band (RSPBA) curriculum, the Piping and Drumming Qualifications Board (PDQB) and the Scottish Credit Qualifications Framework (SCQF).

MUSIC - MILITARY BANDS

This provides training for full bands using various pitched and percussion instruments. The syllabus and instructor qualifications are from the Associated Board of the Royal Schools of Music (ABRSM) and Trinity College London (TCL).

MUSIC - CORPS OF DRUMS

This covers side (snare) drum and bugle only. The syllabus is designed by the ACF and is based on the Army School of Ceremonial Drums Wings syllabus. Instructors need to complete the same training as cadets and achieve the required levels to be able to teach cadets.

CHAPTER TWENTY TWO
ACRONYMS INITIALS & SLANG

CONTENTS:
- Introduction
- General acronyms, initials & slang list

REFERENCES:
- Various publications & manuals

CHAPTER TWENTY TWO: ACRONYMS, INITIALS & SLANG

INTRODUCTION

Throughout the ACF and the Military environment as a whole, there are a lot of acronyms and initials used to reference people, places and processes. There are also many unique words that may cause confusion if not understood.

Over the next few pages are many of the general acronyms, initials and words that may be handy for reference, but it is definitely not a full list as there are far too many to cover.

2IC	Second In Command
2LT	Second Lieutenant
4FGR	Four Figure Grid Reference
6FGR	Six Figure Grid Reference
A&A	Arms & Ammunition
A&E	Accident & Emergency
AAC	Army Air Corps
Ablutions	Toilet & wash block
ABRSM	Associated Board of the Royal Schools of Music
AC	Army Cadet
AC SMS	Army Cadet safety Management System
ACCT	Army Cadet Charitable Trust
ACF	Army Cadet Force
ACFA	Army Cadet Force Association
ACIO	Army Careers Information Office
ACRC	Army Cadet Resource Centre
ACS	Army Cadet Syllabus
ACSO	Army Command Standing Order
AED	Automated External Defibrillator
AGC	Adjutant General Corps
AIC	Advanced Instructor Course
AIP	Authority In Principle
ALM	Adult Leadership & Management

CHAPTER TWENTY TWO: ACRONYMS, INITIALS & SLANG

ALS	Army Legal Services
AM	Ante Meridian (before midday)
AO	Activity Owner
APC	Army Proficiency Certificate
AR	Air Rifle
AT	Adventurous Training
ATC	Air Training Corps
ATC	Authority To Conduct
ATO	Ammunition Technical Officer
AUO	Adult Under Officer
AWOL	Absent Without Leave
BAMS	Bidding & Allocation Management System
BATCO	British Army Tactical Code
BC	British Canoeing
BEL	Basic Expedition Leader
BFA	Blank Firing Adapter
BIC	Basic Instructor Course
BMC	British Mountaineering Council
Bn	Battalion
BNCA	British National Cadet Association
BPM	Beats Per Minute
BRCS	British Red Cross Society
BSA	British Shooting Association
BTEC	Business & Technology Education Council
Buckshee	Spare item got for free
CAA	Company Administrative Assistant
CAM	Camouflage
CAMus	Corps of Army Music
CAPT	Captain
CASP	Cadet Action Safety Plan

CHAPTER TWENTY TWO: ACRONYMS, INITIALS & SLANG

CBN	Cadet Briefing Note
CCAT	Cadet Centre for Adventurous Training
CCF	Combined Cadet Force
CCISTT	Cadet Communication Information Systems Training Team
CDT	Cadet
CE	Community Engagement
CEFO	Complete Equipment Fighting Order
CEMO	Complete Equipment Marching Order
CEO	Cadet Executive Officer
CFATA	County First Aid Training Advisor
CFAV	Cadet Force Adult Volunteer
CFI	Cadet Force Instruction
CFIT	Cadet Forces Instructional Techniques
CFSO	Cadet Force Standing Order
CIS	Communication & Informations Systems
Civvie	Civilian (non-military)
CLAP	Clear, Loud, As an order, Pauses
CLF	Cadet Live Firing
CoC	Chain of Command
COIL	Combat effectiveness, Order of battle, Intentions, Locations
COL	Colonel
Comms	Communications
Coy	Company
CP	Command Post
CPD	Continual Personal Development
CPL	Corporal
CPR	Cardiopulmonary Resuscitation
CQMS	Company Quarter Master Sergeant
CRAM	Clear, Relevant, Achievable, Measurable
CRAVED	Confidence, Rapport, Attitude, Voice, Enthusiasm, Distractions

CHAPTER TWENTY TWO: ACRONYMS, INITIALS & SLANG

CRoW	Countryside & Rights of Way
CSA	Cadet Stores Assistant
CSBTR	Cadet Small Bore Target Rifle
CSM	Company Sergeant Major
CTC	Cadet Training Centre
CTR	Cadet Target Rifle
CTT	County Training Team
CVQO	Cadet Vocational Qualifications Organisation
CZP	Correct Zeroing Position
DBS	Disclosure Barring Service
DC	Detachment Commander
DCCT	Dismounted Close Combat Trainer
Det	Detachment
DGA	Dangerous Goods Awareness
DI	Detachment Instructor
Diffy	Item for exchange
DIN	Defence Information Notice
DIO	Defence Infrastructure Organisation
DLE	Defence Learning Environment
DLF	Defence Logistical Framework
DLSR	Defence Land Safety Regulator
DofE	Duke of Edinburgh Award
DP	Dual Purpose
DPM	Disruptive Pattern Material
DRAB	Danger, Response, Airway, Breathing
DS	Directing Staff
DSA	Defence Safety Authority
DSTL	Defence Science & Technology Laboratory
DT	Drill & Turnout
DTE	Defence Training Estate

CHAPTER TWENTY TWO: ACRONYMS, INITIALS & SLANG

DTG	Date Time Group
DZ	Drop Zone
EASP	Event Action safety Plan
ECO	Event Co-ordinating Officer
EDIP	Explain, Demonstrate, Imitate, Practice
EFAW	Emergency First Aid At Work
ERV	Emergency Rendezvous
ES	Extreme Spread
ESTC	Expedition Supervisor Training Course
ETA	Expected Time of Arrival
ETD	Expected Time of Departure
ETS	Education & Training Services (Army)
EXP	Expedition
F&M	Fire & Movement
FA	First Aid
FAAW	First Aid At Work
FC	Fieldcraft
FCO	Fire Control Orders
FOB	Forward Operating Base
FRV	Final Rendezvous
FTX	Fieldcraft Training Exercise
Gash	Rubbish
GCHQ	Government Communications Headquarters
GP	General Purpose
GPS	Global Positioning System
GR	Grid Reference
GRIT	Group, Range, Indication, Type of fire
HDT	Home to Duty Travel
HE	High Explosive
HPS	Highest Possible Score

CHAPTER TWENTY TWO: ACRONYMS, INITIALS & SLANG

HQ	Headquarters
HSE	Health & Safety Executive
IA	Immediate Action
IAW	In Association with
IIC	Intermediate Instructor Course
IOT	Initial Officer Training
ISR	Intelligence Surveillance & Reconnaissance
JCIC	Junior Cadet Instructor Cadre
JESIP	Joint Emergency Services Interoperability Programme
JI	Joining Instructions
JSP	Joint Service Publication
KA	Keeping Active
KFS	Knife, Fork & Spoon
KGVI	King George the Sixth (leadership course)
KM	Kilometres
LCPL	Lance Corporal
LEL	Lowland Expedition Leader
LLA	Lowland Leader Award
LRF	Local Resilience Forum
LT	Lieutenant
LT COL	Lieutenant Colonel
M	Metres
Maj	Major
MEL	Main Event List
MK	Military Knowledge
ML	Mountain Leader
MMTTR	Mechanised Moving Target Trainer Range
MOD	Ministry Of Defence
MPGS	Military Provost Guard Service
MPI	Mean Point of Impact

CHAPTER TWENTY TWO: ACRONYMS, INITIALS & SLANG

MSO	Medical Support Officer
MSSC	Marine Society & Sea Cadets
MTP	Multi Terrain Pattern
MWIS	Mountain Weather Information Service
NAAFI	Navy, Army, Air Force Institute
NATO	North Atlantic Treaty Organisation
NAV	Navigation
NBC	Nuclear, Biological & Chemical
NCO	Non Commissioned Officer
NGB	National Governing Body
NNAS	National Navigation Award Scheme
NOK	Next Of Kin
NSN	Nato/National Stock Number
NSP	Normal Safety Precautions
NSPCC	National Society for the Prevention of Cruelty to Children
NSRA	National Small Bore Rifle Association
NUV	Non Uniformed Volunteer
O' Group	Orders Group
OC	Officer Commanding
OCS	Obstacle Course Supervisor
OIC	Officer In Charge
OP	Observation Post
Ops	Operations
ORP	Operational Ration Pack
OS	Ordnance Survey
PARQ	Physical Activity Readiness Questionnaire
PCS	Personal Clothing System
PI	Probationary Instructor
PLT	Platoon
PM	Post Meridian (after midday)

CHAPTER TWENTY TWO: ACRONYMS, INITIALS & SLANG

PME	Public Military Event
POA	Point Of Aim
PoC	Point of Command
PPE	Personal Protective Equipment
PPPP	Pose, Pause, Pick, Praise
PPPPPP	Prior Planning & Preparation Prevents Poor Performance
PDQP	Piping & Drumming Qualifications Board
PRC	Portable Radio Communications
PRR	Personal Role Radio
PSS	Permanent Support Staff
PT	Physical Training
PTT	Push To Talk
QARANC	Queen Alexandra's Royal Army Nursing Corps
QBO	Quick Battle Orders
QM	Quartermaster
RA	Royal Regiment of Artillery
RA	Risk Assessment
RAC	Royal Armoured Corps
RAChD	Royal Army Chaplains Department
RADC	Royal Army Dental Corps
RAFAC	Royal Air Force Air Cadets
RAMC	Royal Army Medical Corps
RAMP	Raise, Activate, Mobilise, Potentiate
RAPTC	Royal Army Physical Training Corps
RAVC	Royal Army Veterinary Corps
RBL	Royal British Legion
RC-Cdts	Regional Command Cadets
RCAC	Royal Canadian Army Cadets
RCO	Range Conducting Officer
RE	Royal Engineers

CHAPTER TWENTY TWO: ACRONYMS, INITIALS & SLANG

Recce	Reconnaissance
REME	Royal Electrical & Mechanical Engineers
Reveille	Wake up time
RFCA	Reserve Cadet Forces Association
RLC	Royal Logistic Corps
RMP	Royal Military Police
RPOC	Regional Point Of Command
RQMS	Regimental Quarter Master Sergeant
RSD	Range Safety Document
RSM	Regimental Sergeant Major
RSPBA	Royal Scottish Pipe Band
RTR	Return Fire, Take cover, Return appropriate fire
RTU	Returned To Unit
RV	Rendezvous
SA (K)	Small Arms 'K' Qualification (range duties)
SA (LR)	Small Arms (Longe Range)
SA (M)	Small Arms 'M' Qualification (blank firing)
SA (SR)	Small Arms (Short Range)
SAA	Skill At Arms
SAAI	Skill At Arms Instructor
SAO	Senior Activity Owner
SAR	Search And Rescue
SB	Small Bore
SCIC	Senior Cadet Instructor Cadre
Scran	Food
SF	Special Forces
SH	Shooting
SI	Sergeant Instructor
Sig	Signaller
SITREP	Situation Report

CHAPTER TWENTY TWO: ACRONYMS, INITIALS & SLANG

SLO	Schools Liaison Officer
SMART	Specific, Measurable, Achievable, Relevant, Time-bound
SMI	Sergeant Major Instructor
SML	Subject Matter Lead
SO	Staff Officer
SO	Standing Orders
SO1	Staff Officer In Command
SO2	Staff Officer Second In Command
SOC	Security Operations Centre
SOP	Standard Operating Procedure
SPO	Senior Planning Officer
SPS	Staff & Personnel Support (Army)
SQF	Scottish Qualifications Framework
SSI	Staff Sergeant Instructor
SSI	School Staff Instructor
SST	Safe System of Training
SUSAT	Sight Unit Small Arms Trilux
SyOps	Security Operating Procedure
TCL	Trail Cycle Leader
TCL	Trinity College London
TEWC	Tactical Exercise Without Cadets
TIBUA	Training In Built Up Areas
TIWAF	Training In Woods And Forest
TMH	Trigger Mechanism Housing
TO	Training Officer
TOPL	Training On Private Land
TRF	Tactical Recognition Flash
TSA	Training Safety Advisor
TSM	Training Safety Marshal
UIN	Unit Identification Number

CHAPTER TWENTY TWO: ACRONYMS, INITIALS & SLANG

UXO	Unexploded Ordnance
VA	Voluntary Allowance
VCC	Volunteer Cadet Corps
VP	Voice Procedure
Wdr	Withdraw
WGL	Walking Group Leader
WHT	Weapon Handling Test
WO	Warrant Officer
WO1	Warrant Officer First Class
WO2	Warrant Officer Second Class
x	Yards (Yds)
YPS	Youth Proficiency Scheme